Urban Land Policy

Issues and Opportunities

A WORLD BANK PUBLICATION

Contributors

Harold B. Dunkerley, Senior Adviser, Urban Development Department, The World Bank

Alan A. Walters, Economic Adviser to the Prime Minister of the United Kingdom

William A. Doebele, Professor of Advanced Environmental Studies in the Field of Implementation, Harvard University

Christine M. E. Whitehead, London School of Economics and Department of Land Economy, University of Cambridge

Donald C. Shoup, Graduate School of Architecture and Urban Planning, University of California, Los Angeles

John M. Courtney, Urban Development Department, The World Bank

Malcolm D. Rivkin, Rivkin Associates, Inc.

Urban Land Policy

Issues and Opportunities

Harold B. Dunkerley
coordinating editor
with the assistance of
Christine M. E. Whitehead

65301

PUBLISHED FOR THE WORLD BANK
Oxford University Press

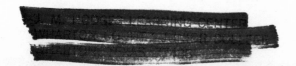

Oxford University Press

NEW YORK OXFORD LONDON GLASGOW
TORONTO MELBOURNE WELLINGTON HONG KONG
TOKYO KUALA LUMPUR SINGAPORE JAKARTA
DELHI BOMBAY CALCUTTA MADRAS KARACHI
NAIROBI DAR ES SALAAM CAPE TOWN

Edited by Jane H. Carroll; figures by S. A. D.
Subasinghe; binding design by Joyce C. Eisen

Library of Congress Cataloging in Publication Data

Main entry under title:

Urban land policy, issues and opportunities.

Bibliography: p.
Includes index.
1. Land use, Urban. 2. Urban policy. 3. Land
tenure. I. Dunkerley, Harold B., 1921-   . II. Whitehead, Christine M. E.
HD111.U7   1982   333.77'17   82-20247
ISBN 0-19-520403-4

First printing, January 1983

Contents

Preface

THE URBAN LAND ISSUES now facing developing countries are necessarily of concern to the World Bank. The availability and price of urban land affect project design and the relation of economic and social costs to benefits. Conversely, the projects supported by the Bank often have a significant influence on the supply of, and demand for, urban land—and hence affect land prices. Wider considerations of land utilization are involved in the quest for more efficient spatial patterns, more employment opportunities, and a less uneven distribution of income and wealth between the rich and the poor. As the U.N. Habitat Conference in Vancouver demonstrated, many of these urban land issues are of almost universal concern, not least the rapidity of the rise in urban land prices, the potential for capturing publicly created land values, and the developmental problems inherent in the rights of ownership and land use. For this reason, these chapters, initially designed for use by World Bank staff in urban project and program activities, are being made available here, in a rather different form, to a wider audience.

The origin of this book in the urban project work of the World Bank explains its format. The introductory chapter provides a context, or perspective, for more detailed consideration of the urban land issues that most clearly impinge on the preparation and implementation of urban projects and programs. This overview serves as a starting point for the following chapters on major problems of urban land by various authors with long experience in their respective fields. The second chapter deals with the economic valuation of land, based on the opportunity cost of using land for one purpose rather than another, and with the underlying relationships behind shifts in the provision of services. The third chapter provides perhaps the most thorough discussion available of different types of urban land tenure in relation to objectives of equity and efficiency. The following short chapter links these issues to the rationale for government intervention and to the forms that such intervention may take. A fifth chapter discusses measures to influence the allocation of surplus values created in the development of urban land, including various forms of land taxation and government acquisition and development of land. Finally, two chapters deal with other forms of regulation of land use, the general limitations to which they are subject, and the characteristics of individual regulatory tools.

Urban land problems are inherently complex because of the many interactions between land uses, locational specificity, and the deep roots of land rights in legal and social systems. The subject is poor in accepted theory and rich in controversy. In developing countries conditions vary greatly, and the data base is generally extremely poor. In this context it was recognized that a comprehensive and fully consistent treatment of all the problem areas was not possible. Readers should not therefore be surprised to find some differences of opinion among authors, particularly on the relative merits of different solutions to the problems. Although generalized recommendations are of limited use in this field, the analyses presented should nevertheless refine and illuminate many of the urban problems that confront the authorities of developing countries and provide some practical guidance to suitable and adaptable approaches for dealing with them.

The program as a whole was directed by Harold B. Dunkerley, senior adviser of the Urban Projects Department, who also wrote the overview chapter. He was assisted by Douglas H. Keare, chief of the Urban and Regional Economics Division, Development Economics Department, and by Suzanne M. Snell, who surveyed actual experience with land problems in urban project work. Alan A. Walters, William A. Doebele, Donald C. Shoup, Malcolm D. Rivkin, and John M. Courtney contributed the original supporting papers. Acknowledgment is also due to many World Bank colleagues, particularly Orville F. Grimes, Johannes F. Linn, Callisto E. Madavo, Rakesh Mohan, Maurice Mould, Anthony J. Pellegrini, and Bertrand M. Renaud, who helped review earlier drafts and whose constructive suggestions have been largely incorporated in the present texts. Particular recognition is due to Christine Whitehead, who carried out the arduous task of editing the original Bank-focused papers and added a short connecting chapter to make the presentation more suitable for a wider audience.

ANTHONY A. CHURCHILL
Director, Urban Development Department
The World Bank

Urban Land Policy

Issues and Opportunities

1

Introduction and Overview

Harold B. Dunkerley

THE PHENOMENON OF THE RECENT extraordinary growth of
cities and towns in the developing world is by now familiar. It is still
difficult, however, to grasp the magnitudes involved. More than 400
million people were absorbed into the urban areas of developing countries other than China between 1950 and 1975, a number almost equal to
the present urban population of the industrialized countries of the
Western world. One billion more are expected to be added between 1975
and the end of the century. By then, probably as many as forty cities in
developing countries will have populations exceeding 5 million inhabitants (in 1950 none had reached this size) and ten or eleven cities are likely
to exceed 15 million. Well within the lifetime of most persons being born
today, the majority of the population of the developing countries is likely
to be urban.[1]

When this explosive urban growth is set against the paucity of
resources to provide housing, workplaces, schools, roads, water supplies, transport vehicles, and the many other requirements of urban life,
the conflict between the pressures of urbanization and the means available
becomes clear. Two-thirds of the population of the developing world live
in countries where annual output per head still averages below US$500;
annual net saving for all types of investment, even at this level of income,
is usually well below US$75 per head. The scarcity of skilled administra-
tors for policy direction and implementation is an equally critical constraint. The task of directing and coordinating the wide variety of
activities that interact in the process of urban development is inherently

1. Urban areas are generally defined as population centers exceeding 20,000 habitants. In
some countries, however, a population of 5,000 or more is considered urban.

difficult; the rapidity of change, social as well as economic, greatly enlarges the institutional problem.

Against this background, the absorption of such a vast increase in urban population in so short a time, without much higher unemployment and mortality than now exists, is as extraordinary as it was unanticipated. It should not be surprising that the unprecedented urban growth has also produced many seemingly intractable problems, in particular the proliferation of slums and squatter settlements in which living conditions are deplorable and incomes low and precarious. The great and growing interest of developing countries in the supply, price, and allocation of urban land reflects this unprecedented growth of their towns and cities and the severe social and economic problems they face. Unfortunately, there is no corresponding corpus of accepted theory, of analysis of experience, or usually even of minimally adequate statistical material, against which to test the possibilities for improving conditions.

The use of urban land poses serious problems in all countries simply because the supply of serviced land is limited and subject to many competing claims. Dissatisfaction with the emerging urban forms is almost universal. But in the developing countries, where towns and cities often double in area as well as population within a decade, these land problems are most critical. The quality of life in towns and cities, the environment and conditions under which the inhabitants live and work, and the possibilities for recreation are heavily dependent on the systems now being developed for servicing and allocating urban land and on the adaptability of these systems. The effective supply of urban services, such as roads and public utilities, in turn largely depends on the effective collection of revenue from beneficiaries, through general land taxes or special levies on land benefiting from public projects, or the collection of costs via public ownership of urban land.

The U.N. Habitat Conference of 1976 identified sharply rising urban land prices as the most serious of the many problems facing developing countries in this urbanization process. But rising prices are only symptoms, and attempts to forbid price increases, without dealing with underlying causes or weighing the economic consequences of removing price signals, can do more harm than good—as evidenced by the experience with rent controls in many countries. Securing for the community the rise in urban land values caused by community action, such as the provision of infrastructure, or by general urban growth is also fraught with problems, however logical and equitable such a move may appear. And the widely advocated solution of public ownership of urban land or detailed control of its allocation cannot of itself ensure efficient, equitable, or harmonious patterns of urban land development.

This is indeed a field in which simple solutions are suspect. Land problems are inherently complex both in theory and in practice, particularly because of the interdependencies of land use, the specificity of locational advantages, transfer costs, social taboos and inhibitions, and many other market imperfections, not least the opportunities land transactions provide for corruption. Empirical information on land markets, prices, and total transaction costs is grossly inadequate. Local geography, history, social and legal systems, and general economic policies are too diverse in their effect on land to permit easy generalizations even when evidence is available. Land rights, moreover, are deeply embedded in the social and legal structure and are often the source of family and community cohesion. In consequence, they can be developed and transformed only with difficulty, and major changes are likely to be impractical within a short time.

The situation is made still more complex by the variety of objectives that land policies are supposed to further and by the limitations, interactions, and side effects of the instruments that can be used. The objectives generally put forward for urban land policies, each of which must be considered within the dynamic setting of rapid urban expansion, can be summarized as:

- An appropriate supply of urbanized land for dwellings, for community and recreational activities, and for productive activities, including the provision of basic urban services
- Harmonious urban spatial patterns that minimize the use of resources relative to economic and social benefits
- Greater equity in wealth and income, including access by low-income families to adequate shelter
- A spatial distribution of population and activities at regional and national levels consistent with general national priorities.

The trouble with such objectives is not only that they overlap and raise familiar conflicts between efficiency and equity, particularly in the short term; they are also too vague to be useful. They do not define the concepts needed to determine operational priorities and to adjust these priorities to rapidly changing conditions. Desirable urban patterns are particularly difficult to define with precision; many value judgments are involved and must be made in ignorance of long-term effects and of changes that will occur over the long lifetime of what is now being built.

In such a setting, this initial outline of the field attempts no more than an overview of the issues involved. After a brief look at some salient characteristics of urban land, subsequent sections deal with groups of issues related to the implementation of large-scale urban projects, including tenure, valuation, the allocation of surplus land values, and the control of land use. Some general conclusions are drawn in the final section to reconcile the multiple objectives of urban land policy and the instruments that appear to offer the greatest opportunities for meeting these objectives in developing countries.

The Rising Cost of Urban Land

The unprecedented expansion of urban population in most of the developing world is causing an exceptionally rapid increase in the demand for urban land. Land location is specific, and existing urban plots cannot be reproduced. Thus the rising demand for urban land tends to be met primarily by converting rural land at the periphery of the existing built-up area. The subdivision of agricultural holdings and the provision of access roads is followed by the extension of other services. This expansion of total urban area—many cities are more than doubling in area in a decade—is accompanied by higher economic values for the more central sites; their locational advantage is continually increased by their enlarged access to a growing number of people and by a corresponding growth in expenditures. Higher values in turn increase the pressures for economy in land use, so that part of the expanded demand for urban land is met by increasing the density of activities on the more highly valued land in the central areas.

The basic pressures toward higher urban land values are derived from the increasing demands of a rapidly growing urban population and are accentuated by factors constraining the supply of urbanized land. Some constraints are physical—mountains, swamps, or the sea, for example. Others relate to the lengthy and costly processes of the transfer of land and the establishment of title; these may bear particularly heavily on the supply of small plots for low-income groups.

At present more important constraints in developing countries are probably the shortage of financial resources and the lack of capacity to provide urban services on a scale that matches the growth in the number requiring services. These shortages are typically amplified by design standards that are unrealistically high in relation to the ability of most of the population to pay for them, and often by charges below the costs of supply to those actually receiving the services. Unclear or contested ownership of land may also hold up the provision of services. The net result is an aggravated shortage of serviced land, in the sense that people would be prepared to pay the full cost of considerably more services than are made available. Such serviced land as is available can hence command a premium; the user pays a higher rent and the benefits go largely to the landowner.

The total supply of urban land, or the supply for particular purposes, may also be constrained by excessive "holdouts" and other monopolistic practices, particularly if a small group of landlords is in collusion or there is no effective power of expropriation. It is, however, difficult to ascertain how far practices of this nature exceed the legitimate economic function of holding land ready for a more valuable economic use that will be feasible only later. (Neutze, 1973, pp. 14-15, discusses some of the issues involved.)

Land use controls may also limit supply both in general and for specific purposes—though the latter may have the effect of increasing the supply available for other purposes. Communities almost always exercise some control on urban land use, if only to reserve land for public purposes such as roadways or to reduce hazards such as fire. Often these controls bring added costs and delays because of the need to prepare and submit applications for specific approval of uses of new urban land or new uses of existing urban land. Moreover, land controls can be readily diverted from their stated purpose, for instance to reinforce the exclusive nature of some neighborhoods by effectively denying residence to certain groups, particularly low-income groups.

The increase in the economic value of land in and near urban areas that results from these various forces is unlikely to follow a smooth path. For any site, jumps in value are likely to occur at certain transitional points, often associated with the provision of infrastructure and other urban services. Of these, the most important transition for the rapidly expanding cities in developing countries is usually the initial transfer from rural to urban use.

In anticipation of the increase in rent and capital values, prices of rural land near urban areas will start to rise several years before the change in use. The length of time in which this rise will occur and the rate of increase will depend on the size of the expected "unearned increment"— that is, the rise in annual value from the change in use, net of any costs falling on the owner—and on the alternative rate of return on investment of comparable risk. The higher the level of real interest rates and the greater the risks associated with the land transaction, the shorter will be the time and the faster the rate of increase in the value of the land during the adjustment period preceding the change in use.

After the initial change from rural to urban use, the value of the now urban land will continue to rise, but more slowly, as the city expands and the locational advantages of the plot increase. At some later stage, however, there may be another sharp jump in annual value and consequent capital value, brought about, for instance, by the addition of urban infrastructure, such as a nearby bus terminal, or a change in restrictions that permits a more valuable use of the land. A similar sharp rise in value will then occur in advance of the change in use, becoming more rapid as the time of change approaches (see figure 1-1).

Three elements of the rise in land values can be distinguished. One

Figure 1-1. Changes in Annual and Capital Values of Land with Changes in Land Use

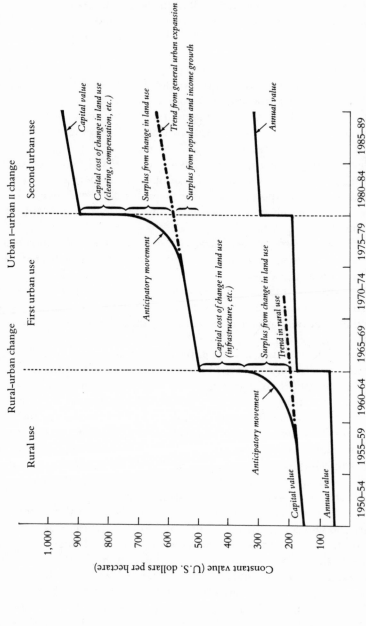

Note: In this illustrative example, capital value is three times annual value under stable conditions. Value changes owing to general inflationary trends are excluded.

8

derives from investments made at the time of the change in land use, including those for preparatory work, various costs of subdivision, the provision of urban services (whether public or private), and other activities such as clearing the land and relocating the original occupiers. The second element derives from changes in permitted uses, and the third from changing locational advantages as towns and cities expand. These last two elements are not the result of capital investment specific to the plot, but are generally classified as "socially created."

Market values, though fundamentally based on economic rents, also depend on the extent to which an acquirer or user of the land is entitled to the full economic rent. Some part of the economic rent may go to others as a result of rights to multiple uses of the land, or taxation. More precisely, the amount an acquirer will be ready to pay is determined by the expected return from the land, net of any expenses, compared with the return expected from other investments. Thus, the existing restrictions on use and the taxes on output or rent lower the present and prospective rents received and are automatically taken into account in lower market values. Expectations of higher future taxes (including, in extreme cases, expropriation) will be discounted to produce lower present market values. Expectations of changes in restrictions may work to raise or lower anticipated future returns.

Market values are also affected on the demand side by the availability and cost of finance for the acquisition of land and buildings and the availability of other forms of readily marketable securities for the alternative investment of savings. Most developing countries lack a capital market that provides an easy and reliable avenue for the domestic investment of savings. Financial instruments are scarce and provisions for safeguarding holders' interests are weak. Interest on bank deposits, regulated by the authorities, is often below the rate of inflation. By contrast, loans on the security of land may be obtained at low or negative real rates of interest by persons with the requisite standing and collateral. Accordingly, the institutional framework may tend to increase demand, thereby creating an upward pressure on market values of land.

The pressures on land prices just described are superimposed on the general rise in prices. Thus the overall rise in land prices may be very sharp in the cities of developing countries, and the rate of increase will normally exceed that of the general price level. However, if savers and asset holders had adequate knowledge and rational expectations, one would expect the yield on holding land for conversion into urban land use, or from one urban use to another, to approximate closely the yield on comparable forms of investment. But the generally accepted view and some evidence, spotty though it is, suggest that real land values in or near most urban centers have in fact continued to rise at a rate providing net yields substantially in excess of market rates for comparable investments. Among the possible explanations for continuing high returns are:

- The future growth of city populations, areas, and incomes and hence of the benefits accruing to landholders from public expenditure and enhanced locational advantage may be underestimated. The "urban explosion" is relatively recent and still far from being fully understood.

- Similarly, for individual holders of land awaiting future development, the perceived risks of confiscation, changing master plans, building code restrictions, delays in obtaining permits, and the like may be greater than for the community as a whole.

- The skills of developers may be in short supply.

- The anticipation of high yields may itself induce holdouts and higher prices and thus become self-fulfilling at least in the short run.

- Market imperfections may increase the spread between the price of undeveloped and developed land. In particular, insiders with a privileged position can extract a larger yield and reduce risks as a result of their personal connections with the decisionmakers who administer the provision of services or land use controls.

In contrast, the real costs of development by private developers may well be underestimated—and the "unearned" increase in values consequently overestimated. Part of the growth in land values and apparent yields may reflect the high transaction costs of changes in land use, including determination of title, taxes, and payoffs to officials. The yield on alternative investments may also be greater than generally recognized. Finally, it is possible that the news media play up exceptional increases in market value, particularly in cases of a change of use, so that the perceived upward movement is exaggerated. Averages of prices of actual transactions in land are also heavily influenced by such cases. (See chapter 2 for a fuller analysis of these factors.)

When the price of land rises much more rapidly than other prices, and the high profits cannot be justified by private improvements to the land, there is an obvious case, on grounds of equity, for capturing part or all of these profits for the public purse—particularly if this can be accomplished without adversely affecting efficiency.

More fundamental in the long term, however, is the reduction of the underlying causes of excessive land prices, particularly the political and institutional constraints that contribute to the shortage of serviced urban land. The high land prices and rents that derive from this scarcity effectively exclude large and often growing segments of the poorer population of developing countries from legal occupation of a minimum dwelling plot in cities. The consequence, almost inevitably, is illegal invasion of land, particularly public land, and illegal subdivision of unserviced private land. Over one-third of the population of many cities in developing countries is now housed in settlements of at least dubious legality. And although these settlements often succeed in providing rudimentary services and allocation systems, the resulting physical lay-out, tenancy arrangements, availability of services, and general living standards are often far worse than they need be. Better conditions can be realized at less cost with a more rational approach to the provision of urban land and services.

Within this general framework of rising market values of urban land the following sections take up specific issues that affect the efficient and equitable use of urban land and the effective implementation of large-scale urban projects.

Tenure and Transfer of Urban Land

The prevalent forms of land tenure in any area have a profound effect on physical urban patterns and their flexibility in adapting to the pressures of rapid growth. They exert a basic influence on population densities and the ability of the poor to find adequate shelter. Tenure systems largely determine the ease or difficulty of land acquisition and assembly. They may make expansion of the urban area difficult and raise transfer costs to levels that poor groups cannot afford. They affect the attractiveness of the landholdings offered through projects such as industrial estates or site-and-service schemes. The potential for covering project costs or raising municipal revenues by land and property taxation depends largely on the existence of clear titles to landownership and to rights of land use. A highly skewed distribution of wealth may be promoted by past and present tenure systems.

Despite the need for data on the forms of tenure and their influence on urban expansion, and for analytic frameworks dealing with these issues, little of such material has been forthcoming. This lacuna can be mainly attributed to the diversity and complexity of the many forms of tenure and to their historical roots in cultural, religious, and legal institutions. The evident difficulty of introducing changes in tenure systems in a short time has deflected interest from tenure as a longer-term policy tool. Yet many issues simply cannot be avoided; they concern, for example, the acquisition of land for projects, changes in tenure form prior to the sale or lease of project land, the relation of tenure to the ability to raise local finance for projects, and its long-term effect on urban physical patterns.

The very wide variety of forms of land tenure, often overlapping and imprecise, throughout the developing world defies easy classification. At one extreme are various types of private ownership, with almost exclusive rights of use and disposition, such as are found in much of South America, where the underlying concepts are closely related to freehold tenure in North American and European countries based on Roman law. At the opposite extreme are often ill-defined rights to limited tenure determined by tribal customs or the precarious tenure following illegal invasion of public or privately owned land in squatter settlements. In between are systems ranging from complete public ownership and control to Islamic religious concepts of nonalienation by chosen families and an enormous range of customary, often overlapping, but unrecorded rights to limited use. (See chapter 3 for a more detailed discussion.)

The precise legal form of tenure may be less important than how it is perceived by the occupants, and theoretical advantages are in any case subject to practical limitations. Hence, many of the formal distinctions—for instance, between freehold and leasehold—may become blurred. A short lease that is by custom always renewed may provide greater security of tenure, as perceived by the holder, than a longer lease or freehold ownership that may be subject to arbitrary public acquisition. The theoretical advantages of private ownership are marred by market imperfections. Public ownership provides the opportunity not only for more rational land uses, but also for abuses. Clearly no individual tenure system can be expected to meet all requirements. Each form of tenure involves tradeoffs between objectives such as security, flexibility, and equity. Nevertheless, certain issues stand out as of particular relevance.

Security of tenure appears to be essential to stimulate the individual initiative necessary for the provision of adequate dwellings for a large part of the urban population of developing countries. In the prevailing conditions of rapid urban growth and lack of resources, plot holders will normally invest in building or improving their dwellings only if they are assured adequate security of tenure. The provision of rights to secure tenure is consequently a central consideration for the success of site-and-service projects or the upgrading of squatter settlements.

Formalizing the existing situation in squatter settlements—giving titles where none existed before—creates major problems. In the process of regularizing the de facto situation, rights of existing legal owners, public or private, are extinguished. This gives rise to questions of appropriate compensation as well as other important issues such as whether further illegal seizure of land will thereby be encouraged.

Fortunately, though such issues arouse great concern, they are often less serious in actuality than they appear in the abstract. Often the land is publicly owned and the grant of title can be regarded as a fully justifiable distribution of public assets to the poorer elements of the community.

Eventually, the improvement of land and the resulting increase in property values will create a higher tax base and more public revenue. Regularization of tenure also facilitates charging for services. As for the invasion of other urban land, such action is more likely to be deterred by an adequate supply of urbanized plots with reasonable services and at reasonable cost, for example through site-and-service projects, rather than stimulated by the regularization of tenure (see World Bank, 1974*a*, p. 29, on this issue).

When serviced sites or upgraded areas are in short supply, it is often suggested that tenurial rights in such projects be restricted so that tenants are protected from influential speculators and other pressures. Tenants are often required to sell back to the agency when they move away, to try to ensure that higher-income groups or moneylenders do not acquire the improved land and that benefits do not go directly to landlords via increased rents. Similar considerations relate to tenancy of serviced industrial sites.

To the extent—often limited—that such restrictions can be enforced, they unfortunately reduce the mobility of plot holders and may therefore reduce their employment opportunities. The implementation of restrictions also entails considerable costs of salaries and skilled manpower. Various compromises are possible; for example, rights of tenancy might be increased over time, with the right of free disposition after a certain number of years. Compensation for investments made by departing tenants is also of obvious importance for mobility.

Tenure arrangements as well as infrastructure should be designed to facilitate changes in land use as they become needed. This further complicates the design of projects, especially in rapidly growing urban centers. Apart from the obvious difficulties of deciding how much provision the original layout should make for further subdivisions and services in the future, there is the dilemma of choosing between relatively short leases to facilitate changes in urban structure and long leases to provide security of tenure and stimulate savings and investment. The relative strength of these opposing considerations depends greatly on local conditions and the sector involved. Industrial sites, for instance, may need long leases to justify the high capital costs of plant installation.

The regularization and liberalization of tenure are normal features of urban shelter projects and industrial and tourism projects which offer to lease or sell to private investors. Experience indicates, however, that in most urban projects the problems of tenure are more likely to be recognized than resolved. Yet it is at moments of transition in land use that changes in land tenure can most readily be instituted. The potential for changing tenure arrangements in association with major urban projects therefore deserves explicit consideration in project preparation. The effects of the regularization of tenure and subsequent transfers of title on the distribution of income and wealth should command attention, as should the problems of changing certain forms of communal land.

The tenure forms prevailing may also have important implications for the cash requirements of the project. The outright sale of rights, approximating freehold, tends to produce the largest immediate cash flow to the seller and helps guard against the erosion of real values by inflation; likewise, the outright purchase by a project agency maximizes its immediate cash requirements. Annual rents conversely tend to involve the smallest immediate financial transfers. However, these considerations may generally be subordinated to others more essential to the project, such as security of occupancy. Exceptions occur where land costs are a high proportion of total project costs.

The immobility of land, its permanence, value, and locational uniqueness make it attractive as a tax base. The same attributes also make it extremely useful as collateral for loans. Both uses are of particular importance in developing countries. In both cases, however, the ownership and rights of personal use must be clear, the land value must be appropriately related to the amount of charges, and foreclosure must be possible to cover debts. Leaseholds, particularly if the remaining life is short or subject to curtailment, are generally much less acceptable as collateral than freeholds. Traditional forms of tenure based on tribal concepts pose great difficulties when raising finance.

"Cloudiness" of title is unfortunately widespread in developing countries, in some cases because of the form of tenure, in others because of the lack of adequate cadastral surveys and up-to-date registers of landholdings. Titles can often be cleared rapidly only through an official expropriation procedure, which allows a "quick take" and later compensates the various claimants.

Acquisition of Project Land

The early acquisition in the open market of land for a project has many advantages. Prices are lower because the new use has not yet increased the value, there is a wider choice of sites, and existing owners have less power to hold out for higher prices when the transfer of title is not mandatory. Against these arguments is the considerable cost incurred in preempting public funds, usually very scarce, that could have been used for other purposes in the interim.[2] Moreover, the best location and size

2. This problem is reduced when land can be rented out during the interim. However, the real costs, in terms of the benefits lost from holding unused land in the "public patrimony," are rarely evaluated.

for the site may not be readily identifiable until an advanced stage of project preparation. Early choice may thus mean a far from optimal location.

The timing of the acquisition of project land becomes more of a dilemma the longer and the more difficult the legal process of transferring title, and the more important the precise choice of site is to the efficient functioning of the project. The latter characteristic is usually sector-specific: the exact location for a telecommunications center is, for instance, likely to be less critical than for a link in a transport or utility network. There are hence significant variations in the tradeoffs between the risks of project delays and the costs incurred by advance acquisition of sites.

Most, but not all, countries have legislation permitting public condemnation of land required for public purposes, although the details and length of the often complex procedures vary greatly. Sometimes the threat of instituting proceedings is sufficient to expedite purchase; in other cases it is ineffective. In a majority of developing countries, however, such legislation needs fairly drastic revision if it is to ensure the timely acquisition of land at reasonable cost for public projects during periods of rapid urban expansion.

The paucity of reliable cadastral surveys further complicates the initial choice, but it can be fairly readily remedied for chosen sites. More serious is the lack of an up-to-date register of titles, which makes it extremely difficult to determine who may be adversely affected by forced acquisition and to whom compensation should be paid. To avoid the consequent delays it is generally necessary to provide for the legal settlement of disputes after the transfer of rights to the public agency.

To avoid the problems and costs of possible delays, land is usually acquired in advance of project presentation, negotiations for loan finance, or even project appraisal in the case of major installations, particularly those dependent on external finance. Exceptions sometimes occur, as in some site-and-service projects, where land is acquired for only the first phase and assurances are obtained for later acquisitions. It is rare for easements for water supply pipes, for example—or land acquisition for this purpose—to be required in advance of project approval; and insofar as the networks are laid in existing public rights-of-way, problems are avoided. Additional land outside public holdings is usually purchased on the open market by the local agency concerned, thereby avoiding lengthy legal procedures—but possibly incurring substantial financial costs.

In practice, most countries place a premium on choosing sites for public projects from land already in public possession. Administrative convenience on the one hand and the danger of delays and the high cost of acquiring new land on the other tend to limit the consideration of other sites. As a result, economic and social costs and benefits of alternative sites are often inadequately analyzed. Even where public holdings are extensive or all land is nationalized, it may be difficult for one agency to acquire land held in surplus by another.

The assembly of large sites at a given date from a variety of current landholders presents particular problems. Because of the pattern of landholdings, projects such as new ports and airports, site-and-service projects, or industrial estates may depend on whether there is adequate power for the public acquisition of land. Even when sufficient tracts of land can be acquired for an initial project without the use of such power, replicating or extending the program over much larger areas may necessitate condemnation procedures to save both time and cost. The availability of such power is therefore relevant to the rationale of the initial project.

In the course of land acquisition, existing users may be displaced. Port extension, road widening, and many other projects may force the removal of squatter dwellings. The provision of alternative, reasonably well-located sites and structures for such displaced users should be taken into consideration in the appraisal of the original project and may require land in addition to that needed for the project itself. Similarly, the potential use of land released when resiting takes place may be an important consideration in the choice between extension of an old site or substitution of a new one. These secondary effects have, in the past, often received little attention—at least until public concern has disturbed the course of project implementation.

Evaluation of Urban Land Costs and Benefits

The valuation of project land in balance sheet and financial flow analyses raises several groups of issues. The first group affects the calculation of the profitability of the project, the value of its assets, and the contributions of the local agency. The second concerns the economic valuation to be put on land inputs in project analysis. The third centers on the economic evaluation of project benefits as reflected in the values of project sites and neighboring land. The theoretical and practical problems of measurement are relevant not only in calculating rates of return but also in figuring the appropriate intensity of land use and hence in planning the physical design of the project. Widely varying local accounting practices present further difficulties in ensuring consistency in project presentation.

Financial Costs

Even when the project site is purchased freehold for cash on the open market at the time of the project, the method of financial accounting is not without problems. It is still necessary, for instance, to include all costs, such as legal fees and interest paid on funds borrowed for the land acquisition. If land is acquired in excess of that needed for the current project, the excess must be treated as a separate component.

More debatable is the issue of revaluing the land in the balance sheet over the course of the project. Insofar as account is taken of the effect of inflation on financial values of other components, this principle should also be applied to land. Similarly, if the land is acquired leasehold, account should be taken of the declining asset value of the lease over the life of the project.

When the land is acquired in advance of the project or is provided without a cash transaction by another government agency, the financial treatment becomes more complex. Few countries maintain an adequate registry of landholdings of public agencies, and few public departments maintain capital balance sheets that include landholdings. Historic costs, when these can be ascertained, require substantial updating to allow for holding costs and increases in market value. If the site is part of a substantially larger tract, the assignment of cost among the different parcels or plots may be difficult. Partial disposals, under differing tenancy conditions, may add awkward complications. In these circumstances, it will generally be more appropriate to secure an independent valuation based on market prices of roughly similar sites.

More difficult still is to decide what to do when all land has been nationalized and is treated in the accounts of the agencies concerned as having no financial—or, for that matter, economic—value. Similar problems arise when land is appropriated for the project at substantially less than market value. The lack of a cash outlay equal to the value of the land should not obscure the fact that a valuable asset is used and withdrawn from other possible uses.

The valuation of land in such circumstances is treated in chapter 2. Here it may be noted that simply taking account of cash outlays by the agency can mean that financial comparisons between different projects become misleading guides to relative cost and profitability. For example, the inclusion of market rent for land (or interest on its purchase price) in one airport project and the exclusion of any charge for land in another make direct comparison impossible without adjustment but may strongly affect the calculation of landing charges needed for financial viability. Inclusion of imputed costs may also cause problems of interpretation. For example, in site-and-service projects charging tenants for land donated by the authorities can be readily justified on grounds of replicability, but it will produce apparent surpluses for the agency, which are not realistic measures of profitability. The evaluation of the contribution of local agencies will differ significantly according to whether any land provided by them is valued at market price or, for instance, treated as of zero cost. Much more important, the location and size of the project site may be affected if the financial accounts obscure the true asset value of the agency.

Much remains to be done to improve the financial accounting of land costs in projects in developing countries. Many technical issues hinder the adoption of uniform procedures, not least among them is that revaluation is often contrary to local accounting practice. Often, when the land is already in the hands of the agencies concerned, the local practice is that some site costs are not recorded at all. At most, an addendum to a financing table may indicate the value of a contribution of land already in the agency's or government's possession. Updating historic costs or allowing for the reduction of unexpired leasehold periods over time appears to be exceedingly rare. Partly as a consequence, land costs often appear as only a small item of total project costs, generally not exceeding 5 percent of total project costs or 10 percent of physical components, excluding contingencies. In some cases such as shelter projects and industrial estates, however, the land costs that are included are routinely of the order of 10 to 15 percent of total costs and exceed this level significantly in some cases.

The fact that land costs appear small, as at present accounted; does not mean that they are low in reality. Still less does it mean that the valuation of land costs is insignificant in influencing the choice of site, its size, or decisions on recovery of costs. Even when the true financial value of the land is relatively small, its inclusion or exclusion may appreciably affect the calculation of local contributions.

Consistent and easily interpretable estimates of financial costs require a detailed examination of how local, and perhaps national, accounting practices should and could be adjusted. Such an examination should lead in due course to guidelines for the financial analysis of projects. Basic data could be improved by better inventories of public land, cadastral surveys, and general land registration. Technical assistance in this area could be particularly productive.

Economic Costs

The economic costs of inputs of land in urban projects pose even more severe problems of evaluation than do the financial costs. Of theoretical relevance is the opportunity cost: the outputs forgone, net of contractual outgoings, that could be expected from the land in its most likely alternative use. (Distinctions between "the most likely alternative use," "the best alternative use," and "the expected value of the probability distribution of alternative uses" are here ignored.) The difficulties lie in assessing the alternative uses, the net output from that use judged most likely, and the appropriate rate for discounting the future stream of net output.

When deciding the best alternative potential use, expected future restrictions on the use of the land as well as current development plans must be taken into account. In the rapidly changing political, social, and economic conditions of most developing countries, predictions of this type are particularly difficult. In considering the value of output from the alternative use, problems arise in evaluating any externalities, such as the extent to which the alternative use may reduce or increase the value of adjoining properties. Fortunately, the dangers of faulty prediction are narrowed by discounting future output to obtain present value, since output in the near future, which has the main influence on present value, can generally be predicted with more accuracy.

When deciding whether to do a project the economic value of the land to be employed should be based on the predicted value without the project. However, when deciding the amount of land to be used, evaluation of marginal increments should be at their value with the project in operation. (See chapter 2 for more extended treatment of this issue.)

In some circumstances the present market value of the project land will provide a good basis for calculating its opportunity cost. If, however, the market value already capitalizes the expected net output from the proposed project, this value cannot be used when deciding whether to undertake the project. It may be more fruitful, in estimating land value in the next-best alternative use, to look for guidance from the value of similar land elsewhere. Moreover, market values reflect varying tax liabilities and may therefore differ substantially from values based on economic rents. Even where a free market exists, land prices should generally be treated as no more than the starting point for the calculation of economic costs.

If land is nationalized or has an arbitrarily assigned accounting price, the calculation of opportunity costs presents different problems. Widely varying criteria underlie national valuations and priorities for the use of land. The very concept of aliention of land is foreign to some communities. In several countries, such as Tanzania and Zambia, land is nationalized or transferred at a nominal or zero cost. In others, government holdings are so large that they dominate the market for land, and dispositions are often made at zero value or at historic costs which bear little relation to economic values.

The problem then becomes one of estimating the value of net output from the most likely alternative use of the project area, and of choosing a suitable discounting procedure for expressing time preference. When land is transferred at zero cost but a market for property exists, land price can sometimes be estimated as a residual by deducting building and associated costs. Unfortunately, socialist countries do not seem to have made much progress in developing suitable planning prices for land. Planning imperatives rather than output forgone have been generally used as a basis for decisions. For want of any better approach, it may be necessary to use world or local prices to value output from the project land under alternative uses, combined with a discount rate based on estimates of the opportunity cost of capital in the country. Valuations derived from comparable uses elsewhere are problematic, however, since different communities may place dissimilar values on such urban land uses.

In many cases, refinements in the calculation of economic costs are unlikely to influence significantly the outcome of calculations of net present value or cost-benefit ratios of a project on a given site, though these refinements cannot be reasonably excluded for individual projects and sectors that make extensive use of land. As in the case of financial costs, however, variations in the methodology can have important influences on the calculation of relative advantages of locations and the dimensions of the site. Unfortunately, it is rare for an adjustment to be made to market prices for land in calculating economic costs and not exceptional for land costs to be completely neglected in the case of free transfers. The whole subject clearly deserves much more study, particularly with regard to free transfers and to interdependencies such as those between zoning, transport, and land values.

Effect of Project on Land Values

In calculating the economic benefits of the project, both the project site itself and other land affected must be considered. In the main, the other land will be in the immediate vicinity of the project. On occasion, however, effects on more distant land cannot be reasonably ignored; for example, when the choice of a particular site may lower the value of another already in use or being considered for a promising alternative. The extent of more diffuse repercussions on the value of land where development has not occurred and the possibility of zero-sum changes in total urban land values as a result of specific investment are debatable, though possibly these issues are more relevant to developed countries with relatively static urban populations.

In the majority of cases, the change in value of the project site as a result of the project can be ignored in the evaluation of project benefits—though not in the selection of site location and dimension—since the benefits are already accounted for in the evaluation of project-produced outputs. To include increases in the value of project land would involve double counting.

In cases such as site-and-service or industrial estate projects, project output is largely in the form of services provided by the land and structures. Here changes in the value of land—or of the plots plus dwellings or other structures—may be the clearest indication of the minimum valuation to be put on project benefits. More generally, they can be used as a proxy for site-specific benefits not otherwise measurable. Land value changes may also serve in the distribution weighting of benefits. If a facility is relocated, as in some airport projects, it is necessary to take into account the resulting value of the vacated land.

It is usually more important to include among project benefits the effect of the project on the value of surrounding land than its effect on the value of the project site. A sewerage scheme, an urban roadway, or a metro station, for example, may raise local land rental values substantially because of increased services and accessibility. However, double counting must be avoided. If, say, reductions in factor costs and the value of increased net output are reflected in the increased value of surrounding land, both the output benefits, such as reduced transport costs, and the higher land values reflecting such output must not be included. Reductions in off-site land values arising from the project should be treated similarly.

Customary measures of discounted benefits from the output of such projects often do not fully reflect their actual and potential value, as indicated by the increased price of neighboring land. If benefits are, for example, based directly on prices paid for services, some part of the total consumer surplus may be excluded or some categories of beneficiary missed because of difficulties in identifying indirect benefits or their recipients. In airport projects, for example, the project may not only produce benefits in the form of transport services but also induce other, less frequently accounted benefits in industrial and commercial activities in the vicinity of the project. In such cases, the increased values of surrounding land, net of disbenefits in the form of any lowered land values, may be used as proxies for spillover benefits.[3] They may also better indicate the extent to which such benefits reach various households and income groups for purposes of social analysis.

In practice, the effects of urban projects on neighboring land do not

3. The increase in the market value of land may also undervalue total benefits in the form of consumer surplus created; some landholders might be prepared to pay more than the revised market value.

appear to be evaluated adequately nor, indeed, are even rough evaluations generally attempted. One reason for this failure to use changes in land values in assessing benefits is the difficulty of separating increases due to the project from those due to other causes. In addition, the effects will generally be capitalized into the value of the land well in advance of project implementation. These practical difficulties appear to explain why only in fairly extreme cases, such as that of a new metro station or an upgrading scheme, is it at all usual to find a detailed analysis of changes in the value of nearby land. Much more often the surrogate of savings in user costs is preferred, though this too presents serious methodological and practical difficulties.[4] Once again, the subject would appear to warrant much closer study. The difficulties of estimating increases in land values are easily exaggerated. Where there are many real estate brokers, and changes in value are large—so that errors in preproject valuation are of less concern—reasonable estimates are possible and would probably provide more comprehensive and accurate measures of benefits than alternative procedures.

Allocation of Surplus Value of Urban Land

The control of urban land use and the public capture of "unearned" increments in land values—more succinctly, "surplus value"—are closely connected. It is convenient to consider the surplus value issues first, although a full evaluation of alternative approaches must take account of land control. The capture of surplus value may theoretically not alter the total charges paid for the land, and hence the allocative function of the market, but it may do so in many practical circumstances. The level of charges on surplus value and how they are administered may also affect the total supply of urban land. Finally, the overall framework of property and land taxes needs to be considered (see chapter 5).

It is important to clarify which of the several customary definitions of surplus value is to be used. Here it is roughly defined as that part of the increase in urban land values over the period considered that, with allowance for general inflation, is in excess of the increase attributable to capital invested in the land by private holders, including a normal

---

4. Under World Bank auspices, Bahl, Coelen, and Warford (1973) examined the possibility of using changes in rental value as a basis for evaluating the benefits of water supply projects. They concluded that other methods for measuring benefits were to be preferred because of the difficulties of separating changes due to the water project from other influences. Also relevant are World Bank (1974b and 1976).

allowance for holding costs, enterprise, and risks. It may be considered as an increase in annual value, or rent, or as an increase in the corresponding capital value. The capitalized stream of increased values resulting from public projects such as roads and water supply is included gross of any charges made for these services; these charges are considered as one of the instruments for capturing the surplus value created. An alternative definition would include these values net of charges. However, since many services are provided free of charge or charged at rates unrelated to either cost or value, the first definition allows easier comparison with other approaches.

The major sources of such surplus value are public infrastructure projects, the general growth in urban areas and incomes, "artificial" land shortages induced by monopolistic practices or failure to provide services for which a demand exists at the cost of supply, and, for particular plots, private investments made on neighboring plots. Recent international discussions have served to underline the widespread conviction that these surplus values should accrue to the public, since they are produced mainly by public or community efforts and are unearned by the private holders (see, for example, United Nations, 1976).

The extent to which surplus value is captured affects both project preparation and implementation. High urban land prices are often a serious constraint on municipal projects; but the projects themselves may contribute to this high cost if the surplus value created is not captured by the community. If users are not charged for services provided, for example, by urban roads, large benefits may accrue to adjoining land-holders. In such cases, the propriety of supporting the project raises difficult distributional issues. Replicability is also affected since land and property taxes or more specific charges on the betterment produced by the project may determine the extent to which project costs are recovered. The overall growth in urban land value, as cities expand, may increase receipts from general property or land taxes and thus also contribute significantly to municipal finance for projects.

Three broad types of instrument can be used to capture surplus value: charges for services, taxes on land, and public participation in land development. In each case, it is necessary to consider how far the public authorities can preempt surplus value without serious adverse effects on private incentives, on the supply of urban land, and on its allocation and, an often neglected point, without serious inequities between members of the same income group.

Charging for public services is a common way to retrieve part of the surplus value created by some public investment, such as that for water and electricity supply, but not other such as that for primary education. Charges may in principle cover, or be less or more than, the costs of providing access to the services—but in practice charging more is rare. Lump-sum charges for access, though benefiting the cash flow of utility agencies, may prove too heavy for poor groups to bear in a single payment. Partly for this reason, charges for access, or connection, are frequently included in a single tariff that also covers actual use and operating costs. Access charges are rarely related directly to the resulting increase in value of the plots or at all closely to the varying costs of providing services to different sites. When "rates" for water supply and sewage disposal are based on assessments of property value, charges may relate more closely to land values than to the costs of providing the service.

In addition, or alternatively, part of the surplus value (in theory even the whole) may be appropriated by land taxes. The two main types are taxes applied to the value of urban land or property in general and betterment levies or special assessments that are based on increases in the value of land or property judged to be within the zone of influence of individual projects. Although both types are often advocated for their theoretical advantages, there are many practical difficulties. Experience in developing countries, particularly with special assessments, is very limited.

If land taxes and the various forms of charges for access to public service are fully anticipated, their imposition does not inflict arbitrary burdens on current landholders or owners. Their imposition will already have been taken into account in the current market price of the land, and failure to implement the charges would indeed result in windfall gains. Conversely, if the future surplus value has not been anticipated at all, taxes or charges on the surplus value can be announced without causing a reduction in present prices and hence losses to present holders. Such situations are rare, however, and serious problems arise with the introduction of taxes or charges based on flows of surplus value that are already occurring or anticipated. In these cases, strong opposition is to be expected on grounds of unfair treatment and losses to particular groups.

The third group of instruments for the capture of surplus value is the public acquisition of land or development rights. One method often advocated is the public purchase at market value of land to be developed later. In this case, however, payment is in fact made for the present value given to the whole stream of anticipated future surplus value, net of expected taxes, as well as to the current use. Only value sufficiently far in the future or so unanticipated as not to affect present prices is captured by the public authority. The appropriation of anticipated surplus value requires the use of power to pay a "market price" based on similar land that is without benefits from the development project. The outlay and expertise required for large-scale public acquisition, management, or disposal at prices that recoup the surplus value are generally beyond the capacity of public authorities, even in more developed countries. To reduce the financial and administrative burdens, the authorities may instead focus on acquiring relatively small parcels of land, purchasing them close to the time of the development expected to produce large surpluses.

Public purchase of land outside the urban periphery can also avoid some of the costs. Such land may be priced close to its present rural-use value, or may be cheap relative to its future surplus value, because of uncertainty as to the timing and extent of development. Even so, there are likely to be heavy holding costs. Another, theoretically attractive variant is to purchase development rights only, so that the value of current use is excluded. Various Nordic countries have had success in doing this. Although this method is considerably cheaper than outright purchase, it presents greater procedural difficulties, and future surplus value that is already anticipated still has to be paid for.

One way out of the basic dilemma of how to capture surpluses that are already reflected in the price of land is to increase charges or taxes on surplus value gradually over time. Low initial rates and the discounting of future increases will then limit the immediate impact on prices and lessen opposition. Potentially more attractive is to make known that surplus value arising after a certain date will be appropriated. With the usual high discount rates, benefits, say, ten years in the future have so little present value that current market prices would not be much affected. Surplus value currently reflected in market prices would then go to present owners, but surplus value arising further in the future could be captured by public authorities without causing an unanticipated decline in market prices. Numerous modifications of this basic scheme appear possible.

Recovery of the Value of Project Land

When the project agency retains the site acquired for a given project, to what extent should the agency endeavor to recover the cost of the land over the life of the project as part of general cost recovery? Since the land is not destroyed or generally worsened by the project, the recovery of current rental value, or the leasehold value if equated with the life of the project, seems appropriate. In practice, since the land will normally represent only a minor part of total asset value, it seems probable that the choice between methods will not significantly affect cost recovery for the project as a whole, although there may be timing problems.

Other issues regarding ____ ite values arise when the project land is ____ leased to users. It must then be decided whether recovery should be limited to part or all of the costs incurred for land and development, or extended to any additional surplus value created by the project, or whether it should capture the full market value of the site, including any surplus value arising from other influences such as general urban expansion. In principle, the full market value should be captured unless there are specific reasons to the contrary. Otherwise the pressures of demand are likely to mean that much of the surplus will be pocketed by individuals who are in a position to influence the allocation of the land; distortions in design may also result. If the policy has been made clear well in advance, it should minimize inequities between members of similar income groups caused by landholding. Exceptions to the general principle may be warranted when it is possible, as in site-and-service schemes, to ensure that the surplus value benefits disadvantaged or poor groups. Serviced land may be priced differently for different income groups for greater equity. A case can also be made for drawing on surplus value for short-run promotional purposes, as in some tourism projects. In such cases, it will probably still be desirable to recover full project costs eventually, or at least to an extent that makes replication possible.

Capture of Increased Value of Neighboring Land

When the project significantly increases the economic value of land other than that acquired for the project, a different set of considerations prevails. In some public utility projects, for instance, it may be possible to recover total project costs by charges based on the cost of providing individual connections or increased accessibility, by charges on the actual or expected use of the facility, or by various charges on the increase in land values.[5]

Many issues are raised by the choice between different charging systems. Charging by use has much to commend it, but may absolve owners of vacant land from payment even though the land has been provided with services. Whether such cases should be dealt with by, for example, two-part tariffs may depend on the existence of other taxes on vacant serviced land. Special assessments on benefited land, such as the valorization tax of Bogotá, have had some success in taxing surplus value when sufficient care has been taken in devising the formula for assessing gains, which should take account of location and frontage. The costs of providing services as varied as road construction, sewerage, urban

5. For particular aspects of charging, see Bahl, Coelen, and Warford (1973); case studies of urban land taxation and controls in Colombia and Korea by Doebele and Grimes (1977) and William A. Doebele, "Land Readjustment as an Alternative to Taxation for the Recovery of Betterment: The Case of South Korea," in Bahl (1979); ongoing case studies of property taxation and municipal finance in eight cities by Johannes F. Linn and R. W. Bahl; and Bahl (1977).

renewal, parking lots, and preservation of historic areas have been effectively recovered by basing charges on a proportion of the estimated surplus value produced by the projects, even in the poorer quarters of the city. Clearly, the more the created land values exceed the cost of a project, the easier it is to apply a betterment formula for recovery of costs (see Doebele and Grimes, 1977).

There is no conceptual reason such taxes should not be used to capture the full project benefits, insofar as these are reflected in land values, rather than merely the project costs. There are, however, practical difficulties in determining the before-project and after-project values, since both have to be imputed. Unless the tax is fully anticipated, the immediate before-project value is likely to contain an element of the anticipated surplus value, which needs to be eliminated when calculating the surplus. The after-project value on which the betterment charge is levied has to be calculated by estimating the charge that would leave the basic market value unchanged. Nonproject influences should probably be excluded because they would introduce inequities in relation to land not affected by the project. Because of these problems the authorities must usually aim to recoup appreciably less than the full surplus or risk the dangers of overcharging some individuals and deterring development of the land concerned.

Public participation provides other ways of capturing the surplus value of neighboring land arising from the project as well as from socially created nonproject influences. One such method is "excess condemnation" under which land contiguous to the project is purchased at a controlled price, often approximating current use value, and sold or leased at the much higher current use value prevailing after the project has been developed. This is fundamentally the system used for financing the railways and the Tennessee Valley Authority (TVA) in America. If it is known well in advance that the affected land will be acquired at its initial use value, such an approach has much to commend it. Even then, raising sufficient finance to pay for the land may prove an intractable problem in many developing countries. Similarly, proposals for more general acquisition of development land, either by public agencies or in association with private developers, are likely to founder on the initial costs.

A potentially interesting variant is for the authorities to develop basic services on land belonging to a group of private owners; in return, a portion of the developed land is ceded to the government in payment for the public investment in the services. The provision of scarce basic facilities not otherwise available is an inducement to private investors to come into the scheme. This variant, often called land readjustment, has been used with success in Korea and Japan. It has the advantage of limiting the authorities' finanical outlays to the cost of providing services—but the disadvantage of leaving the surplus value of the land in the hands of the landowners. However, there appears no theoretical reason the authorities should not also retain land corresponding in value to a part of the remaining surplus, so long as there is still sufficient incentive for private landowners to enter the scheme. (See chapters 3 and 5 for discussion of these and related approaches.) One danger is the temptation to ration development permission so as to increase the surplus value of land that is acquired by excess condemnation and is subsequently to be released for development. Such practices may result in higher land values and some inefficiency.

General Considerations

Policies to capture surplus value are best considered on at least a municipal level so as to preserve parity of treatment between projects in the same municipality. The extent to which taxes or special assessments on surplus value are suitable for individual projects must also depend on the level of existing taxes on land and property and their impact on different income groups.

Improving the lot of low-income groups and obtaining adequate funding so that public agencies can replicate projects point to the need to capture, within the general tax structure, the surplus value arising from urban expansion. General land taxes can bring in a fairly steady and expanding flow of revenue in contrast to specific betterment levies, which depend on the priorities and timing of specific projects and on special collections. Overall, revenue from land can account for a large proportion of municipal income.

The form of tax liability is also important. Annual charges to capture the flow of benefits as they occur will depress market prices to the extent of the discounted future liabilities to tax. Lower prices may make it easier for those without ready access to credit to acquire dwelling plots. Lump-sum taxes on capital gains that fall on the existing holder will tend to have relatively little effect on subsequent market prices and may in some circumstances increase them. Capital gains taxes collected when the owner dies or sells the property can have other important effects on the timing of the release of land for development.

The accurate assessment of liability presents particular difficulties, not only in calculating changes in valuation, but also in determining which owners or holders have benefited. The effectiveness and acceptability of surplus value taxes may depend on whether there are adequate records so that delays and inequities can be avoided. The need for cadastral surveys and the registration of titles accordingly deserves further emphasis. Fortunately, new methods such as aerial photography and computer techniques of numerical and graphical identification and assessment can be of considerable help.

The complexities of the theoretical issues and the practical problems of implementation and coordination have deterred active consideration of ways of capturing surplus value. Despite the obvious importance of supplementing local tax revenues, almost all public projects in developing countries attempt no more—and often less—than the recovery of direct financial costs. As a rare exception, the full market value is charged for some components to provide funds for lowering charges on others.

Yet the technology now exists to acquire cadastral information much more cheaply than in the past, and innovative techniques, ranging from land readjustment schemes to valorization taxes, could enable administrators to charge land much more fully for publicly provided benefits. Successful experiences need to be publicized, particularly those that are within the administrative capacity of developing countries. The present failure to capture surplus value particularly affects the urban poor, who suffer most from lack of access to public services—services they could afford, given appropriate levels of service and the adequate recovery of unearned surpluses.

Control of Urban Land Use

Of parallel concern is the need to ensure that urban land is used in the general interest of the community. With this objective all communities at all times have imposed some controls on land use; in addition, most cities publicly own or effectively control large tracts of land. One reason for this involvement is that land is needed for public uses, such as roads, hospitals, schools, and open space. (See chapter 4 for the rationale for this widespread intervention.) Regulations are also required for fire prevention, public safety and health, and a modicum of order and efficiency in the extension of public services. Without some standards for land subdivision and building, market forces will often produce patterns of development that increase the cost of providing public services. Such increases in costs cannot be readily related or charged to the individual actions which caused them. Incremental development by individuals, for instance, tends to reinforce monocentric urban patterns and add to congestion; public assembly of land and the concerted development of infrastructure may be needed to stimulate more efficient growth along corridors or in a multicenter pattern.

Because land uses interact, the precise use to which any plot is put affects the locational advantage and hence the value of surrounding plots. Significant differences between private and social interest can occur as a result of these interactions, or externalities, which for practical or political reasons cannot be readily offset by compensating charges.[6] Industrial or commercial use of a plot may increase the value of surrounding plots for similar or complementary productive functions, while lowering the value for residential purposes. The wealthy tend to buy or build homes near others of the same income group, thereby raising the value of land in the neighborhood. Prohibition of commercial use in one area may lower land values in that area but raise values in alternative commercial locations.

Because of these various externalities, the unfettered use of land by the highest bidder may not be considered the most socially advantageous. Indeed, the existence of a market for land does not by itself ensure that the uses selected will be the most economically efficient or the most generally desired—whether on grounds of aesthetics, general urban form, or equity—by future as well as present generations. Limitations on urban land use to avoid unwanted and uncompensated interference with neighboring land or to safeguard historic sites for posterity are common to almost all countries. In the light of the many reasons for public regulation of urban land, it is not surprising that a pure market system of urban development probably does not exist.

General Limitations

The wide variety of control systems reflects the varied development of social systems and ethics. In consequence, what is appropriate and works to the best public advantage in one city generally cannot be transferred with similar results to another city, even within the same country. The importance of the historical and physical context may explain why the fairly comprehensive compendium of land controls in different parts of the world (see in particular U.N. Department of Economic and Social Affairs, 1971 and 1975) has not been matched by evaluations of their effectiveness or explanations for their success or failure.

Nevertheless, both market systems and public controls have serious practical deficiencies. Although uncontrolled market mechanisms permit the development of inefficient urban patterns and antisocial land uses, the suppression of land markets tends to stifle private development and to remove signals that are useful for the efficient allocation of land. Information required for efficient administrative decisions is rarely available, particularly in the rapidly growing and changing towns of developing

6. Theoretically, many but not all of the externalities could be rectified by appropriate private agreements or by taxes. The practical difficulties of arranging covenants and the hardships they impose on present landholders or low-income groups, however, severely limit their potential application.

countries. Also controls may be easily subverted to serve the interest of politically influential groups, thereby producing inefficiencies and inequities. The question thus becomes one of how to limit the deleterious effects of land use controls while preventing, correcting, or offsetting the shortcomings of the market forces.

In choosing among the various instruments, it should be remembered not only that the interaction between market forces and government regulations and activities is complex, but also that the market for land is fragmented. Residential, commercial, and industrial properties are held for a variety of reasons, pose widely differing problems, and are not readily substitutable. The same applies to vacant lots as opposed to those with buildings. Government regulation and intervention serve interrelated and sometimes conflicting objectives, such as the efficient provision of public services, the prevention of adverse externalities, or the achievement of particular urban patterns. To improve a set of controls and regulations account needs to be taken of a wide variety of interactions between the multiplicity of markets, instruments, and aims.

One further, often neglected point deserves emphasis. The efficient implementation of controls on urban land depends not only on institutional capacity and political will, but also on the strength of the countervailing pressures and the account taken of them in the control system. Despite strong legal sanctions and enforcement agencies, for instance, it may not be possible to implement density controls if the population is expanding rapidly but the supply of urbanized land is tightly constrained. Regulatory measures slow the rate at which urban land is supplied and hence increase pressures to subvert them. Conversely, increasing both the overall supply of urbanized land and the supply of particular types in particular locations may create the conditions that make land controls more effective.

The relation between natural locational advantages and planning controls has an important effect on the economic value of land. Some urban locations have clear natural advantages for certain uses as a result of geography and communications networks; for other uses, differences are less pronounced. Where inherent advantages for a given use such as housing are weak, planning and other regulatory controls affecting such uses may readily influence location without great economic consequences. In such cases the designated uses and standards largely determine the relative value of the plots concerned. For other uses, particularly industry and commerce, however, the locational advantages of a particular site arising from communications, inputs, and markets may be much more significant. Planning decisions may then have much greater economic consequences.

In cities in developing countries, where the pressures on land are strong and administrative capacity is low, it is to be expected that strong restrictions on land use will tend to be circumvented. This increases the need to consider packages of controls, taxes, and investment policies and programs that are consistent with the real prospects for implementation and take account of both the long-term and the immediate position.

In this context, two broad categories of controls on land use can be distinguished. The first comprises plans, rules, and regulations that set a framework within which the activities affecting urban land use must take place. The second comprises the actions of public authorities that directly determine land use, such as development by public agencies. These two categories do not automatically strengthen one another. Public agencies often fail to conform to the framework, or else they stimulate changes that accommodate their own projects but are not necessarily in the general public interest. Moreover, even in socialist countries with nationalized land, operational agencies in fact compete for urban land. Such agencies exercise independent and often strong influences on land use in much the same way as do large private developers.

The Framework of Plans and Regulations

A wide variety of planning systems, zoning ordinances, building regulations and bylaws, permits and inspections, fines and other penalties exist in most of the large towns and cities of the developing countries, and some of them even in the smallest (see chapter 6). What they have in common, with rare exceptions, is limited implementation. This is not to say they have no effect on land use, but their impact is frequently very different and much more limited than stipulated. Residual advantages may then be outweighed by direct costs and other disbenefits.

Almost all towns of any size have land use plans, varying from simple maps setting out broad categories of desired land uses to highly detailed master plans which carefully relate land uses and densities to transport and public utility services for some fixed date in the future. Such sophisticated plans are, however, followed even more rarely than in developed countries. Incorrectly estimated growth patterns, political pressures for change, and failure to provide the indicated public services are common causes of this poor record. In view of the dynamic conditions of developing countries and their rapidly changing social structures, it is open to doubt whether the future can, even theoretically, be gauged with sufficient precision to give much meaning to such master plans.

Nevertheless, master plans do generally have both direct and indirect influences, particularly on the location of public investment and the direction of urban expansion. Unfortunately, they may also have serious negative effects, causing delays and unproductive expenditures in the process of securing exceptions or spurious conformity to the plans.

Much the same is true of zoning ordinances and bylaws, which set out densities, uses, building specifications, and plot ratios in greater detail. Such ordinances, often borrowed with little adjustment from already outdated Western models, ignore local conditions and limited administrative capacity, but nevertheless exercise some modifying influence. For example, some open space, if not the ordained total, may be secured in private subdivisions. Unfortunately, the regulations also create serious problems of delay and corruption. The rights to developed land are intrinsically very valuable and the bureaucrats generally poorly paid. Moreover, as noted, compliance with land use regulations is not an automatic consequence of public ownership of land, since it is still necessary to leave much of the detail to the local government and individual initiative.

Perhaps nowhere, however, is the distance between precept and practice greater than in the regulation of materials and construction standards in building codes. These, too, have often been derived from codes in the developed world. They are generally out of date and inappropriate, not taking full account of local materials and, above all, of the standards that can be generally afforded. Though widely ignored, they may nevertheless prove a stumbling block to the adoption of more appropriate standards, not least in publicly financed projects where formal variation from official standards can less readily be condoned.

Fortunately, there are indications of new attitudes toward land use planning and regulation. The older types of master plan are giving way to a more flexible approach relating planning and implementation more closely at the metropolitan or regional level. Institutional reform and the development of integrated decisionmaking and financing of projects are major elements of the new approach. Development budgets and operating expenditure of the main public agencies can then be considered against the background of overall resource constraints and alternative patterns of future urban growth. Urban planning is beginning to become more indicative, or "structural," with greater focus on "critical areas." There is growing recognition that planning is a continuous process, requiring periodic review of actual accomplishments and changing requirements and a pragmatic approach to meeting the multiple objectives with the very limited means available—not least, those for implementation and enforcement.

Direct Intervention by Public Authorities

The most direct public control of urban land use comes from public agencies taking over the task of supplying land for specific purposes, such as roads, schools, hospitals, or parks. Other methods already noted include excess condemnation, land readjustment schemes, and advance purchase for subsequent resale with or without the addition of infrastructure.

Such controls will normally be in line with the desire to capture surplus value, although they may in certain circumstances reduce the collectible amount. Whether acquisition augments or reduces the effective supply of urbanized land depends on how long it takes for acquisition, assembly of sites, and development, how fast and for what purpose the land is released, and the restrictions placed on other suppliers. Although direct public participation in the supply and development of land is potentially the most effective method for its public control, the extent to which this potential can be realized depends on the institutional framework.

Of particular interest is public intervention in the supply of urbanized land for dwellings for the poor. Such intervention may be either negative, as in the all too common example of the demolition of squatter settlements, or positive, as in the acquisition and development of specific areas for site-and-service schemes. The preparation of projects to increase the supply of serviced land for dwellings should take into account the effects of demolitions elsewhere. Difficult choices are nevertheless bound to arise when it appears desirable to eradicate some settlements in the context of overall plans for special development.

More generally, public acquisition of land for controlled uses requires very large financial resources unless limited to a few key sites. Once the land is developed, renting or leasing it rather than selling outright will retain control but will further increase the financial resources required. Few municipal authorities in developing countries have much borrowing potential. Even where government agencies already hold large tracts of urban land, as in India and many countries in Africa, the capacity of local authorities to control land use by this method is limited.

The basic features to be sought in government land development are well expressed by Neutze (1973, p. 3):

(a) land should be purchased without development rights, compulsorily if necessary, and disposed of with those rights specified, and development required within a specified time;

(b) enough resources should be available so that the government can set the price in the market, and supply enough developed land to maintain the price established, and

(c) price should be set to cover acquisition costs and the cost of development.

Such a program can keep the price of new land down by increasing the supply, can remove market stresses on land use planning, and allow the government to cover the cost of local services using revenue from developed land, without the price becoming unacceptably high. After the government has developed the land it can enforce land use controls more readily, "borrow" the cost of some services from private developers, collect a share of postdevelopment land value increments, and organize redevelopment more readily and economically, if it leases development sites rather than selling the freehold. The important characteristics of such leasehold tenure are the conditions attached to the lease and frequent revision of the rent.

A lesser degree of control over private development when used in reinforcement of other measures can be exercised by providing or withholding public utilities and improved access to them. Although public authorities rarely use this power of persuasion, the potential is especially strong at the time trunk-lines are installed for roads, water pipes, sewers, telephones, and electricity and when distribution networks are provided or extended. The surprising lack of conscious use of this power seems attributable to the tendency to provide infrastructure only in response to accumulated strong demands and to the autonomous nature of many public utility agencies.

Other Influences on Urban Land Use

Among government actions, the policies, regulations, and investment in infrastructure that are specifically directed at controlling urban land use do not necessarily have the greatest influence on that use. Urban sprawl in the United States in the 1950s and 1960s, for instance, was probably more heavily influenced by the interstate highway program, developed in part for defense purposes, and the Veterans Administration policies on housing loans to the families of former servicemen (see chapter 7).

In developing countries, too, national programs such as those for intercity transport and communications can profoundly influence both urban extension (which is particularly attracted to the entry points of highways) and the expansion of smaller urban areas along the highways. Such countries as Turkey, Brazil, and Thailand illustrate the strong effects of these programs. Within cities, transport installations such as bridges or subways also tend to produce large changes in land use—regardless of what the land use plans may have indicated. The subway in Mexico City and the Bosphorus bridge in Istanbul provide ready examples.

The impacts of public investments on surrounding land use are all too often largely unforeseen and unplanned. Rarely is there a thorough investigation of the interrelations with existing land use controls outside the project area, even for such obviously important projects as bridges or ports. Complementary measures to support or offset these effects are provided only tardily and therefore at high cost, if at all. Exceptions occur in tourism projects, which sometimes include controls to diminish land speculation and preserve the amenities of surrounding areas, and airport projects, which increasingly take account of approach areas and their implications for future expansion. These are only limited exceptions to the normally narrow project–oriented approach, and it remains the norm for project evaluations to exclude the effects on overall urban patterns.

Clearly, national spatial planning, regional planning, and urban planning should be compatible with government activities that strongly influence urban form directly or indirectly. Yet this compatibility has rarely been achieved even in developed countries. In developing countries the shortage of professional skills and the urgent need to cope with rapid development diminish the practical possibility of such reconciliation.

Reconciliation of Multiple Objectives and Instruments

As is evident from the foregoing discussion, any attempt to provide an overall policy for urban land is faced with a multiplicity of objectives and interacting instruments that influence the allocation and use of land. No clear methodology is available to reconcile them by offering an optimal solution for even a few of the objectives and instruments. Because of the different weights given to the various objectives and differing views on the efficiency and side effects of the major instruments for achieving them, even in the developed world the appropriate mix of urban land policies and instruments remains highly controversial. In the widely varying local conditions of the developing world, where population pressures are so much greater, resources so much smaller, and implementation capacity so much less, the uncertainties surrounding measures to influence or control land use are greatly magnified.

As pointed out in the introduction to this chapter, the commonly stated objectives (an adequate supply of urban land, efficiency and equity, and spatial balance at regional and national levels), though appropriate to the dynamic conditions of towns and cities of developing countries, are generally too vague to have much operative substance. The objectives overlap and interact. The achievement of efficiency in a socioeconomic sense, for instance, implies a relative improvement in the condition of the poor, but equity considerations can conflict with economic efficiency, at least in terms of short–run production costs. In other words, without specificity of target in a given time frame, it is difficult to assess the relevance of the objectives.

In this situation, the fact that the various objectives are linked by the stringent limitations on the resources available in developing countries assumes a particular importance. Indeed, the mobilization of resources becomes, for practical purposes, an objective in itself. Consideration of the overall program of public investment and policies for taxation and charging for services is probably the most effective way to breach the circular interrelation among urban land objectives and bring the discussion down to earth. Even more than in developed countries, the confusion among urban land objectives and instruments and the variety of local conditions needs to be countered by a pragmatic incremental approach, which uses instruments and resources that are relatively quickly available and which emphasizes reasonably clear and specific improvements to manifestly unsatisfactory conditions.

Such a limited approach should, however, be combined with institution building, training, and the development of more appropriate methodologies, instruments, and policy responses, so that more options are available for the ensuing period. An integral and quite feasible part of the program should be to eliminate or drastically simplify existing regulations that are inoperative or obviously inappropriate, and to concentrate on those most effective in restraining incompatible urban developments. As remarked earlier, emphasis on performance rather than detailed technical specification would seem called for in the current conditions in most developing countries. Particular attention should be given to ensuring that low-income households are not excluded from services and housing by standards designed for high-income groups. In many cases separate standards may be appropriate for central business areas, high-income residential areas, and low-income peripheral areas.

A closer look at public holdings of urban land and their management is also necessary when considering the sequential development of individual sites, the interrelations of different sites, public project requirements in both the short and long term, and their total effect on urban structure. The management of public land development is a function that exceeds but encompasses the interests of individual municipal departments, though this is often barely recognized. Authorities frequently ignore the interdependence of different public land sites in working for the general objectives of open space and densities. Keeping records of physical holdings of public land and their possible uses, and relating a structural planning process to holding costs and resource availabilities would further improve the management process. All such activities, as well as the land tax system, could benefit from the development of greater local expertise in land appraisal and valuation than is usually encountered.

With improved regulations, controls, and public land management, the authorities can more readily take account of the tendency for many policy instruments to reinforce or conflict with one another. Charges on surplus value reduce pressures for devious manipulation of land use controls but, if too heavy, may retard private investment in land development. Measures to increase security of tenure tend to conflict with others to adapt urban patterns to the dynamic conditions of very rapid urban expansion. Rent controls to protect the poor may end up as effective subsidies to the middle class. Plans may help formulate objectives more precisely, but also cause delays and increase costs of implementation. National spatial or macroeconomic policies often conflict with what is being attempted at the local level.

In general, land use controls (direct and indirect) can best be approached as related primarily to efficiency, and land taxation and charges as related to greater equity in income and wealth distribution. Instruments of either group, however, need to be considered in relation to their effect on all objectives. Land use controls, for instance, have strong social and political implications that modify distribution, while land taxation can significantly affect both the overall supply of land and its supply for particular uses.

It is unfortunately difficult to assess accurately the major direct, let alone indirect, contributions of the available instruments to meeting the various objectives. In many cases, given the complexity of land tenure and local land market restrictions, it is not even possible to identify the ultimate beneficiaries, let alone their relative shares. The extent to which regulations can be applied is subject to wide margins of error. This does not mean, however, that some indication of the general direction of benefits or disbenefits and some idea of relative magnitudes cannot be derived, but rather that these will inevitably be rough, and the risk of overlooking important side effects will remain. Hence, high priority should be given to monitoring the actual effects of policies, comparing them with predictions, and reviewing progress as a basis for further adaptation of the instruments.

Above all, however, in view of the inherent conflicts in the use of the various instruments, increasing the total quantity of serviced urban land needs continuing emphasis. This is the only way to accommodate the urban population explosion and alleviate the greatest deficiency of both market and state systems: that the allocation of land use tends to favor a small minority distinguished by wealth or influence. With a larger supply of urbanized land, less regulation can have greater success in attaining objectives and limiting any adverse interaction between them.

Despite the difficulties of developing sensible urban land use policies, the rapidity of change in the developing countries provides opportunities that should not be overlooked. On the one hand, the rate of growth of urban populations and consequent need for serviced land make it imperative to do something about the situation. On the other hand, large-scale projects to cope with infrastructure and other services provide a vehicle for introducing new policies and adapting old regulatory instruments. Given the political will and advance preparation, laws and other statutory instruments can probably be more readily changed in most developing countries than in most developed ones. In brief, the developing countries, in their urban affairs, are probably more acclimatized to change than the developed countries.

The policies discussed in this chapter have the potential to bring about a more efficient and equitable use of urban land. The possibilities include:

- Simplifying the existing complex, and in large part unworkable, framework of planning and regulatory controls; it may be possible to do this when large investments are undertaken either publicly or privately, or as a result of separate studies.
- Introducing betterment levies either on urban land in general or on land within the zone of influence of individual projects, so that the benefits of community action may be captured for the community as a whole
- Introducing charges for urban services that relate directly to the cost of providing them and to the benefit to consumers, thus providing incentives for the more efficient use of these services as well as the finance to expand the services to meet demand
- Realizing the objectives of both equity and efficiency from the public acquisition of urban land to help implement investment projects and again capture the surplus value for the community. Variants here include the purchase of development rights only, concentration on strategically placed sites, and excess condemnation of land bordering project land.
- Instituting partnership schemes between government and private landowners, such as land readjustment projects, to help overcome the difficulties of parceling land and to allocate the benefits of improvement more equitably
- Reforming laws and statutory instruments governing the public acquisition of land and the payment and timing of compensation
- Developing cadastral and registration systems for urban land, to help clarify title and provide a suitable tax base.

This list is by no means exhaustive. It does not cover, for instance, the considerable opportunities for influencing spatial development at national, regional, or local urban levels through policies to increase the supply of serviced land. Opportunities for constructive change tend to be greatest when the rate of overall urban expansion is high. The following chapters examine in more detail some of these opportunities.

2

The Value of Land

Alan A. Walters

IT HAS BEEN WIDELY ASSERTED, for instance at the U.N. Habitat Conference of 1976, that rising urban land prices are one of the most serious problems facing developing countries. Moreover, it has often been stated that these prices are "too high" and that they have risen or are rising "too rapidly."

Here I examine these assertions by looking first at how prices might be defined and changes measured. Next it is argued that for decisionmaking the relevant concept is in any case not the price but the opportunity cost of land. I discuss how this might be ascertained for different types of decision and under different institutional conditions. Rents are sometimes useful points of departure, but they are often regulated and, even when market-determined, do not necessarily reflect social values. Capital values, which can also be used, are affected by the same factors as well as by difficulties in assessing the value of future rents and the risk of their loss. Finally, this chapter analyzes some reasons for the allegedly rapid rise in the price of urban land in developing countries, including the effects of administrative and financial restrictions on the supply of urban services and the high rate of return required on risk capital.

The Rise in the Value of Land

The complaint that prices are "too high" is usually made against urban land or land about to be brought into the urban area. Usually there is the joint complaint that prices have risen too rapidly. These are two quite distinct allegations and logically both cannot hold true for all periods of time. If, for example, the rate of increase of land prices were to be always higher than that of all other prices and at present the level were judged too high, then, necessarily at some point in the past the level of land prices must have been too low relative to the level of other prices. To clear the ground, discussion here is restricted to the proposition that land prices have been rising too rapidly. Such a rise is normally considered relative to the rise in the general level of prices. Here the discussion is limited to the contention that land has risen at too fast a rate relative to the rate of inflation, as measured by the general price index or the value added in the domestic economy.

Even with this definition there are difficulties in determining the base from which comparison should be made, because of the specificity of land. Each plot is different. Presumably, the assertion applies to some sort of average plot. But if the city retains the same boundaries and the population is growing, the assertion that average land prices are increasing rapidly is neither surprising nor very interesting. Presumably, therefore, the definition of "average" must cover all the expanding built-up area. Such an average price for the growing urban area cannot be said, by definition, to be increasing at a rapid rate. Clearly the expansion of the city will bring in low-priced land on the periphery, which will modify the increase of price within the existing boundaries.

Asset Price as a Standard

It may also be argued that the general price level is not the best standard of comparison. Since land is an asset, it may be more sensible to use the price of other assets, for the asset holder (the saver) has the choice of holding his wealth in the form of land or in some other form such as bonds or real capital. Each form of asset has an expected rate of return consisting of an income (which may be zero or even negative) and any expected change in its price.[1] Given freedom to purchase land and other assets, there is no reason the expected yields on land should differ substantially from the expected returns on other assets.

If average expectations are justified, the rapid rise in the price of land relative to the price of other assets simply reflects the fact that it has a lower current income than other assets. The more rapid price appreciation, relative to other assets, thus makes up for this lower income flow. In addition, events may turn out quite differently than expected. The land price rise may not have been generally anticipated, in which case the actual return may be higher than elsewhere.[2] But this explanation for

1. See appendix A to this chapter for a formal statement of the relation between the current yield and the capital value of an asset.

2. The reader may find it difficult to credit this proposition, since allegations of rapidly escalating prices of land appear to have always been around.

increases, though it may apply to certain short periods, clearly does apply to the long run; people do learn from history. For instance, the dramatic fall in prices for land and urban real estate generally in 1974–75 brought about near catastrophic losses to many institutions and people. This is likely to have considerably affected expectations. In the long run, the average price of land may not have risen dramatically, although the price in many cities with active land markets may indeed have risen at very rapid rates. Thus the dispersion around the average may be substantial.

Unserviced Land as a Standard

It may be alleged, however, that the increase in the price of urban land should be judged relative to the price of a particular asset, namely, nonurban land. This at least appears to be the implicit presumption in some discussions. It is natural to compare the rate of increase of the average price of urban land with that of agricultural land. The main objection to such a comparison is that urban land usually includes services such as water, sewerage, electricity, and roads, and the value of urban land will reflect the relative scarcities of these facilities. Even if urban land is unserviced, its price will reflect the likelihood of services being installed. It is therefore difficult to ascertain which changes are specific to the land.

The Income (or Wealth) of the Poor as a Standard

A final standard of comparison for the rise of land prices might be the rate of growth of the income or wealth of the poor. Much of the concern expressed at Habitat, for example, about the expense of urban land arises from the supposition that the urban poor cannot afford to buy a plot of land and so are encouraged to squat illegally. This comparison seems, however, to be inappropriate. There is no reason the acquisition of land as an asset should be in their interest. If, as argued above, the rate of return on land is low because of the expectation of a rapid appreciation in price, it may well be in the interest of the poor to hold other, higher-yielding assets.

Perhaps the most useful comparison is, therefore, not between the income of the poor and the price of land but between that income and the escalating rentals of dwellings occupied by the poor. Land is only one input into the provision of shelter, the final service that affects their material standard of living. In assessing the impact of higher land prices on the urban poor, one must assess the extent to which the poor can substitute other things, such as plentiful labor and capital, for land to provide low-cost shelter. Thus a comparison between the price of some standardized equivalent unit of shelter (but not with fixed land input) and the incomes of the poor is the obvious measure of the effect on material well-being. The increase in the price of land will affect this price of shelter, but less than proportionately.

One important element in the cost of land and shelter for the urban poor is the frequently large and fixed transactions costs, consisting of legal fees, registration, and search fees, as well as the ordinary hassle of red tape. Since these do not vary proportionately with the size of the plot, the true market prices for small plots are considerably higher than those reported for large plots. Such transaction costs may be a significant deterrent to subdivision and the development of small-scale shelter.

Statistical Evidence

So far as I can discover, there have been no carefully designed statistical studies of the price of land that would shed light on the various measures discussed above. Nor is this surprising. Even where there are well-developed systems of data collection, as in the United States and western Europe, the difficulties of definition, comparability, and sequencing are daunting. Yet the poor statistical base for statements about escalating land prices has not prevented the widespread propagation of the thesis of the rapid inflation of urban land prices. Proponents have, quite properly, relied on direct observation and experience. Reports of the price at which land changes hands, the experience of the government in acquiring land at "fair market price," and the rapid increase of prices of buildings on certain select sites—all have been adduced as evidence of the speedy progression of land prices (see, for example, Wong, 1975). Such evidence, valuable though it is, must be examined and interpreted with care and reflection; appearances are often deceptive.

First, there is a natural *selectivity* in reports of land prices. Since land prices emerge only when sales take place, the more frequent the sales of particular types of land the more frequent the reports of prices. (Even if the reported "prices" of land are in fact based on assessments or appraisals, these would normally be geared to actual land transactions.) Further, it seems likely that plots for which use has often changed will be on the market more frequently than other sites. Consequently, the evidence from direct observation will tend to be weighted by such change-use prices (which are likely to have a rate of increase higher than that of prices on the average plot).

Second, there is likely to be *reportage* bias. The news media and interested agencies and politicians are likely to select stories of a dramatic increase in the price of land and of massive windfall gains. Stable or gradually increasing prices and small gains are not news and are unlikely to be useful for persuasive argument.

Third, there is the *existence* bias. In some countries land has been nationalized by the government, with or without compensation, and private sales have been declared illegal. Since land cannot be freely bought, there are no observations of its price. "Prices" in the form of capitalized rents may exist in one form or another, but the proscriptions on use make such prices of little or no use for comparative purposes. If, say, the land held by private owners were completely expropriated, its value to them falls to zero and this zero value is the appropriate "price" of land. Such situations in certain countries counterbalance the remarkable price increases of land in countries that have not experienced expropriation or are thought unlikely to do so. There are, of course, many observations of land prices in such free-market countries. Judging the general trend of land prices from countries such as Singapore, Brazil, and Mexico, however, is as misleading as estimating the rate of return on horse-race betting, ex post, only from the odds on the winner. And the greater the risk in investing in land, the higher the rate of return must be on the successful (and widely reported) cases. All these factors suggest that the land prices that have increased more than average are the ones more likely to be reported.

The Opportunity Cost of Land

Rising land prices are only symptoms, they are not themselves the cause of urban problems. The critical attribute of land that distinguishes it from most other resources is that, with minor exceptions, it is nonreproducible and spatially specific. Although land may be extraordinarily valuable in the center of a city, it is impossible to produce more of it; the amount must be taken as given. The only recourse is to make different use of the existing stock of land. Hence the choice of use is of particular importance.

To determine this choice, the value of using the land in different ways must be ascertained. The price of such land is often an unsuitable measure of this value, and it is necessary to look at the underlying concepts. This section examines these concepts in relation to the specific problem of measuring the effects of a large urban investment project.

For most large public projects, such as the construction of highways and housing, land is a necessary input. In the calculation of the consequences of adopting that project, such land should be attributed a cost. The simple principle is that the cost of land so absorbed is the opportunity cost. For an all-or-nothing project, this is defined as the stream of future outputs from the land, gross of taxes but net of contracted inputs, in its most likely (not the most efficient) use without the project. Since this is a stream of future values, each of which is uncertain, one should calculate some function of the likelihoods multiplied by the associated future outputs; but this problem is deferred until a later section.

The opportunity cost is a residual value and can be expressed only in terms of some numeraire such as money.[3] And since the opportunity cost occurs year after year, the money calculation will be dated for each year. Changes in the annual opportunity cost (or net output forgone) reflect variations in the productivity of land owing to changes in preferences, production, and technology, and in the legal and regulatory environment.

The first three items are taken into account in the normal process of predicting the consequences of technology and tastes, characteristic of all forms of economic activity. The only distinguishing feature of land in this context is its longevity—land is, in the main, a nondepletable resource, whereas most other assets run out or wear out in a few years. This longevity, together with the virtual nonreproducibility of land, also partly accounts for the fourth item, since legal and regulatory constraints and changes in such conditions are more important in determining the opportunity cost than in the case of most other assets. Under a regime of private ownership, the law, for example, may prescribe the use to which the land may be put, or more likely proscribe illegal uses. Alternatively, the use of the land may be determined by a central planning authority through the exercise of executive power or by tribal custom and indigenous ritual. And changes in these laws, regulations, or customs can affect the opportunity cost.

This concept of opportunity cost is quite independent of the institutional structure of society. Whether land (or any other asset) is privately or publicly owned, the concept of cost is the same. Of course the actual measure will vary according to the institutional structure since the proscriptions and opportunities will differ. For example, if a planning authority or a tribal taboo specifies that certain tracts of land shall be used exclusively for a single purpose (say, housing) and the quantity of land so designated greatly exceeds the amount actually used in this way, the land used for additional housing will have an opportunity cost near to zero. But the principle of opportunity cost is the same.

3. "Bushel of corn *minus* labor" epitomizes the sort of calculation of the residual opportunity cost required. An alternative to money, commonly suggested in Marxist and socialist societies, would be labor units; thus converting "bushel of corn" into labor units would give the opportunity cost in terms of these units. Then the expression over time would be in terms of labor at different dates in the future.

This example illustrates another common misconception. The opportunity cost is not the net output of the land in the next most efficient use; that is, "efficient" in the normal sense of having the highest net output. Constraints may prevent such an arrangement. One must in fact measure what occurs (or, strictly, what is likely to occur) rather than what might occur under some idealized system. Thus the opportunity cost may change when constraints are varied, even when the most efficient use remains constant, and may similarly vary between different institutional settings.

Which Opportunity Cost for Project Evaluation?

Many large urban projects require considerable land. For example, new port facilities may use many acres. The installation of the facilities normally changes the opportunity cost of land (ignoring, for the time being, the "one-use" planning restrictions referred to above) both on- and off-site. Land which was an unusable swamp, for instance, may become highly productive when a port is constructed on its periphery. Thus there are two opportunity costs of land—one without the project and one with the project completed. Which is the appropriate opportunity cost for the land that is absorbed in the project?

At first sight, the answer seems obvious: clearly it is the without-project opportunity cost. The community is giving up whatever net product the land would have produced in the absence of the project, and this is the opportunity cost of the land for the port. This is the relevant answer to the question, usually the most important one in project evaluation, of whether the project is worthwhile. This is an all-or-nothing question, or possibly simply one of location: whether to erect the port at A or at B. In this case, the port calls for a specific package of investments with specific commitments of land.

But there is a second problem to consider. Whether or not the port is worth building, does it have the right amount of land? Many technologies can be employed in port operation, some of which use a great deal of land whereas others may use little land but rather larger amounts of capital. (A common example is the use of multiple-stacking containers; low versus high-rise housing is another.) The question is how to assign an opportunity cost to land when considering the different port complexes. Clearly the low without-project opportunity cost is not relevant to this decision. The relevant opportunity cost is the high with-project value. Land used up in the port complex would not be available for industry, commerce, or housing—all of which would find it advantageous to locate near the port. In determining the optimal use of land, one should therefore make the port "compete" with other with-project land uses. For this purpose, the productivity of the land as used in the port should be compared with its productivity in industrial and other uses after the port is installed. Note that there will be a difference in the with-project and without-project costs of the port land only if there is some freedom of entry into the port's hinterland.

It may seem paradoxical to require two radically different opportunity costs for the same tract of land. There is, in fact, an essential difference. In the first case, the issue is port or no-port—an all-or-nothing proposition for a lumpy piece of investment. In the second case, the concern is with marginal increments of land to the port complex to adjust, at the margin, between port use and other uses. Thus is the paradox lost.

In principle, one should answer the second question before addressing the first. One should find the most efficient configuration of the port before asking whether it is worthwhile to build a port at all or choosing between possible sites. However, many complicated interactions have to be taken into account when estimating the opportunity cost of land with the port in place. In practice, it is often convenient to reverse the order and first decide whether to build a port. This issue is usually so clear-cut that the appropriate design of the port can be left to later study. Only in a few critical cases will the issue of port or no-port be determined or influenced by such subtleties. The choice of location may, however, be more strongly influenced by design factors.

The port will give rise to substantial increases in the rents of plots that are affected by the new accessibility (and will also generate some reductions in rents of land surrounding superseded port facilities). These increases in land value are undoubtedly part of the benefits of the project and are the mirror image of the decline in transport costs occasioned by the opening of the port (see Walters, 1968, chap. 5). Again, however, in deciding how much land to use for access roads, water reservoirs, or any other land-using project, the appropriate cost is the high with-port value.

Institutional Conditions

So far, all commentary applies to any economy, whatever the form of its institutions. It applies to a communist, centrally planned economy as well as to the capitalist, free enterprise system; it applies to an African society that may not use the concept of the alienation of land as well as to the highly developed landlord-tenant systems in certain Asian cities; it applies to state, communal, or cooperative ownership as well as to private ownership and control. The principle of opportunity cost remains valid whatever the institutional framework. However, because communities differ markedly in the relative importance ascribed to various land uses and the value of the outputs therefrom, the measured opportunity costs will differ. The critical problem is how to estimate such opportunity costs.

SOCIALIST ECONOMIES. For a centrally planned economy, there seems to be no rational alternative to the detailed calculation, year by year, of the potential net outputs either in money or in some other approved standard numeraire, such as labor units. These dated values may then be converted to present values by employing the planning rate of discount for each period. The present values may then be used as accounting prices in the formulation of plans for highways, enterprises, and housing.

The complexity of such calculations is enormous, particularly because, as already noted, opportunity cost is a residual value and thus particularly subject to error. It involves forecasts of land use and of the associated outputs and inputs with their planning values for many years ahead. Even when rigid plans are enforced, they usually do not extend beyond a five-year horizon; and in most socialist economies, there is some flexibility built into the planning process and thus uncertainty about opportunity cost values.

It is not surprising that almost all socialist developing countries make no attempt to calculate the planning price for land. In practice, land is allocated on the grounds of planning imperatives or rules of thumb (and, as such, is a practical application of the political process) rather than on some calculation of its value in alternative uses.

In project analysis in socialist developing countries the best that is likely to be obtained is some estimate of what the land would be used for in the absence of the project. This information can be obtained only by close liaison with the planners both at the central level and in the local political cadres. Following the Little-Mirrlees (1974) or UNIDO guidelines, one would try to value the output forgone at world prices, if there is a world market. For urban projects, however, such a convenient price will probably not exist; conventional domestic prices may be the only ones available, although problems arise when these are not freely determined.

No economy can be characterized as purely a centrally planned social system. Even the most centrally controlled system will have sectors or subsectors in which people negotiate more or less free contracts with one another, thus using some form of price system. Virtually all systems might be described, more appropriately, as mixed economies, although clearly the strength of the market system varies enormously. Economies in which the vast majority of decisions are left to the free interplay of individuals and firms, and only a small element is socialized, might be characterized as the other pure type in a taxonomy: the free-market economy.

FREE-MARKET ECONOMIES. In a free-market economy property rights are well defined. Contracts are freely entered into whereby these rights may be transferred from one person to another, and the state provides a framework of law which recognizes contracts and the right to redress if the contract is violated. In the extreme version of this free-contract system, the owner can employ the land in any activity he likes (provided it is consistent with the law) and is entitled to the residual income therefrom. If the right to this residual is freely sold on the competitive market, and if the period over which this right is to be exercised is also specified in the contract (say, one year), the price of that right will tend to equal the annual opportunity cost. This price is often referred to as the true or economic (annual) rent.

There are two distinctions from the socialist cost-of-land concept: (1) The economic rent emerges from the individual's assessment of the privately most advantageous use of that land. If he miscalculates he pays the costs of his wrong decision, so there is considerable incentive to get it right. (2) The economic rent reflects the highest private assessment of the productivity of land, and this in turn reflects the valuation of labor and other products on the markets.

This economic rent may differ from the opportunity cost because of incorrect individual assessment, as in socialist economies when forecasts turn out to be wrong. But the main complaint against the use of the economic rent as the opportunity cost is that the prices of outputs and inputs that determine the economic rent do not reflect the social values of either resources or outputs. Instead they measure private profit and productivity. The deviations between social values and the values that would emerge in a free market are alleged to be large and significant. Whether they are or not is a matter of fact.[4]

One manifestation of such social costs—urban highway congestion—is particularly important in developing countries. The rental value of plots depends primarily on the land's accessibility by road. The costs of access consist largely of the private expenses incurred by users of urban highways. But unless a congestion levy is exacted from consumers, the private costs of using the road will be considerably less than the true social costs.[5] The value of an accessible location will therefore be less than the true social value. This suggests that the market will considerably underestimate the rental value of accessible urban land, and the greater the congestion the greater is this underestimate. Other social costs, such as noise and air pollution, may be important in certain areas since they involve high transaction costs if externalities are to be offset through private contracts.

Another important cause of the difference between market or eco-

4. See Coase (1961); and Baumol and Oates (1979). The main point that emerges from these studies is that, granted the government allows free contractual arrangements, and abstracting from income distribution effects, there is a marked divergence in surprisingly few cases.

5. See Walters (1968). However, the backward-bending case must be excepted in the argument that follows.

nomic rent and the opportunity cost is that the government may impose differential taxes, subsidies, or controls (such as quota restrictions or rationing). In principle, these measures may indicate what the government deems to be the divergence between private and social cost and so help determine the correct opportunity cost. But in most cases, taxes, restrictions, and rationing serve primarily other goals (such as revenue raising) and take little account of such factors. Similarly, institutional arrangements may inhibit the prices of outputs and inputs into the land-using process from reflecting their opportunity costs. In principle, the opportunity costs for each year could still be calculated from the market transactions by setting shadow prices and following the UNIDO guidelines and Squire and van der Tak (1975). In practice, this involves significant forecasting problems.

So far, the discussion has illuminated reasons for believing that market rents may be less than the true value of land. Perhaps the main reason for supposing that they may be too high is the existence of monopolistic landowners in certain developing countries. A monopolist (or cartelized group) may withhold land from development in order to maintain the rents on existing developed plots. Although in this case the market value is indeed "too high" relative to what it would be in a competitive environment, the market value of this restricted quantity of developed land still represents its true rental value. The landlord obtains the true economic surplus of his plots of land; he also ensures that the supply of such plots is so restricted that he earns a monopoly profit therefrom. But it also follows that the opportunity cost of the (restricted) developed plots is considerably less than the market value. The monopolistic landowner exploits the urban resident.

However, the landowner often does not receive all this economic surplus. Some may be transferred to others, particularly the government. It is useful to have a nomenclature for the extent to which a landlord actually acquires the true economic surplus generated by his property. I call it the appropriation ratio (AR) and define it as:

$$AR = \frac{\text{Net rent received}}{\text{Net surplus generated}}.[6]$$

The appropriation ratio will never knowingly exceed unity (unless there is extortion) and will presumably never be less than zero. The net rent received is therefore the product of the net surplus and the appropriation ratio. This is the actual appropriation ratio that holds for a given year.

6. The size of the surplus is itself a function of the institutional framework and other constraints.

There is correspondingly a series of expected appropriation ratios that are thought to apply in future years, and these obviously play a crucial role in determining capital values.

Capitalization of Surpluses and the Price of Land in a Market Economy

So far, the discussion has been limited to contracts for outputs and land occupancy rights for a specified short period. But owing to the longevity of land the rights may be alienable for much longer, in some legal environments in perpetuity. The value of ownership of stipulated rights in perpetuity—in short, the price of the land—is equal to the estimated present value of the expected future appropriations of rents.[7]

Additional difficulties in determining this capital value include: (1) uncertainties about the net rent to be received, which in turn can be decomposed into uncertainties about the appropriation ratio, the net surplus generated, and any interactions between them; (2) uncertainties about the rate of inflation of the net value added of land compared with the rate of price increase of other "typical" baskets of goods and services; and (3) uncertainties about the rate of interest for various term structures in future years.

Uncertainties about Net Rent

The landowner's net rental income (after tax) may be money income, income in kind, or the imputed income of an owner-occupier and may vary between these over time. In forming expectations of what the income will be in the future, the landowner first estimates what the net surplus generated by the land is likely to be. As in the estimation of opportunity cost, the landowner must take account of changes in technology, the prices of output and inputs into the land-using process, and restrictions on the use to which his land may be put, together with any likely change in those restrictions.

Perhaps more than any other single factor, however, it is the expected changes in the appropriation ratio that affect the level and changes of land prices. Although all assets are subject to some extent to changes in the appropriation ratio—cash held on deposit in numbered Swiss accounts is

---

7. See appendix A to this chapter for a discussion of the relationship between the current yield of an asset and its capital value, and appendix B for analysis of some of the effects that government policies may have on this yield.

probably the only asset that has a 99.9 percent security rating—land is probably more subject than other assets to such changes, even to the extreme of outright expropriation ($AR = 0$). Land is immovable, perpetual, and visible and is more directly subject to the government's control than most other assets. Furthermore, expropriation or high and specific taxation of the landowner has been politically attractive to many governments. Consequently, in countries where the AR is high, one might expect future expropriation ratios to be considerably lower in anticipation of a historical drift toward land reform.

The main conclusion is that the price of land will probably underestimate the true capitalized value of the surplus generated by future uses of the land. The opportunity cost will be higher than the market value, and the markup will depend on estimates of the future AR values. Furthermore, the AR and expected changes therein may interact with the actual use to which the land is put. For example, if the state is expected to nationalize, with low compensation, all undeveloped urban land, the rush to put some buildings on plots will ensure that very little such vacant land is left. One interesting example emerged in Cheung's study (1979) of Hong Kong: rent controls applied to existing, but not new, residences resulted in substantial and wasteful new building and the destruction of many serviceable existing structures.

By affecting the AR the government may reduce the price of land as low as it likes—subject to political and administrative constraints. For example, a 100 percent tax on income, including imputed income, from land in perpetuity will ensure that land is virtually valueless to the private taxpayer. Conversely, ownership of land may be accompanied by tax breaks that amount essentially to subsidies (and so an AR exceeding unity); but probably few cases of this occur in developing countries. In certain developing countries the market price may exceed capitalized opportunity cost because of large land monopolies or cartels, but in the absence of these it is perhaps wise to regard the market price of land as the lower limit of the capitalized opportunity cost.

Uncertainties about Inflation

So far, the assumption has been that the general level of prices does not change and is not expected to change, so that the money value of a contract approximates its real value. If, however, the general level of prices in money terms is expected to rise, the money value of land will rise to reflect the expectation that future surpluses will be worth more and more in terms of money. (In this sense, land is similar to an indexed bond, and the price of land reflects this implicit indexing.) In many countries, the high price of land relative to the value of its current surplus reflects the expectation of high inflation rates and the absence of a supply of other inflation hedges, such as indexed bonds or assets denominated in foreign currency.

Again, however, one must be careful about what else is being held constant in this valuation. Experience suggests that as inflation gets under way the authorities are likely to institute or more rigorously enforce price control and regulation. In the inflationary surge of 1973–74, for example, many developed and developing countries either pursued rent control policies or allowed the rent control legislation to have a more effective bite. And in the great German inflation of 1919–23, by virtue of rent control only 0.4 percent of a family budget was spent on rent (Bresciani-Turroni, 1937). Thus a landowner who proposes to rent his property must also take into account the likelihood and extent of changes in such controls in an inflationary environment.

In principle, all streams of real claims, as distinct from nominal or money claims, will be capitalized in money terms to reflect the increase in prices. In most project work, the analysis is carried out in constant prices, and the capital value must be converted into an inflation-free figure. Various procedures are possible: (1) extrapolating past trends in inflation, choosing a price index as closely related as possible to the asset in question; (2) using the difference between yields on indexed bonds and nominal bonds where these are issued (as in Brazil); and (3) using forecasts for expected short-term inflation and extrapolating accordingly. The uncertainties in all these procedures are considerable. Probably the second method is best, but unfortunately few countries issue indexed bonds or have a free enough market to enable the use of the quotations as indicators of expected rates of inflation. Extrapolation of past trends is the method that must normally be used. But current policies that may modify, arrest, or even reverse the trends of history should also be taken into account, and a large degree of uncertainty is sure to remain.

Uncertainties about Interest Rates

The price of land will reflect the cost of finance (sometimes called the supply price of capital) and expectations about the cost of finance in the future. The cost of finance is closely related to the rate of interest, but in most developing countries institutional or governmental constraints on capital markets create artificial interest rates that do not reflect the true costs of capital. Nevertheless, asset owners may expect substantial changes in these costs, for either institutional or political reasons. (There is no reason to expect this private cost of capital to reflect whatever the government or the planning agency may decide is the appropriate social rate of discount.) Again, if the capital is specified in money terms, the cost will reflect the expected future rate of inflation.

Land Values, Rents, and Taxation

Another factor that affects the relation between rental and capital values is taxation. Taxes on land may be imposed on rental income and on capital value or capital appreciation. When the real rental stream is known with certainty, there is an exact equivalence between a tax on rents and a capital tax. Consider the simple stylized example in which the rent on land becoming serviced increases from $1 to $2, and the capital value increases from $3 to $6. The authorities may impose a tax of $1 on rents for serviced plots, or they may levy a capital tax of $3 at the time the services are installed. In the case of a rental tax, the price of land will continue at $3 even after it is serviced. In the case of the capital tax payable on servicing, the price of land will rise from $3 to $6, and after the tax is paid it will remain at $6 per plot. In both cases the rate of return, after tax, is still 33.3 percent.

Although formally the same in their incidence, the two types of taxes have markedly different effects on capital values: the capital tax induces oscillations in the price of land, which the rental tax avoids. In practice, this may be a crucial difference—for instance, because of the way variations in the cost of finance affect different segments of the population. Lower-income groups may find it difficult to provide the necessary collateral for raising loans, whereas wealthier members of the community tend to have relatively cheap credit readily available. Similarly, it may not be a matter of indifference to the government whether it receives $3 per plot once and for all, or $1 a year in perpetuity. Since the government can usually borrow at a cost lower than the supply price of funds to the private sector, the rental tax may be more valuable to government than the "equivalent" capital levy.

Planning Restrictions in the Free Market

Even in free-market economies such as Hong Kong, there is rarely complete freedom of contract with respect to land and real property. The law (or some extralegal body) may specify the uses to which the land may be put, or it may stipulate that the land must be let to a sitting tenant at a specific rent. Some controls, such as zoning or planning constraints, may be rationalized as maximizing the total net surpluses of assets, including nearby property. But these controls artificially restrict the use of land and create additional scarcity, particularly of land for industrial or residential use as opposed to agricultural use.

It is often claimed that zoning arrangements ensure that the resultant high scarcity value of industrial land, for example, merely reflects the net locational external diseconomies, such as pollution and the visual disamenity of industrial plants, in contrast to the pleasant net external economies of green fields. The higher price that industry pays for its land is then merely a measure of its greater disutilities. Even if these locational disbenefits are correctly measured, however, this argument may neglect the external economies of industry which are not specific to location. These may be particularly important in developing countries. For instance, industrial employment supplies significant external benefits of training both in particular skills and in general. Governments often acknowledge this by their subsidies to industry and training, but may not when determining land use controls. Similar arguments may be advanced in relation to residential zoning.

Moreover, studies of zoning and planning in practice, as distinct from theory, show little, if any, correspondence between the externality rationalization suggested above and the facts of planning.[8] Rarely does the rational calculation of externalities intrude on this form of intervention. It is a political process, and planning issues are normally decided in a political context.

By whatever means and criteria zoning arrangements are made or planning permissions allocated, they do affect the gap between the economic rent and the opportunity cost of land. For instance, the economic rent with restrictive industrial zoning may be very high, but if that land were not employed in industrial pursuits it would be devoted to farming; the opportunity cost is then the net output in agriculture. The appropriate value for purposes of project evaluation is thus the opportunity cost of the net farm surpluses.[9]

There is another, more sophisticated argument for suggesting that the appropriate value is not the opportunity cost in agriculture but is, in fact, the market rent for the scarce industrial plot. To secure the scarce and valuable zoning permissions, people will spend real resources to demonstrate "need" (or meet other planning criteria) up to the point at which the marginal cost of the procedures to secure zoning changes equals the

8. See, for example, the monumental work of Hall and others (1973); and for an alternative approach, Siegan (1972).

9. This assumes it is not possible to demonstrate that the net external costs of industry are equal to the zonal premium. If the externalities can be measured and shown to equal the zonal premium, it will then be appropriate to use the artificially high economic rent for the land.

marginal advantages of zoning so gained.[10] Then the appropriate value for the land in projects is the industrial value, since that tends to measure the opportunity cost in real terms.

This principle of quantity control is very similar—but opposite—to traditional systems of rent control. Rents may be regulated or constrained by law, by extralegal tribunal, or by some customary system of rights. For instance, in many tenure arrangements an implicit acceptance of a status relationship is associated with a certain security of tenure. A low rent may reflect a customary equity held by a *de jure* tenant; he will be in part a *de facto* landlord. The nominal rent is only a fraction of the true opportunity cost of that property, and the latter is the appropriate value for project evaluation. Again, however, the argument in the preceding paragraph may apply. A valuable tenancy will have many people competing for it, and they will use up real resources in the process. Thus, the true economic rent, including these real resources rather than the amount of money changing hands, would be the appropriate opportunity cost (see, for example, Cheung, 1974).

The Effect of Servicing on the Value of Land

It is commonly observed that there is a "shortage" of serviced land in the cities of developing countries. A shortage implies that, at the existing prices, taxes, or service charges levied by the authorities, the demand for services exceeds the supply that the (monopolistic) authorities are willing to make available. But the shortage of serviced land is reflected in the high price that such land will fetch in the open market. This price will exceed the sum of the price of unserviced land and the price of the services.

A shortage of urban services relates to an excess demand for those services at a certain price. A landowner with raw land cannot simply pay the stipulated price and ensure that services be installed. Even when the price charged for the services is above the marginal cost of providing them, if the authorities do not supply services to those who are willing to pay for them, the shortage will persist. And serviced land will still command a premium. The authorities must then have some process of rationing the installation of such services—perhaps a queuing system, but more usually some other administrative measure for deciding the location

10. If there is simply a transfer of money from the applicant to the authority there is no real cost; it is merely a transfer payment to those who dispose of the proprietary rights of the zoning ordinances. But, of course, there would then be a considerable incentive to use real resources to acquire such a profitable sinecure.

of the next servicing investment. But either method of rationing is likely to give rise to considerable external diseconomies, absorbing resources that could be put to more propitious use.

It is, however, more probable that the authorities charge prices considerably below the cost of supplying the services. Underpricing will increase the shortage (and thus the premium on serviced land) for two reasons. First, for a given supply of serviced land, the gap between its value on the market and the price paid for the services will be the greater. Second, the subsidies for servicing will constrain the amount of investment that can be financed. Lack of funds often appears as a rationalization for restricted urban services in developing countries. Yet the subsidization of servicing exacerbates this shortage and enhances the gains from the provision of such facilities.

It might be supposed that there would be a sudden and very steep increase in the price of land with the provision of services. This would be the case only if the proposal were a bolt from the blue, completely unanticipated and unforeseen. But in practice the process of urban development—particularly the provision of services, which often lags far behind—is well anticipated. The date at which land will eventually be serviced is usually known, although not with certainty. The market is also aware that the rental value of the plots will rise dramatically once the services are installed.

In a stable price environment, these prices and rents must be such that the annual rate of return on holding serviced land is equal to the rate of return on unserviced land. Since the landowner gets only a very low rent from the unserviced land, the capital appreciation because of the rise in price of the land about to be serviced must be sufficiently steep to compensate for the lack of any substantial income. After the services have been installed, however, the rental value of the land will rise suddenly and the capital appreciation will cease; the price of serviced land will again be constant.

Consider the stylized situation in which a plot of land has a constant rent of $1 an acre in agricultural use. At a specific time, however, it is known with certainty that services will be installed and the rental value of that plot, net of the payment for services, will rise to $2 an acre. In the stable price environment of this Utopia, the value of $2 an acre is expected to persist in perpetuity.

The capitalization factors for these income streams will be determined by the degree of risk of expropriation and by the rate of return and risk on alternative investments. If the risk of expropriation is the same in agricultural and urban uses, then the capitalization factors will be the same. If they are both 3, so that the rate of return on this investment is 33.33 percent, then the rent and price per acre of this land may be plotted

Figure 2-1. The Effect of Servicing on Land Prices: A Stylized Example

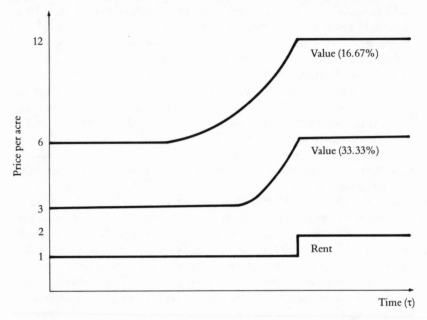

as in figure 2-1, which shows the appropriate path for that rate of return and state of risk. (The relationships are further developed in appendix A to this chapter.) It also shows a path of capital values when the rate of return is 16.67 percent (that is, when the capitalization factor in the steady state is 6).

Several effects of servicing may be seen immediately. First, the value of land must be $3 an acre in the before steady state with a 33.33 percent rate of return and $6 an acre after the services are installed. Second, the anticipation of the increase in rent does not have an appreciable effect on capital values until a few years before the day of conversion (τ) when the capitalization factor is 3. The rate of discount (33.33 percent) of future earnings is so large that the effect on capital values is small until four or five years before the date of conversion. Third, by contrast, the rate of growth of capital values (but not the absolute increment in values) is considerably slower for the 16.67 percent example than for the 33.33 percent one. The general rule is that the higher the risk, the lower the capitalization factor, and the higher the rate of return, the more rapid and sudden is the rate of increase in the price of land.

There is a nice paradox. Any event or policy that reduces the capitalization factor—that is to say, anything that reduces the price of land in relation to its current use or rental value—will make the rate of increase of land price in response to a new use correspondingly steeper and compressed in time.

There are, of course, many other implications. The date of development is not known with certainty. Some asset owners will find it profitable to spend money to acquire knowledge of the plots to be developed. The rate of return from that knowledge is likely to be considerably greater in the lowly capitalized developing countries than in developed countries. The sudden and sharp movement of values enables fortunes to be made quickly from correct knowledge, and this may be one rationalization for the widely expressed need to control land speculation.

A further variation on the general theme may be of some practical interest. It has been assumed, in the example, that the risk in holding land is the same per acre whatever the size of the holding. This is often not true. The likelihood of expropriation or severe limitation on the rights of land may, for example, be much less acute for large landholders with established title than for smallholders and peasants with only customary rights. Once title is established and the element of uncertainty eliminated, the value of the land held by peasants or squatters may shoot up at an accelerated pace.

This analysis helps explain the often rapid rise in the price of raw land that is considered ripe for development. In practice, however, the price may escalate with greater rapidity than this argument can account for, while in other cases there is a lower price increase. This dispersion is often brought about, in part, by uncertainty and an apparent arbitrariness about the provision of services. Buying raw land in the expectation that it will become serviced is often a gamble. The winners enjoy very rapid escalation of price and the losers suffer an erosion of their values.

Conclusions

The basic conclusion of this discussion is that, under free-market conditions, one would expect the price of land to be such that, on average, land earns a rate of return in the long run roughly equal to that on other assets of similar risk and characteristics. Unlike most other assets, however, serviced urban land is limited, often not by the normal rules of the profitability of supply, but by the institutional, administrative, and financial ability of the authorities to install desired services. This shortage is often exacerbated by the convention of fixing prices for such services below the cost of installation and supply. The land supply may be further limited by planning restrictions and various rationing or allocation arrangements deemed in the public interest. Such restrictive mechanisms ensure that any urban land that is marketed commands a much higher price than would occur in a free market, even when spillover effects are taken into account. This may well be the source of much of the concern about the scarcity and high price of urban land.

APPENDIX A. The Relation between Current Yield and the Capital Value of an Asset: A Mathematical Note

First it is necessary to explore the relation between the capital value of an asset and the expected earning stream. Let the value of the asset at time t be $V(t)$, the expected earnings in period t be $y(t)$—this is the net rent— and let the supply or price of capital (in the sense used by Tobin, 1969) be ρ. Then the fundamental relationship of capitalized values is:

$$V(t_0) = \int_{t_0}^{\infty} e^{-\rho(t-t_0)} y(t) \, dt.$$

A well-known solution of the integral, where the earning or rental stream is expected to expand at a constant rate λ, is:

$$V(t_0) = \frac{y(t)_0}{P - \lambda}$$

where $0 < \lambda < \rho$, or in words:

$$\text{Price of a plot} = \frac{\text{Initial rental value}}{\text{Cost of capital} - \text{Rate of growth of rental value}}.$$

If the rental value is not expected to grow, the formula reduces to the normal capitalization equation, where the reciprocal of the cost of capital is the number of years' purchase of the plot.

To avoid misunderstandings, it must be emphasized that all these money measures are in nominal or current magnitudes. Thus the rate of inflation is absorbed into the calculation. Similarly, the supply price of capital (ρ) is the rate of return that the landowners require in order to absorb the existing stock of land into their portfolios. (See appendix B for a discussion of the portfolio effect and its relation to government land policies.) It is closely related to, but not the same as, the long-term interest rate or the marginal efficiency of capital. The interest rate is the price of funds, whereas the marginal efficiency of capital is concerned with the rate of return on a small *increase* in the capital stock. The supply price of capital is, at all times, equal to the rate of return on land.

Differentiating $V(t_0)$ with respect to t_0, we obtain:

$$\frac{dV(t)}{dt} = -y(t) + \rho V(t)$$

where we have switched the notation to describe the limit of the integral as t rather than t_0. Rearranging,

$$\frac{1}{V(t)} \frac{dV(t)}{dt} = - \frac{y(t)}{V(t)} + \rho,$$

or in words:

Rate of change $+$ Current rate $=$ Supply price
of price of plot $\quad$ of return $\quad$ of capital.

The stable-state situation emerges immediately from this equation by writing $dV(t)/dt$ as zero. Then the current rate of return is equal to the supply price of capital.

For developing countries, another extreme case is probably more useful and relevant. Suppose that the current return in agriculture is zero, that is, $y(t) = 0$, but that the value of the land is not zero since it is confidently expected that at some future date the rental value of the land will rise substantially. Then the $V(t)$ must move over time such that:

$$\frac{1}{V(t)} \frac{dV(t)}{dt} = \rho.$$

This is quite consistent with common sense; it says that if no income is currently received from the land, then to induce people to hold it, the capital value must appreciate at the same rate as the supply price of capital.

In interpreting the equations above, one must be careful to note the sequence of events. If it becomes expected that at some future date the rental income from a plot will rise, this will affect both V and dV/dt. With the supply price of capital (ρ) fixed, the *rate* of increase of the price of land will move to exactly the same absolute extent as the current yield; the latter will sink because of the increase in the price of the plot. This follows since:

Rate of change of $=$ Supply price $-$ Current rate
price of plot $\quad$ of capital $\quad$ of return.

Thus, calculating all rates and ratios in annual time units, the result is that, with ρ constant at $1/3$, for example, and no change in price, the last term must also be equal to $1/3$. But suppose that, because of anticipated higher incomes in the future and thus capital appreciation of the plot, the current yield declines to $1/4$. At this capital value (that is, at the 33.33

percent appreciation on the original capital value) the rate of inflation of land prices must be $1/12$ or 8.3 percent:

$$1 dV/V dV = 1/3 - 1/4 = 1/12$$

where $\rho = 1/3$, current rate of return $= 1/4$.

This one-to-one relationship between the current yield and the rate of increase of the price of the plot does depend on the assumption that the supply price of capital is unaffected by the rate of inflation of land or any other prices. The argument for this supposition is that it is determined by the willingness of portfolio holders to absorb the current stock of real assets in the private sector, and land is only a small fraction of total assets.

APPENDIX B. Portfolio and Savings Effects

The stipulation of private proprietary rights in land creates or perpetuates an important asset for the portfolios of the private sector. Policies of governments concerned with either taking over those rights, severely circumscribing them, or eliminating them entirely are bound to have some effect on portfolios, on asset preferences, and on savings and incentives. At one extreme, the government may decide to nationalize the land and issue appropriate compensation in the form of cash made available by the central bank. (I leave aside the case of a corresponding government bond issue, since markets for such long-term government paper are very rare in developing countries.) As the private sector attempts to adjust its portfolio, this would increase the price of the remaining assets, which may be privately held. Furthermore, in the long run, a marked increase in the general price level would ensure that, by the depreciation of the currency, the financial cost of the rationalization program would be borne by holders of cash balances. Clearly such an increase in the price level would have some effect on private savings and also on the disposition of residents to hold domestic financial assets.

In many developing countries, land and real property serve as an acceptable and generally preferred collateral for loans and advances from financial institutions to the nonbank private sector. Severe circumscription of land rights, or the nationalization of land or its threat, without a corresponding type of long-term marketable asset in the hands of the private sector, may severely affect the mobility of capital. In particular, the flow of industrial long-term capital in the private sector may be constrained by the lack of suitable collateral.

3

Concepts of Urban Land Tenure

William A. Doebele

INSTITUTIONS FOR DEFINING THE RIGHTS of ownership and use of land (tenure) have been a concern of every organized human society and have frequently been interwoven with fundamental social structure and religious belief.[1]

In all socioeconomic classes in all countries, land tenure (or its lack) touches deep emotions. It often plays a critical role in the individual's sense of participation in a society, as well as in the investment of labor and capital likely to be made on any land parcel. In most parts of Asia and Latin America, rural and even urban populations see landownership as the basic difference between perpetual dependence and marginality, and between security and some degree of economic independence. Even in western Europe, land has been viewed as a mainly marketed commodity, owned by private individuals, only since the decline of feudalism. In spite of the general spread of European thought and institutions in the colonial period, an enormous variety of views still persists about the nature of land tenure.

Land tenure is a basic instrument of overall development policy, performing both an indirect, facilitating role and a direct and active one. It interacts strongly with other elements of the urban economy, being closely linked to the mortgage market, which takes a substantial proportion of borrowed funds in most countries; it is a major determinant of the local tax base and significantly affects the quality and return of investment undertaken in land and structures. The objectives of urban tenure policy

1. For a much more complete discussion of the nature of property ownership and tenure, see U.N. Department of Economic and Social Affairs (1975), vol. 7, *Global Summary*, particularly sec. C, "Concept of Land-Ownership and Regional Variations."

must, therefore, be viewed within the setting of more general policies concerning urbanization itself.

To discuss all aspects of land tenure in all countries and to evaluate them according to various policy criteria would be an almost impossible task. Here, the attempt is to give only some indication of a possible intellectual framework within which the subject can be fruitfully approached, and to lay out a disciplined and organized way of thinking about this rather unfamiliar subject.

Although there is a considerable and growing literature on urban land use controls and related subjects in both the developed and developing countries, very limited attention has been given to tenure as a specific and independent variable. Not only has there been little study of the economic and social effects to be expected from various tenure arrangements, but even in the case of projects with important tenure components, evaluations have tended to concentrate on other aspects of project design. This chapter will therefore have to proceed from a very thin base of well-documented material.

I first discuss some qualities of land and land tenure that distinguish it from other goods. I then examine certain policy objectives, define the major types of tenure, and examine the advantages and disadvantages of each with respect to these policy objectives. After discussing problem areas related to the effective operation of a given tenure system and the value of large-scale investment projects, I suggest areas where further investigation would be of value.

Some Special Characteristics of Land and Its Tenure

Virtually all societies have recognized the dual nature of land as both a public and private good. It has a public nature in that:

- It is permanent. It cannot—except very marginally—be created or destroyed. Since no generation can consume it, each has a moral duty to use it with a view to those who follow.
- It is one of the three classic elements of all production. In agricultural societies it is the most important source of goods. In urbanized societies relationships are more complex, but productivity still depends on sufficient and appropriate locations.
- Its value, particularly in cities, is created to a considerable degree by the social phenomenon of urbanization.

On the other hand, it has a private nature in that:

- There are deep psychological needs for the security that has traditionally been associated with ownership of land and a house.
- Urban land markets are so complex that even the most centralized

states, such as the Soviet Union and the People's Republic of China, have delegated certain areas of decision about land and its use to local and individual levels.[2]

- In developing countries, reasonable security of ownership (or even possession) has been able to evoke capital investments in housing which notably could not be mobilized by any other institutional device.

One way of stating the problem of determining an optimal system of land tenure may therefore be that it is the task of finding tenure arrangements most capable of reconciling the contradictions between the public and private natures of land.

Differences in Cultural Frames of Reference

A professional trained in the European tradition is likely to think of land tenure as a set of rather tidy categories which, in a specific situation, define a relationship that is reasonably clear and familiar to the parties concerned. These assumptions are by no means valid in many developing countries, which frequently have systems of land tenure that are neither clear nor commonly understood. C. W. Rowling, for many years Nigerian federal adviser on lands, described the traditional land tenure system as one in which rights of individuals

> ramify into those of others, and into fields we may not suspect. Nor will they fit neatly into our own legal categories; indeed, these may be wholly irrelevant. By dealing with him and his rights in isolation we ignore those ramifications, and maybe, set in train changes we neither intend, nor desire, and they will quite probably appear in a seemingly unrelated context. We may also create unnecessary difficulties in the way of changes or controls which we do desire, since we are likely to ignore weapons which lie to hand. The traffic is moreover two-way: while we mistake our methods, he may mistake our intentions and will certainly not apply our ordinances according to the "objects and reasons" we publish.[3]

Confusion of Titles

In addition to this generic problem, the land registration and recording systems of many countries are still primitive or nonexistent. In many

---

2. Pragmatic descriptions of urban land allocation systems in socialist countries are rare. For an interesting account, see Reiner and Wilson (1978).

3. C. W. Rowling, "Land Tenure Supplement," *Journal of African Administration* (October 1952); quoted by Okpala (1977), p. 82; see particularly chap. 2.

parts of Africa, in Indonesia, Iran, and Turkey, for example, it is frequently almost impossible to determine the actual state of the title to a piece of land because it is so clouded with a variety of familial and societal claims. Many of these claims are founded on religious, tribal, customary, or inheritance principles or rights of possession, none of which are recorded in written form relating to the contemporary urban setting. Thus, any project requiring the acquisition or transfer of land may be forced to face the thorny and frustrating problem of equitably and expeditiously clearing title before the substantive program can be effectively addressed.

Tenure as a Legal Status and a State of Mind

Although tenure is generally considered a legal concept, it fundamentally involves the occupant's perception of his security in relation to the investment contemplated. Thus, in Africa, a renewable license to occupy may give enough feeling of security to persuade its holder to make substantial housing investment. In Latin America, a twenty-five or forty-year lease may not be sufficient to elicit a similar response (given general political instability and other factors). With respect to commercial uses, a three-year term for a stall in a market may seem a very long commitment, while a ten-year minimum term may be necessary for activities requiring a simple structure, and a twenty-story office building may demand a very long leasehold or even a freehold tenure. Similar factors apply to industry. Yet in squatter areas in particular, the amount of investment seems to be closely correlated with the perception of risk of removal, irrespective of the technicalities of legal title.

Dynamic Aspects

Another pronounced characteristic of urban land in the cities of developing nations is the dynamism of the forces (government and market) which act upon it: squatters upgrade; low-density residential districts, formerly on the outskirts, find themselves centrally located; once viable commercial streets become clogged with traffic; industries originally safely located on the periphery become major polluters as residents engulf them. Under these conditions flexibility and adaptability are extremely important in any calculation of tradeoffs—more so than in cities in the developed world, in which growth has traditionally been slower. The productivity of land is a matter not only of establishing optimal outputs at the outset, but of having tenure and other arrangements that permit the parcel to be readily adapted to different uses over time. Productivity therefore is a dynamic, not a static, concept, and tenure arrangements must be able to take this into account.

This requirement of adaptability may well conflict with the sense of security required for investment and may elicit compromises such as those used in some site-and-service projects, in which rights of occupation slowly mature into full title. The occupant can then be given a promise of security, based on the performance of certain obligations (such as a specified amount of construction or the maintenance of regular payments for a given time), while the project's management retains a high measure of control.

Fungibility

Another consideration of major importance is that land is a nonfungible commodity.[4] Since one square meter is not the same as another, ensuring an adequate supply of land for all the uses required may be much more complex than ensuring an adequate supply of rice or potatoes. Consideration must be given not only to the market as a whole, but also to the specific characteristics and location of each major parcel, and to the timing and density of its development, all of which affect its productive capacity. These factors are particularly difficult to formulate in the conditions of very rapid growth that prevail in the large cities of developing countries.

Tenure in Relation to the Market and to Land Use Controls

What happens to a given piece of urban land is a product of three basic forces: the market, land use controls, and form of tenure. One definition of policy is that it is the function of finding the optimal balance of these elements in a specific situation.

The first two are discussed in detail in chapters 2 and 6 (see also Grimes, 1976, chap. 4). Of relevance here is that although the market can be highly flexible, it is subject to important limitations, which may tend to make it inefficient. These limitations include:

- Existing buildings are often not easily converted in response to new market pressures.
- Information is imperfect.
- Decisionmakers are often dependent on credit.
- Individual decisions are affected by unpredictable externalities, such as public decision with respect to transportation and infrastructure and the actions of adjoining landowners.

4. "Fungibility" refers to the ability of one thing to be legally substituted for another. One unit of currency is perfectly fungible with another. One bushel of grade A winter wheat is fungible. However, since every piece of land is unique (at least in location), it is generally considered in law and economics as a nonfungible good.

Land use controls may try to solve these problems, but lack of information and slow adjustment still present difficulties. Moreover, the controls themselves tend to be inflexible, are often negative, pose serious enforcement problems, and are hard to individualize to specific sites.

Tenure controls, exercised through deed restrictions or lease provisions, usually have certain advantages over land use controls:

- They are generally more powerful than land use controls since they are based on certain property (or ownership) rights being held by the government. Violation may therefore result in the loss of the property, whereas violations of land use controls normally result only in fines or less dramatic remedies.
- Tenure controls can be individualized, since the ownership retained can be varied in each case, while land use controls normally apply to an entire district.
- Tenure controls permit a wider range of response to policy, since constitutional limitations on land use controls frequently do not apply where the government has legitimately acquired a share of the ownership itself.

There are disadvantages, however:

- To the degree that controls are individualized, administrative complexity is greatly increased.
- Temptations to graft and manipulation are greater, since the negotiations are individualized and hence less subject to public scrutiny.
- Tenure controls can be potentially more stifling to private initiative than land use control systems, which do not interfere with basic ownership rights.

Market, land use, and tenure forms of control can also be differentiated by their different transaction costs, considered below.

The Importance of Moments of Transition

In the typical cycle of land utilization, public intervention is easiest at moments of transition, when the market, land use controls, and tenure options are in a fluid state. The first and most important moment of transition is when agricultural land is transformed into urban land (usually, but not always, signaled by the division and sale of urban-size lots). Normally, this is when the highest single increments in capital value are realized and land use and tenure are likely to be committed for many years to come. At this stage an important problem is whether the agricultural forms of tenure in the outskirts of cities are suitable for conversion to urban uses.

A second significant moment occurs when major urban infrastructure—a water system, sewers, a subway stop, and so on—is installed at or near the property. Market values and potential uses are again open to substantial change, and since the infrastructure is generally the work of some government agency, the possibilities for public intervention are correspondingly high. Another arises when actual building starts; here again major changes in market position occur, land use controls (such as zoning and building codes) are particularly critical, and intense calculations are made as to the possible permanence of occupation (that is, tenure). Other moments may appear when there is reassembly and reallocation of existing land or buildings through the process of redevelopment (including certain kinds of upgrading). Again, the same considerations are involved.

Policy Objectives and Types of Land Tenure

This section considers the policy criteria by which given tenure systems may be judged and then defines these systems. The objectives include efficiency, equity, compatability, and continuity.

Efficiency: Does the system encourage a smoothly functioning land market that permits the maximum productivity of land as a resource;[5] that is responsive to rapid increases in demand, allowing the assembly of land as needed to meet such demand; and that is responsive to major changes in urban form, whether they result from market forces or government policy?

Equity: Does the tenure system provide reasonable access for all groups (particularly those of low income) to land for housing, business, and other needs? And does it enable the government to recapture increments in land value when it is socially desirable to do so?

Compatibility: Does the tenure system integrate well with other policy instruments dealing with economic development and urban land, such as national, provincial, and municipal planning, taxation, and the management of public service systems?

Continuity: Does the tenure system avoid, where possible, abrupt breaks with the cultural and political system which led to existing arrangements?

Of these four criteria, the first two are obviously of a different (and

5. "Productivity" is used here in a nontechnical sense: Does the tenure system facilitate investment in uses and structures which yield the highest total amount of goods available to the society in ways that do not harm the ability of others to make similar use of their land? (See chapter 2 for a further comment on the concept of productivity in this context.)

perhaps more fundamental) character than the others. For simplicity, however, all four will be considered, in sequence, in each case.

Forms of Land Tenure

Internationally, land tenure exists in an enormous range of forms. In Anglo-American law alone, there are easily fifty well-recognized forms of rights over land, and the major legal systems of continental Europe have a similar array. This high degree of flexibility is, however, to some degree related to the commercialization of society, and in many developing countries the options may be far more limited. In Venezuela even recently, leases were limited to five years, although with options to renew (Doebele, 1969, pp. 292-93). In African countries the persistence of tribal traditions often restricts alienability or establishes different market prices for tribal and nontribal purchasers (Okpala, 1977, especially chap. 2). In many British colonies a dual tenure system was established, in which Crown lands (generally the areas of colonial settlement, mines, ports, and the like) were governed by English law, while the territorial reserves (often 80 to 90 percent of the country) continued to be governed by ancient tribal custom. This was frequently unwritten and ill-defined and varied greatly from one tribal area to another.

This mosaic of ownership concepts still exists, even in major urban areas, in many African nations. In Francophone Africa, tribal concepts have been modified by the Napoleonic Code, particularly Article 554, which states that ownership is "the right of absolutely free enjoyment and disposal of objects, provided that they are not in any way contrary to the laws or regulations." This is generally considered to give greater powers of control over land than English law, although it is obviously ambiguous and is differently interpreted in different countries. In the Middle East and parts of Africa influenced by Islam, landownership is defined by concepts codified in the Ottoman Land Law of 1858. This divides landownership into four categories: *mulk* (private), *miri* (state), *musha* (tribal and collective), and *wagf* (charitable and religious). This last category is particularly significant: it comes from the phrase *mawguf lilah* ("stopped" for God) and includes land for libraries, schools, and, on occasion, housing for indigent families. Although some countries (Iraq, Jordan, Lebanon, and Syria) have departments for the review and administration of such lands, the state does not have the power to change their use. This can become a critical problem in urban investment or major public projects such as highways.[6]

6. For a much more complete summary of tenure systems, see U.N. Department of Economic and Social Affairs (1975), paras. 263–325.

Operationally, it is probably most helpful to use the Anglo-American concept: property in land consists of a bundle of rights, which can be distributed in an almost infinite number of ways to different parties. Within this structure a simplified set of tenure categories is examined, which appear most relevant to the needs of developing countries.

Basic Proprietary Categories

NONFORMAL, DE FACTO TENURE. Land occupied and used without permission from its owner—a form of tenure known as "squatting"—represents a high proportion of the residentially occupied area of most major cities in developing countries. Such tenure is of course not recognized in law (although some legislation, such as that in Peru, provides for its easy conversion into legal title under certain circumstances). Its economic value to the squatter depends in large measure on the risk of removal and potential loss of value of any structures, which in turn depends on the political and historical situation of the particular area.[7]

Security of possession varies greatly from country to country and in some cases within a single nation. In some countries, national policy has discouraged all squatting by the most stringent means. In others, policy has been strict with respect to private land, but less so in relation to public property. In still others, policy has wavered or evolved with the passage of time. For instance, in a careful study of the barrios of Caracas, Karst, Schwartz, and Schwartz (1973) observed increasing integration into the formal system. Therefore, although nonformal tenure is treated here as a single proprietary category, it covers a broad range of reality.

PRIVATE FREEHOLD. The most familiar form of tenure is private freehold, in which a private individual or corporation owns outright, and market forces dictate land use and disposition, except to the degree that public controls apply. There may be significant differences between freeholds held clear of debt and those in which the individual or firm has only an equitable interest, that is, a holding subject to a mortgage. In some developing countries a considerable portion of apparently freehold tenure is in fact equitable ownership. In most legal systems the equity owner can do with the property very much as he likes, as long as he does not impair its financial value to the mortgagee; in others the mortgagee may have powers over land use. These systems are, however, beyond the scope of this chapter.

---

7. For an interesting and thorough study of the legal position of squatters in Brazil as of 1967, see Conn (1969).

PRIVATE LEASEHOLD. In private leaseholds a private owner leases to a private individual or firm for a given term of years, possibly with restrictions on certain uses or activities. It includes the so-called rental market and can be applied to all categories of property: residential, commercial, and industrial.

PUBLIC FREEHOLD. Public freehold exists when a government agency is full owner of the land. In an urban context, it generally applies to land directly used by the public, such as parks, roadways, and sites for public buildings. Nationally the government may own vast areas of the country for forestry, conservation, mineral resources, recreation, or other uses. Examples include *baldios* in Latin America and *ejidos* in Mexico, which give clearly defined rights of occupancy and use to small farmers. As urban areas spread, these nationally owned areas, once considered completely rural, may take on great importance for orderly urban development. One problem, therefore, in many countries is to establish institutions that will permit the efficient transfer of such public land into urban areas when appropriate.

Another form of public freehold ownership of some importance is related to the construction of new capital cities, such as Canberra or Brasília, or new towns, as in Great Britain. A public agency may acquire the total site, hold it during major construction, then dispose of it, for example, through public leasehold, to allow further private development. Another example of mixed private-public ownership is the "company town," but it is dying out almost everywhere.

PUBLIC LEASEHOLD. When a public agency owning land leases or rents to a private individual or firm for a specified period of time, the tenure created is called public leasehold. One of the most frequent proposals for tenurial reform is that most developable urban land should be held in this type of tenure. Public agencies may also lease from private owners, but this rarely occurs.

COMMUNAL OWNERSHIP (TRIBAL). Probably the oldest form of land tenure is communal or tribal ownership. Territory controlled by the tribe is considered the personal property not of any firm or family but of the group as a whole, with the tribal chief allocating specific sites for housing and agriculture to individuals and resolving any disputes. With the consolidation of tribes into feudal domains and eventually nation-states, the idea persisted, and the king was seen as the universal landowner, granting specific rights to certain areas in exchange for certain duties. While the concept has changed radically, overtones still remain in the doctrine of expropriation and in modern arguments that all landownership is a type of stewardship, a public trust under which private persons must have due regard to the general rights of society (Bosselman, Collies, and Batta, 1973). This applies particularly when other national resources are involved.

In many African cities, however, a more pressing problem is that tribal traditions have carried over into urban areas, particularly when tribes remain concentrated. In such cases, there are often strong pressures to alienate land only to other members of the tribe, at lower than market prices, and possibly subject to other tribally imposed controls. Although tribal authority tends to erode under urban conditions, these pressures are often too strong to be ignored in the formulation of effective policy, particularly for low-income groups.

COMMUNAL OWNERSHIP (NEIGHBORHOOD). A small but possibly growing phenomenon in developing countries is that of low-income neighborhoods' pooling landownership and giving control over alienability and price to some self-created neighborhood organization. Ethiopia, for instance, has adopted a radical and universal form of collective ownership of all urban land and buildings. Some organizations, such as Barrio Policarpa in Bogotá, have roots in sociological ideology. Others act as a defense against land speculation, particularly when middle-income families buy into more attractive low-income housing areas, possibly displacing the poor. In still other cases, control over tenure and land use have arisen as part of the community-perceived need for a highly unified organization in the face of external threats, especially from government.[8]

Division of Tenure Rights

IN SPACE. Thus far, the discussion has been of basic proprietary categories as applied generally to a given parcel. In urban areas, particularly when there is high-density development, each parcel may be divided into different elements with different rights attached. One example is "horizontal property," or condominium, which gives full ownership of a horizontal portion of a building but shared ownership in the common facilities such as stairs, service systems, and garden. A variation is "air rights," in which ownership is divided by horizontal layers whether or not there is a building at the time of division.[9] The concept of private

8. For an interesting set of case studies, see Magaven, Thomas, and Stewart (1975), pp. 45–111.

9. See Doxiades (1973), especially pp. 25–30, for a definitive discussion of the benefits of the approach.

rights fading into national airspace is now well accepted in all countries. Some governments are also considering the use of a floor area ratio (FAR, that is, the amount of floor area in a building in relation to the area of the site) to specify rights. A FAR of one would be assumed on all land for private purposes; land with higher ratios would be considered as public property, which could be obtained only by some form of purchase.[10] This concept is close to the ideas of development rights transfer now under consideration in the United States and Puerto Rico.

BETWEEN LAND AND ADDED VALUE. An even more important distinction is that between land and improvements, that is, all structures and other changes that increase the original value of the land. In cases of squatting, for example, it is all-important whether, upon removal from the land, the squatter will be compensated for the improvements he has made. If, as in Venezuela, the law is relatively generous, there are incentives to construction in squatter areas (Doebele, 1969, pp. 288-90). If the law is strict, such areas are likely to be dominated by minimal shelter investment. Similarly, in site-and-service projects, it may be possible for the government agency to retain significant rights in the land and infrastructure, once it is firmly established that full market compensation will be paid for all improvements if it becomes necessary to move any of the participating families.

BETWEEN DEVELOPMENT AND USE. Use rights relate to the use to which land and existing structures are currently put. Development rights relate to the benefit from converting land or structures to a more profitable use, greater density, and so on. Use values are present and can be readily capitalized. Development values, however, necessarily deal with the future, and their capital value depends on expected benefits and the rate of discount, both of which may be uncertain. Because the value of development rights (particularly in urban areas) depends on such things as government installation of infrastructure and transportation, on population growth, and the actions of adjacent landowners, it is frequently argued that much of development value is socially created and therefore more legitimately subject to public control or ownership than are existing, accepted use rights.

10. A FAR of one permits a one-story unit covering the entire site, a two-story unit covering 50 percent of the site, or a four-story unit covering 25 percent. For current Brazilian thinking in this field, see, for example, "O Debate do solo criado," *Veja*, April 13, 1977, pp. 73–74.

Small-scale and Large-scale Tenure

The basic law of property rarely makes distinctions between the size of holdings. In real life, however, it may be important, especially in conditions of rapid urbanization. On the one hand, massive amounts of land in the hands of a few owners at the periphery of a city can create oligopolistic powers and excessively high prices. On the other hand, many modern forms of urbanization can be most efficiently carried out when planning and infrastructure are applied to relatively large parcels. The expense and delay of land assembly can be a significant factor in the ability of both the private and public sectors to supply new locations for all uses at the most reasonable prices.[11]

Advantages and Disadvantages of the Main Forms of Tenure

Private ownership of land is neither good nor bad in itself, but only in relation to its actual effects at a given time and under given circumstances. Moreover, tenure is seldom an isolated and independent variable, and many forms of tenure coexist. Thus, it is typically part of a total package of legal strictures and policies about land use and urbanization that collectively have desirable or undesirable effects. Experience shows that certain forms of tenure tend to be associated with policies that lead to certain consequences, but in few cases can the specific role of tenure be fully defined. Nevertheless, tenure does have significant effects, and certain forms are more compatible with particular policy objectives than others. This section therefore deals with those tendencies, not with verities.

Nonformal, De Facto Tenure

PRODUCTIVITY. At a micro level, squatters make remarkably productive use of the land they occupy, frequently bringing into use hillsides and ravines that the formal market has bypassed. As Perlman (1976, chaps. 1 and 2) points out, the favelas of Rio often represent remarkable achievements in low-cost engineering. Without legal tenure, the psychological

---

11. For a good general discussion of this and a review of the small body of literature, see Evers (1975), pp. 117–29, especially p. 129.

security necessary for investment to take place must arise from each individual's calculation of the likelihood that his capital will be destroyed by action of the legal owner. This complex calculation depends on such things as the pattern of police attitudes toward innovation, the size and degree of organization in the neighborhood and hence the possibility of effective resistance, and the length of time the settlement has existed.[12] In these conditions, official action to legalize tenure, as in the barrio of Las Colinas in Bogotá, is likely to initiate a rapid increase in the quality of housing in spite of the inherent difficulties of the site (Solaun, Flinn, and Kronus, 1974, pp. 152-62). The same effect has been noted in another barrio of Bogotá in which secure tenure was given (Nelson, 1969, p. 56). The process of invasion, squatting, provisional shelter, and legalization of tenure followed by increased housing investment does not, however, maximize productivity, since it forces the squatter to endure uncertainty and lowered investment until his perception of security permits a shift of investment strategy.

An institutional system that gave such security from the beginning would encourage more immediate investment and more productive use of land for housing. This implies a system in which the occupants perceive that if they perform in certain reasonable ways, they will not be removed from the site; alternatively, if they are removed, they will receive prompt and equitable compensation for any lost investment. Legally and institutionally, there are many formulations by which this may be achieved. The key element is not tenure in any specific narrow legal sense, but an entire set of expectations. These principles apply not just to housing but also to commercial and industrial activities where expectations concerning removal are uncertain. (See the excellent study with respect to retail commercial activity in Chandigarh, India, by Sarin, 1976, pp. 79-91.)

While nonformal, de facto tenure (with reasonable expectations regarding nonremoval) may be ingeniously productive at the micro level, from the macro perspective it is not the best means of putting land into its "highest and best use" in a rapidly growing urban area. Because low-income people generally require good accessibility to employment, they tend to invade land that has such accessibility. In Ciudad Guauan, Venezuela, in the growth center of Bandar Abbas, Iran, and in similar

---

12. One of the few specific studies of this subject is that by van der Harst (1975), particularly pp. 129–40 and appendix. The study concluded that tax collection, the provision of, or plans for, electricity, main gutters, paved roads, community water taps, and public street sweepers were the most significant "hope-giving" items. In the settlement with these elements, 41 percent of the houses had an assessed life of twenty-five years and 11 percent of fifty years, while almost none of either life span were found in the unauthorized settlements without hope-giving elements.

projects, this pattern has caused serious problems of relocation and resettlement, since it is precisely the land along highways, at intersections, and near existing industrial and commercial centers that is most suited to expanded industrial or commercial uses or other metropolitan activities. The obvious solution is to create areas in which the productive capacity of low-income persons can be maximized, but to locate them where such activity is consistent with an urban or metropolitan plan, and to protect areas with special advantages for commercial, industrial, or other essential uses. Site-and-service and similar projects are based on just this policy. Policies that move low-income persons to peripheral locations, as has been done in Lagos, Santiago de Chile, and Rio de Janeiro, are thus likely to be unsuitable. In short, squatters must be recognized as having special requirements, particularly access to the transportation system, and this should be included in the value of land (see Beier and others, 1975, pp. 40 and 62; and chapter 2 above).

RESPONSIVENESS TO RAPID CHANGE. Almost by definition, squatting is a response to rapid increases in demand, mainly for residential land, that outstrip supply. These market factors may well be exacerbated by government controls that do not themselves adjust adequately to new conditions. Because of its disadvantages to the public authorities and (usually) to the persons concerned, squatting is not a very satisfactory solution. In another sense, however, it may be effective; for many nonformal settlements quickly create rental subunits within individual houses, increasing the total housing stock available, and often catering to even lower-income groups, who otherwise might not have housing at all (Vernaz, 1973, especially p. 104; and Doebele, 1977, pp. 551-64). In this way, initially nonformal areas may in the long run build up to the high densities appropriate to their location.[13] Finally, as already discussed, nonformal settlements are frequently one of the most serious obstacles to changes in urban form, deflecting both the private market and government policy.

EQUITY. In one sense, the phenomenon of nonformal occupation creates greater de facto equity in the allocation of urban land. (Although occasionally middle-income persons are said to engage in invasions, this is not typical.) The direct costs of squatting, however, can be high for the low-income occupiers, for legitimate property owners, for the city's capacity to plan, for potential alternative users of the site, and for the cost of providing services. Where circumstances permit up-grading or regu-

13. See Ward (1976), an important contribution to the controversy as to whether site-and-service projects are wasteful of land and infrastructure because of their initial low densities.

larization of such settlements at reasonable cost, a net gain in equity may be achieved. Ideally, the land allocation system should provide sites for migrants at reasonable prices and with reasonable security, at locations suited to their need for accessibility. This can involve the cost of reduced efficiency, although site-and-service projects may be one way of achieving greater equity while limiting such secondary costs.

COMPATIBILITY AND CONTINUITY. It is obviously difficult to coordinate other public policies with nonformal, unregulated settlements, but it is possible to conceive of plans that designate areas for informal settlements and direct new migrants to them, as in many site-and-service projects (see Grimes, 1976).

The phenomenon of nonformal occupation is a major break in cultural traditions in countries where land has been subject to individual ownership. It is so regarded by squatters, who invade only when they feel all other means of obtaining sites are closed. Elsewhere, especially in Africa, where land has been traditionally regarded as either "free" or a community good, urban squatting does not represent such a break in continuity. At least one study, in Malawi, has shown substantial investment even in the absence of legal title or very clear evidence of government intentions, possibly because of the African tenure traditions (Norwood, 1972, pp. 135-50). Even with this cultural continuity, many practical consequences of squatting remain.

Private Freeholds and Leaseholds

PRODUCTIVITY. In theory, private ownership of urban land should, as with other commodities, lead to highly productive use. This may not occur, however, because of the special characteristics of urban land markets, particularly in developing countries (see chapters 2 and 4; and Grimes, 1976, chap. 2).

The major drawbacks are (1) an inadequate supply of urban infrastructure, (2) semimonopolistic locational advantages, and (3) lack of alternative investment opportunities. These problems do not occur only where there are private freeholds, but private ownership helps intensify the adverse effects of market imperfections.

1. The effective supply of urban land is very inelastic, since at any time only a certain proportion has services (roads, water, sewerage, and so on). Adding to supply requires the joint effort of the owner and of public agencies. In virtually all countries, public agencies lack the financial institutions to assure a rapid and adequate flow of funds to provide new services (or urban infrastructure) at the enormous rates demanded by the flood of migration.

2. Landowners, especially those with large holdings, enjoy a semi-monopolistic position, because land at the edge of the city at any particular moment is unique in its locational advantage and desirability for the next stage of construction.

3. Land prices in many developing countries generally accelerate more rapidly than other prices because of the lack of alternative investments. The market in industrial stocks in such countries is often weak and subject to manipulation. Bank deposits pay rates of interest which may well not keep up with inflation. The value of urban land, however, appears secure. Thus, there is always a ready flow of new capital into urban land. This in turn creates a self-fulfilling prophecy; as more investment capital flows into a limited resource, prices rise, making it more attractive for further investment capital. Such speculative booms are common in history and have often burst. But in most developing countries the flow of migrants has been rapid enough to keep the pressure up.

Arguments can be advanced that the private market's tendency to "hold out" urban land is, in the long run, economically productive and an efficient allocation mechanism. But the intense speculation in developing countries does lead to short-range distortions in land use and construction patterns in contrast to a system in which other forms of investment are more competitive. This is often taken, by commentators (such as Evers) and governments, to imply a less-than-optimal pattern of urban uses and hence lowered productivity.

In this context, Evers (1975, p. 121) concluded after surveying existing studies, particularly of Penang, Malaysia, and Buenos Aires, that there is a distinction between "institutional" land transactions among speculators and "terminal" transactions between the speculator and the ultimate resident. He suggests that the existence of these two markets helps cause overcrowding in city centers, working class slums, and "leapfrog" development and helps price the middle class out of the land market.

RESPONSIVENESS TO CHANGE. The responsiveness of land markets and construction to increased demand is related to the extent to which individual owners have access to credit. Since capital and credit markets in developing countries are frequently limited and imperfect, responsiveness to demand is likely to be impeded. Other institutional factors such as zoning, subdivision regulations, and building codes also make it difficult for the market to respond to new demand, particularly from persons with low incomes. Where pressures are great enough, land is occupied and houses constructed without the necessary permissions, but this, in turn, raises all the issues discussed in the preceding section.

The very permanence of buildings (or a given configuration of infrastructure on a parcel) makes response to rapid shifts in demand difficult. In rapidly growing cities, older areas, particularly near the center, become ill-adapted to current needs. Major changes in urban form generally involve some restructuring of the basic urban services, including transportation. Moreover, the actions of any single individual are often inhibited because, although all would gain from concerted action, it is to the advantage of no one to make the first move.[14] Thus, the private market finds it difficult to react effectively without collaboration from the public sector. As a result, urban redevelopment in almost all countries is carried out by public authorities, often in cooperation with private owners. Furthermore, there is a growing sentiment that, in rapidly changing cities, peripheral land should be developed with a much greater degree of public intervention than now exists in countries in which the private market is dominant.

EQUITY. For historical reasons, private freehold ownership of urban land is a primary source of economic inequity in many developing countries. This is not because freehold is itself either equitable or inequitable, but because present patterns of freehold ownership often block the access of lower-income groups to land. The solution to this problem lies not in the tenure itself, but in the distribution of the landholdings.

One attempt to deal with this problem, while maintaining a system based to a considerable degree on private ownership, was made in India in the Urban Land (Ceiling and Regulation) Act, February 17, 1976. This act limited the quantity of vacant land in cities that could be owned by an individual. Any excess was to be acquired by the state for industrial, commercial, or residential use deemed in the common interest, or held as a reserve. In addition, there were tight controls over the transfer of land remaining in private hands. Evidence suggests, however, that the act has not yet achieved its ends.

One interesting question is whether, when land is being redistributed or subsidized for equity reasons, it should be given to lower-income beneficiaries in freehold form. This implies a loss of government control and hence greater difficulties in future coordination. Economically, granting land in freehold may also appear to deprive the government of the means of participating in future flows from the property. But there are other considerations: (1) Freeholds are seldom paid for outright. Since the selling agency must permit some method of down payment and installment buying, the flows may not be markedly different from those

14. For the classic article on this subject, see Davis and Whinston (1961), pp. 106–17.

from leaseholds, although a point is finally reached when the payments cease. This ending of income flows is offset by the normally lower level of defaults and payments in arrears. (2) Fewer estate management staff are likely to be needed—an important point in developing countries in which trained personnel are scarce. (3) The politics of leasing tend to make it difficult to raise rents when the government is the landlord, no matter what the inflation rate or other objective factors may be. (4) Granting leaseholds at different times creates visible inequities, which have their own political consequences.

If freeholds or leaseholds are distributed on a subsidized basis the costs may limit the program, frustrating larger concepts of equity since a smaller proportion of the needy will be able to share in the benefits. But as mentioned above, freeholds do not by nature require greater subsidies than leaseholds. The significant economic difference is that with full freehold the recipient enjoys greater control over use and income, as well as greater security, and hence may have incentives to undertake more productive uses and greater investment. In contrast, the phenomenon of disinvestment characterizes the terminal years of leaseholds (see Archer, 1974).

It is sometimes argued (for example, by the Australian Commission of Inquiry into Land Tenures, 1973, pp. 57–58) that, since profits from commercial land are the result of the existence of the community, equity would imply that this type of land be held in joint ownership to allow government to share directly in profitability. To the extent that the total system of transportation, land use controls, and the like creates extraordinary commercial opportunities at certain limited locations, a public policy that limits excessive private profits from government activity might support the Australian view. The point is also relevant with respect to industrial uses.

COMPATIBILITY. Since freehold maximizes individual rights of ownership as against public interests, it appears less "manageable" and more difficult to coordinate with other public policies than forms where the public retains a residual property interest. However, a comprehensive system of land use controls coordinated with taxation devices (as in Sweden) can achieve a high degree of compatibility with other policies.[15]

In contrast, leaseholds give the government additional leverage, which improves its position in coordinating private land uses with other public

15. It has been suggested that Swedish capacity to evolve such a system has been related to the very long dominance (until 1976) of the Social Democratic party in national politics (Doebele, 1974).

policy. Rent control, for example, is effective only when a substantial amount of the housing stock is rented. Whether such interventions increase productivity and responsiveness is unclear and greatly debated.

CONTINUITY. In developing countries in which freehold is an understood and traditional form of ownership, its use poses no difficulties. In other developing countries in which tribal forms of landownership are traditional, the shift to freehold concepts has sometimes been resisted, in part because it hinders the development of social unity and participation.[16]

Public Freeholds

PRODUCTIVITY. Full public ownership of land usually occurs in rural areas; in cities it occurs with respect to specific facilities such as parks, roadways, airports, and sites for public buildings. Although it is impossible to generalize, it is assumed here that most such holdings are used with reasonable efficiency.

Government ownership of large amounts of land near the peripheries of cities may cause problems if bureaucratic consent must be obtained before the property can be converted into urban uses. Some places such as Hong Kong have also held considerable portions of the total housing stock in public tenure. The efficiency of both are specialized questions beyond the scope of this chapter.

A form of public ownership that can be important is the advance acquisition of sites for major urban projects. Such action may substantially lower project costs and contribute to productivity. When a project encompasses a whole new city or town, the matter becomes more difficult, involving complex tradeoffs between the cost of wholly new urban locations and the expansion of older areas (see Beier and others, 1975, p. 31). A similar form of public ownership is so-called excess condemnation, the taking of areas adjacent to public projects to recover for the government the resulting "spillover" increments in values and to establish complete control over adjoining uses (see chapter 5).

Where, as in socialist countries, all land is nationalized, problems of productivity may arise because of the lack of a pricing mechanism to determine optimal allocations. This occurred when Great Britain nationalized all development rights to real property in 1947. It may also be a problem in Zambia where all freeholds have been converted into hun-

16. For a critical examination of Peruvian reforms that gave freehold tenure to former squatters, see Rivas (1972), pp. 229–37.

dred-year leaseholds, although structures and improvements remain freely transferable.[17]

In Sweden and the Netherlands, land is often assembled by public agencies, held until determined to be ripe for development, and then put on the private market, either through leasehold or freehold, for actual development. Alternatively, public landownership may be used, as in the Republic of Korea, Taiwan, and Japan, to assemble land, develop it, and sell it for private construction, with the government retaining a part of the land for sale itself, to recoup costs of urban infrastructure. Both systems may be efficient adjuncts to urbanization.[18]

RESPONSIVENESS TO CHANGE. In theory, tenure systems having a high degree of public ownership could be quite responsive to demand. Experience indicates, however, that agencies such as the Lagos Executive Development Board, which was charged with furnishing land for low-income housing and other necessary uses, may be slow moving and relatively inefficient, especially when faced with budgetary uncertainties and the complexities of tribal ownership (Okpala, 1977). If expropriation procedures are involved, responsiveness may be very slow. In contrast, governments with strong administrative capabilities, such as Israel, Singapore, and Hong Kong, have excellent records in responding to new demands.

The theoretical advantages of public ownership must be traded off against bureaucratic disadvantages. In Brasília and Chandigarh, once the grand design was established, it became very difficult to accommodate informal settlements and commercial activities (an integral part of urbanization in these countries). Evidence does therefore suggest that the adaptability of publicly owned lands is limited by the ability of bureaucracy to remain sensitive to changing social and economic needs.

EQUITY. Public landownership is often specifically established to increase the possibilities of more equitable distribution. Again, little literature exists to document whether this occurs, or whether favoritism and corruption offset the effect when public officials manage such valuable assets. Okpala's data indicate that some favoritism operated in the Lagos

17. For a summary of current Zambian law, see Tipple (1976), p. 151. For a more general discussion of the problems of allocating nationalized urban land resources, see Reiner and Wilson (1978).

18. See chaper 5 for a full discussion of both issues. Some cities, however, have had large supplies of land which they have used up without taking full advantage of its potential. This has probably been unproductive. See Grimes (1976), p. 97. For comments on Karachi, see Government of Pakistan (1974), p. 179.

Executive Development Board (1977, chap. 7 and particularly table 7.9, p. 285).

COMPATIBILITY AND CONTINUITY. Again, the literature is thin.[19] In spite of the potential for coordinating a public land agency with overall planning procedures, there have been tendencies, for example, in Lagos and Karachi, for agencies to act independently. This appears to have been less of a problem in Singapore and Hong Kong. Since a high degree of public landownership is not traditional, problems of continuity have also arisen.

Public Leaseholds

PRODUCTIVITY. Granting publicly held leaseholds to private individuals or firms is a widely recommended form of tenure for developing countries.[20] In theory, it should result in high productivity, but there are substantial practical problems.

First, the administration of leases of public land requires a considerable level of sophistication. Where it dominates a private market, that market is lost as a means of establishing the most appropriate use and level of rent. This has been a problem, for example, in Swedish cities. Although proposals have been made for auctioning leases and other devices to restore a market element, the problem is still serious.

Second, the administration of public leases requires a high degree of integrity in the bureaucracy. Since urban land is such a valuable commodity, and particular locations command semimonopolistic prices, the temptations for corruption and favoritism are great. Even in honest administrations, there is a constant temptation to use favorable lease terms as a hidden subsidy to "deserving" groups or individuals. Such policies may be justifiable in social terms, but they impede the ability of government to calibrate its true subsidy system and may lead to inefficiency.

Third, when leases have fixed rents during an inflationary period, the lessee has an incentive to keep the property in its most productive use. When leases are tied to an inflation index, however, problems arise if the lessee's income does not respond perfectly to inflationary pressures. This applies particularly to dwelling leases.

Fourth, the productivity of leaseholds frequently depends on their being of sufficient length to permit the lessees to obtain credit for the

19. For two interesting publications, see Kehoe and others (1976); and Roberts (1977), which includes articles on the experience of six European nations.

20. For a good discussion of its general advantages, see Archer (1974).

construction most appropriate to the site. These periods can be very long. Archer (1974, p. 232), for instance, recommends a range of 60 to 120 years, with a common leasehold of 99 years. Given the growth rate of cities today, such leases are virtually the same as freeholds, unless certain kinds of residual controls are left to the public lessor. The greater the degree of possible public intervention, however, the less attractive the lease may be as collateral. In addition, when leaseholds near the end of their term, their use as collateral becomes less and less acceptable, and the lessee loses the incentive to maintain the property. This has negative effects on productivity in the next lease period.

These arguments are not intended to suggest that public leaseholds are necessarily less productive than other forms of land tenure. They do suggest technical problems in their use, which are frequently glossed over by its proponents.

Possibly the most thorough and balanced discussion of this issue is the Australian Commission of Inquiry into Land Tenures (1973, particularly pp. 49-56). This document suggests that there should be public acquisition of all future development rights in land, administered through a system of development corporations. After a careful examination of leaseholds for residential purposes, the report concludes that substantial gains can be achieved by granting residential lands in fee simple. It suggests, however, that tenure to commercial and industrial enterprises should be in the form of shared leaseholds. Specifically, all such leases would be joint ventures in which the lessor (the government agency) would receive income attributable to its contribution, the land, while the lessee (the commercial enterprise) would receive all income attributable to its buildings. Although the proposal has obvious administrative complexities, it does open up the possibility of a leasehold relationship that optimizes productivity to a greater degree than forms used hitherto.

With respect to site-and-service projects, the Australian arguments suggest that residential tenure may be limited during the construction period (in ways relevant to the cultural context of the project), but in all cases there would be a definable date at which the participant would receive a fee simple title. A joint venture might be considered where there are significant commercial or industrial land uses. Upgrading projects raise more complex issues of tenure but might also benefit from evaluation in these terms.

RESPONSIVENESS TO DEMAND. In theory, public ownership combined with leaseholds can be quite responsive to demand. But the government must be able to increase its total reserve of land to be leased, and to give out leaseholds at a rate appropriate to the new demand. In this context it is striking that the lowest urban land values in Europe are enjoyed by the

Netherlands and Sweden, the two countries in which public agencies furnish the basic supply (Darin-Drabkin, 1976). This effectiveness depends on suitable processes of negotiation and expropriation, which may cause considerable problems in many developing countries. In addition, income received from land distribution must be sufficient to be rolled over into new acquisitions, so that an adequate inventory is constantly available.

Disposal by means of leaseholds can present serious problems of cash flow, since each year's rent is only a small fraction of the total capital likely to be needed to acquire replacement land for the inventory. When a public agency has been in the land acquisition and leasing business long enough and at a large enough scale, the total flow of rents will provide sufficient cash flow. If the public agency is able to pay for new land in installments, the problem is also greatly reduced. Alternatively, a national financial institution can be established to accept leaseholds as security for loans to capitalize new acquisition. For developing countries with little experience, however, such financial institutions might involve considerable risk, as well as administrative overhead.

Sweden has such an institution, but even there more and more municipalities are selling rather than leasing publicly acquired land. In February 1974, only about 20 of Sweden's 278 municipalities regularly used leasing, and about 10 others used it selectively. The trend, except for the largest cities, was toward the sale of public land reserves, in part because of the cash-flow problem.

The cash-flow problem is a different issue from that of the long-run profitability of leasing as opposed to selling. Profit from leasing residential land is almost always limited by political constraints. Commercial or industrial leases, however, may have substantial profitability, particularly if they can be tied directly or indirectly to an inflation index—for example, by making commercial rents a percentage of sales, a device commonly used for North American shopping centers. (See National Association of Home Builders, 1968.)

RESPONSIVENESS TO CHANGES IN URBAN FORM. In theory, the use of leaseholds puts a public authority in an excellent position to adapt to changes in urban form and land use patterns. As leases expire, the property can simply be released to a lessee who agrees to convert to the most appropriate use. In practice, public leaseholds tend to run for sixty years or more. Thus, their rhythm of renewal is far too slow. Although it is difficult to generalize, one may say very roughly that the suitability of many structures and uses in the central parts of cities in developing countries will require major functional adaptations on a cycle closer to twenty than to sixty years.

An even more serious problem is that where sixty-year residential leases have come up for renewal (as they have, for example, in Stockholm), a "lock-in" effect may occur. People's feelings about their houses become so intense that the public authority cannot, for political reasons, radically alter the existing situation, whether or not it has the legal power to do so. Thus, the original 1907 Swedish legislation called for sixty-year leases of residential property and twenty-six to one-hundred-year leases of industrial areas, at the end of which the municipality could, in theory, reclaim the land. In 1953, however, before the original leases were due, the legislation was changed to provide for leaseholds of an unlimited period. The city had the option of terminating at the end of sixty years if the land was needed for another purpose; otherwise the lease was to be renewed automatically for another forty years. Similar terms related to nonresidential land. In 1967 legislation provided that rents (but not use) could be renegotiated more often.[21] The possibilities of intervention for dramatic changes of use in response to demand, even in a generally favorable climate, thus seem quite limited.

Given the difficulties that most developing countries have had in removing squatters, it is unlikely that the expiry of residential leases will, in fact, provide opportunities for costless reallocation of the land concerned. Industrial and commercial uses might be easier to deal with from a political viewpoint, but from an economic one, since they often require more initial investment, they are assumed to need longer terms, and the opportunities for reallocation are correspondingly impractical for several generations.

EQUITY. At the time of the initial distribution of leaseholds, a public authority is in a position to be quite equitable, and indeed to engage in cross-subsidies toward the lower-income groups. Land banking in Sweden, for instance, began as a primitive form of site-and-service provision, organized to divert poor Swedish families from emigrating to the free land in the American Midwest. But even here, as a result of the inflexible form of lease payment, inflation, and the process of exchange over time, the initially equitable distributional effects have been eroded.

More generally, because the public authorities in developing countries often have great difficulty in adjusting rents upward (even to keep up with inflation) and in modifying rent controls (Mexico City being a classic case, only recently partially corrected), the initial equity effects of public leaseholds tend to become locked into place, adversely affecting new entrants. Even where there is the political power to raise rents,

21. Doebele (1974), p. 10, and private communication from Peter Heimburger, Stockholm.

equity problems exist. For example, if the criterion is to keep up with some index of inflation, the adjustment will be fair to lessees whose incomes have also kept pace with inflation, but not to those whose wages lag behind.

COMPATIBILITY. On the one hand, public landownership with leases to private parties permits a high degree of coordination between a government's general development policies and the appropriate use of land. Not only is it possible to allocate the leasehold initially to the party whose plans are most consistent with overall development objectives, but also the terms of the lease can impose restrictions on future use, which can be individualized and fine-tuned to a greater degree than ordinary land use controls.

On the other hand, if the public authority retains too great a power to intervene, the terms may interfere with the ability of the lessee to obtain necessary credit and thus affect investment incentives. There is therefore a tendency for rigidities to increase over time.

Where the public land agency is local, conflicts with national policies can also take place. For example, Roberts has pointed out that in Stockholm, commercial and industrial leasehold terms are used by municipalities to attract industries away from other, perhaps more suitable, areas to improve the municipalities' tax bases (Roberts, 1977). Okpala's work on the operations of the Lagos Executive Development Board also suggests that independent public authorities tend to maximize their own interests and only secondarily consider compatibility with development goals. But these problems also arise under other tenure forms (Okpala, 1977).

CONTINUITY. In countries, such as those in Latin America, in which private ownership of land has strong roots, public ownership and leasing arrangements would be a major break with tradition, although in a few countries agrarian reform has shown the way. In African and Asian nations, where tribal or other forms of public interest in land use allocations are still strong, the shift may be much easier.

Communal Ownership (Tribal)

PRODUCTIVITY. There are few studies of how the tribal form of ownership affects efficiency. A general impression is that it is ill-adapted to urban conditions and possibly results in less dense development than would otherwise occur. To the degree that allocations are made on the basis of family ties and sales are limited to tribal members, an artificial market is created, which sterilizes the area concerned and prevents normal investment and, hence, presumably more productive uses (Okpala, 1977, chap. 4).

RESPONSIVENESS TO DEMAND. Such sites are unlikely to respond to general demand, since allocations are only to tribal members. If there is significant in-migration of tribal members, increased density in the area would presumably be tolerated to accommodate them, just as high residential densities are more acceptable with members of the extended family than with outsiders. Further, since any major change in land use or sale of tribal land requires the consent of the chief, the council, or in some cases the entire membership of the tribal community, it is obviously difficult for tribal areas to respond to urban pressures. Okpala has traced how the attempts of the Lagos Executive Development Board to make changes were repeatedly thwarted by such customs, even though it had extensive powers of expropriation. Tribal organization could expedite neighborhood changes such as upgrading programs, but again experience is very limited.

EQUITY. The tribal system may rank very high in promoting equity within the defined group. Its tradition is one of allocation of land by need rather than by market and usually at below market price to tribal members. Okpala's study, for instance, gives the tribal form high marks on this score (Okpala, 1977, chap. 7).

COMPATIBILITY AND CONTINUITY. Since tribal units represent more or less autonomous governments within the urban fabric, they will impede general coordination of development policy. Where European-based forms of tenure predominate in urban areas, tribal tenure is discontinuous with the commercialized system around it. This must impose costs. But because the tribal system represents continuity for rural migrants to urban areas, government policies that attempt to impose European concepts abruptly (as in the case of Lagos) are likely to encounter serious political and administrative problems (Okpala, 1977, chap. 3).

Communal Ownership (Neighborhood)

PRODUCTIVITY. When land is regarded as communal property, pro-ductivity on the micro scale is probably quite high, for the local council or other informal government is likely to allocate land and structures in a fairly efficient manner in response to the local demand at any moment. Certainly no land will be held off the market for speculative purposes. Such neighborhoods probably have difficulty obtaining credit from conventional sources, and possibly even from government agencies. Total investment may therefore be restricted. This characteristic may be more than offset, however, by the community's ability to mobilize working groups for mutual assistance in housing and, possibly more important, to make building materials available at very low prices. Relatively little is known about such organizations since most are at political odds with the government and not disposed to reveal organizational details to outside investigators. The conclusions in this section are largely drawn from information I obtained in 1974 about the Barrio Policarpa in Bogotá.

Judged in relation to the city at large, productivity in such neighborhoods may be quite low; that is, the land arguably could be put to a more intensive use or could be of greater benefit to the general public. In the case of Barrio Policarpa, one of the major hospitals of Bogotá could be enlarged if the land were available.

RESPONSIVENESS TO DEMAND AND URBAN FORM. To the degree that such communities tend to regard themselves as beleaguered and subject to infiltration, there may be considerable control over new residents. (In Policarpa, for example, in-migrants are required to furnish two references from persons known to the governing body.) This limits responsiveness to increased demand, although, once newcomers are accepted, the community will undoubtedly use its resources to help them construct minimal housing. At the macro level, such communities are probably not as responsive to new demands as are neighborhoods in which the market operates. Studies of communities such as Villa el Salvador, just south of Lima, Peru, might be useful in discovering if they can operate on a relatively open basis.[22] As political enclaves, operating outside the commercial market, they are unlikely to be responsive to change in urban form, whether arising from government policy or market pressures. In principle, however, the approach might help in projects such as upgrading.

EQUITY. For the low-income persons directly involved, the communal tenure system might well be one of the most equitable in terms of allocation by need rather than financial position (although documentation is thin). It may, via political pressures, also indirectly promote equitable government policies, but such effects are likely to be slight because of the insignificant number of such communal systems.

---

22. For an excellent discussion of the Peruvian experience in the form of a longitudinal study, including some aspects of Villa el Salvador, see Collier (1976).

A more politically acceptable but limited approach to communal ownership exists in many developed countries in the form of condominiums or joint ownership of residential projects by tenants. These apply mainly to middle-class developments. The Banco Nacional de Obras y Servicios Publicos (BANOBRAS) in Mexico runs a modified version, by which even very large moderate-income housing projects are held in trust, to which the participants are beneficiaries. Although this limited form of communal ownership confers few rights during the term of the mortgages (fifteen years), it gives the participants a sort of joint ownership at the end of that period and appears to be working reasonably well (see BANOBRAS, 1969, pp. 69-70, and other volumes in the series).

COMPATIBILITY AND CONTINUITY. Where neighborhood communes are fiercely defending their independence, they are unlikely to fit easily into the overall framework of economic, social, or physical planning. Moreover, they have little continuity with existing institutions. Where this form is regarded as desirable, the legal system probably has some kind of common tenure that could be adapted with high continuity to existing institutions.

Division of Tenure Rights between Development and Use

As outlined above, use rights have to do with the value of land or structures in its present use, while development rights have to do with potential future uses. These concepts are of great policy interest. Future (generally more intensive or profitable) uses are normally made possible by the operation, singly or in combination, of four factors: government action, such as the installation of services, extension of transportation lines, change of zoning, or other land use control mechanisms (see chapter 6); the general growth of urban population, which increases the locational advantages of existing sites; the actions of adjacent owners; and the entrepreneurial efforts of the owners themselves. As development value is fundamentally a result of the first two factors, with the last two merely responses to them, many argue that development rights should be the property of the state.

This proposition was legislated in Britain in the Town and Country Planning Act of 1947, and a highly modified form has been suggested for Australia. Under such systems the use value of the property remains in private hands, but the government acquires all rights to develop. In practice, individuals who wish to develop their land further must obtain a license to do so in line with public interest (as in most countries) but must also purchase the development values from the government. Otherwise, it is argued, development values represent windfall profits to the owner. Further, since development values often arise from some sort of government expenditure, charges for such rights will offset costs and be borne by the individual whose property is benefited rather than by the general taxpayer.[23]

PRODUCTIVITY. Productivity can be seriously impaired if government ownership of development rights reduces or eliminates the entrepreneurial profit in land development and thus sharply limits the incentives for development; or if it interposes a major and discretionary bureaucratic decision into an otherwise direct and private process. Both elements occurred in Britain from 1947 to 1952 when the system was in effect. This can be explained in part by a belief that the system was likely to be short-lived. Similar effects have not been observed to such a degree since the reintroduction in 1975, in a much modified form, of a tax on development values.

To achieve productivity when development rights are vested in the government, it would probably be necessary to permit property owners to share in some portion of the development values (current legislation in Britain takes up to 60 percent of the development value in tax). It would also be necessary to have a highly efficient public decisionmaking process that decides whether to permit development and that sets a price on the development value being transferred. This is hard enough when price can be observed in an external market, but as time passes and all development values are set by public administrators, the system may become more and more arbitrary (Reiner and Wilson, 1978). In Israel where the state owns and markets most urban land, a tendency to use fixed prices has given Tel Aviv a much more uniform density pattern than would be expected from a market situation. In contrast, private land has been developed to very high densities.[24]

Another solution may be to auction rights, although the market may be limited. An alternative proposed in Australia and used for a short period in the late 1970s in Britain would be for the development authority to assemble land at use value and sell it to private persons for improvement at the current development value. In this case, the market is likely to be less thin, although monopolistic problems may remain.

A related problem is that giving administrators broad powers to establish the price of development rights, in a commodity as valuable as urban land, is an invitation to favoritism and corruption. Auctions and

23. For a clear and comprehensive discussion, see Australian Commission (1973), pp. 1–25.

24. Lecture by Morris Hill, Harvard Graduate School of Design, April 10, 1975.

other methods of publicizing and ventilating the procedures may ameliorate but not eliminate this problem.

RESPONSIVENESS TO DEMAND. Public control of development rights could eliminate the "holdout" effects now widely believed to increase the price of urban land in developing countries. A reasonably informed public authority could simply release development rights as demand increased, possibly even cross-subsidizing the low-income segment of such demand. Property owners may well be reluctant to participate, however, especially if they get no development bonus. The alternative is forced land assembly (or the option of cooperation or expropriation, which is politically and mechanically difficult in most countries).

The public sale of development rights, if conducted at market value, does not, of course, reduce final prices, since the private developer who buys the land at use value from its owner and pays the public authority for its development value will obviously pass on both costs to the consumer. The final price may even be higher because of the additional administrative costs. There can, however, be offsetting increased efficiency from the assembly of the land by the public authority.

In the Australian plan, although the final tenure in residential developments will be freehold, in commercial and industrial areas there will be leaseholds by which profits attributable to the land will go to the government and those arising from private investment on that land go to the entrepreneur. Although this formula is of considerable interest, one can readily see many problems in applying it, especially in valuing private entrepreneurial skills. Moreover, the limitation on profits might make the commercial sector less responsive under this system.

CHANGES IN URBAN FORM. Public control of development rights would, in theory, constitute an excellent method of controlling urban form in response to new needs. Its effectiveness would depend on the administrative efficiency of the government authorities concerned and on their ability to keep themselves informed and flexible—characteristics not always dominant in bureaucracies. Once development rights have been allocated for long terms (as would be necessary to ensure investment), responsiveness to change would, however, be seriously diminished.

EQUITY. Public ownership of development rights could lead to cross-subsidies that reduce land prices for projects for low-income groups. In addition, public housing agencies in developing countries commonly undervalue land costs to provide a hidden subsidy when calculating the charges to be levied in such projects.

COMPATIBILITY AND CONTINUITY. One of the great advantages of public control of all development rights is that it permits close coordination with economic, social, and physical planning, if linkages are reasonably good between the planning bodies and the public agencies holding the development rights. Again, this effect is limited to original allocations, although these can be spread over time. Public control also represents less of a break with tradition than full public ownership and is therefore likely to be easier to implement. Furthermore, it is perfectly consistent with the general socialist outlook in many developing countries. But since development value is often the largest proportion of total value of land, taking it into public ownership is unlikely to be politically easy, at least in nonsocialist countries.

Policy Objectives Measured against Tenure Form

The preceding section has laid out in some detail the advantages and disadvantages of each form of tenure in relation to policy objectives. Here the major points are summarized in the converse fashion: the extent to which policy objectives are met by the various tenure forms.

Productivity

In micro terms informal, de facto tenure ranks high in productivity, since squatters frequently make use of land passed over by the market and, within financial and technological constraints, make maximum use of every resource invested. On the urban scale, however, informal settlements may block attempts to use the land in more productive ways.

Under the assumptions of classical economics, private freeholds provide incentives to productivity. Imperfections in the land market, however, especially in the rapidly growing cities of developing countries, may distort such responses. The result is wasteful patterns of land use, particularly when strong speculative pressures are created by lack of alternative investment opportunities.

Public ownership can in principle be as productive as private, but productivity is highly dependent on the efficiency and financing of the agency concerned. These characteristics vary considerably from one country to another. Similar difficulties arise with public leaseholds. Moreover, long-term leases may reduce the incentive to improve productivity, particularly where there is continued inflation, and may adversely affect the capacity to obtain credit as the term shortens, causing disinvestment near the end of the leasehold term. The division of ownership between development and use rights also injects more actors into the decisionmaking process and is heavily dependent on the administrative capability of the government agencies involved.

Tribal-communal ownerships appear less interested in the conventional economic definition of "highest and best use" and, in an urban context, may therefore be less productive. There is little evidence on neighborhood communal tenures, which have some of the same attributes as tribal tenure but, like nonformal settlements, may also use resources efficiently.

Responsiveness to Rapid Increases in Demand

Nonformal, de facto tenure is a typical means of meeting increased low-income residential demand in developing countries and often has a high capacity to produce rental subunits (usually rooms), which may be an important addition to overall low-income housing supply. But its provision is not generally optimal to either the squatters or the public authorities.

Responsiveness of private freeholds and leaseholds is dependent on the degree of market imperfection. In addition, land use controls may reduce responsiveness, limiting construction, especially of low-income housing and, at times, of commercial and industrial buildings as well. The effectiveness of public freeholds and leaseholds depends on strong administration, adequate and dependable financing, and strong powers of expropriation.

Tribal-communal ownership is, almost by definition, unlikely to be responsive to nontribal demand, but is presumably responsive to tribal-specific demand. Neighborhood-communal ownership can hardly be judged. Nor is there enough evidence to assess the division of development and use rights, where the increased ability to assemble land may improve efficiency, but the administrative costs of inflexibility are likely to be high.

Responsiveness to Changes in Urban Form

Settlements with informal tenure are themselves responses to changes in urban form, in the sense that new infrastructure will often trigger new settlements. Established squatter settlements, however, are capable of deflecting market forces, and in some cases government itself, from changes that would otherwise occur. Similarly, both tribal and neighborhood-communal forms of ownership are likely to be resistant to changes in urban form, although for different reasons.

The private market often has difficulty adapting to major changes in urban form because of the existence of buildings, problems of land assembly, and dependence on coordinated public infrastructure investment (although on occasion it can respond, as when a private owner demolishes a low-rise building in a central district to erect a high one). For these reasons urban redevelopment in most countries is attempted through public authorities, usually working in cooperation with the private sector. Public freeholds are in theory less subject to these constraints, but experience in such publicly created cities as Brasília, Chandigarh, and Islamabad indicates that commitment to a rigid planning design may seriously inhibit responsiveness. Public leaseholds are often subject to lock-in effects, since long leases are usual for all types of land use. Strong political pressures may also hinder administrative response, especially in residential areas. Similarly, split development and use rights should permit flexibility in initial allocation, but once rights are allocated, lock-in effects again occur.

Equity

Informal, de facto tenure is, by nature, a reallocation of resources toward the lower end of the income spectrum. It has, however, high indirect costs for occupiers, property owners, and public authorities. Alternatives that reallocate without such costs are obviously preferable. (Site-and-service projects are one, but not the only, possibility.) Tribal-communal and neighborhood-communal tenures similarly should have favorable equity effects toward the tribe or neighborhood, and possibly within the group, but again these may hurt the urban population at large.

Private freeholds and leaseholds could in theory be either equitable or inequitable, but the present reality of most developing countries is that they constitute major sources of inequalities in both economic and political power. The equity effects of land held in public freehold must depend on the integrity of the authority administering it. In the case of public leaseholds, even exemplary civil servants (such as those in Sweden) have great difficulty in maintaining equity over time and in resisting political pressures. Similar problems arise from public ownership of development rights, which would, in theory, make cross-subsidies possible to increase equity.

Compatibility with Other Policy Instruments

A fundamental characteristic of informal, de facto tenure is that it is outside existing legal and institutional norms and thus at odds with other policy instruments. (Whether the institutions causing such illegality are reasonable and necessary is, of course, a separate question.) A fundamental task in many countries may be to find methods for making such informal processes more compatible with other institutions and policy instruments. Similarly, both tribal and neighborhood organizations tend to be independent political or semipolitical entities outside the formal structure of government organization, so that compatibility of their policies with national or municipal ones may be a problem.

With private freeholds and leaseholds, compatibility may be restricted because of legal or constitutional limits on public regulation. Yet countries such as Sweden have been able to exercise a very high degree of coordinated public control over property still technically in private ownership. Whether this is possible in countries that do not have Sweden's exceptional political stability must be considered an open question. Public leaseholds allow, in theory, additional coordination at the time the original leases are given, but may be difficult to adapt to changes in policy. The same problem applies to public ownership of development rights. Finally, the ability of a public agency to coordinate with other public policies depends on the amount of internal coordination possible in the government concerned. National experience on this is mixed.

Continuity with Existing Cultural and Political Arrangements

Private freeholds and leaseholds generally have a high degree of continuity with existing cultural and political arrangements, save in countries where the bulk of the urban population is accustomed to tribal or other collective ownership. Where the government is strongly committed ideologically to collective ownership as the proper path to development, public ownership, public leaseholds, and public ownership of development rights would have higher continuity.

Tribal-communal tenure is obviously continuous for rural migrants used to such a system, but quite discontinuous with European concepts of private ownership and a commercial land market that may have been carried over from colonial time. Neighborhood ownership, by contrast, while possibly echoing cooperative principles often found in industrially less developed societies, is less likely to be familiar in detail. Yet most European tenure systems legally acknowledge many types of collective ownership, and to the extent that they do so, there may be said to be continuity (for example, the use of trust ownership in certain housing projects in Mexico).

Finally, virtually all studies indicate that, except for parts of Africa, informal, de facto tenure is seen by squatters themselves as a severe break with a basic respect for private property, to be entered only when all other alternatives are closed.

Conclusions

In many developing countries existing tenure systems do not produce the most efficient patterns of land use, and they reinforce existing inequalities of wealth and opportunity. In addition, they are mechanically ill-adapted to the needs of rapid urbanization because of cumbersome methods of registration and recording, clouded titles, transfer taxes, lack of adequate powers of expropriation for legitimate public needs, and outmoded institutions. These inefficiencies are particularly burdensome to lower-income groups.

Radical change in tenure systems is likely to be extremely difficult, particularly because of the dual private and public nature of land. There are no easy panaceas or universally applicable recommendations. Some forms of change imply fundamental tradeoffs. Many forms of public intervention, for example, promise theoretical advantages in both efficiency and equity, but in practice may require very large, relatively high-level administrative skills beyond the current capability of many governments, particularly at the municipal level.[25] Thus, while deficiencies and inequalities of existing tenure arrangements are easy to observe, corrective public intervention may have the negative effects of high start-up costs in money, administrative time, litigation, and so on. Mixed public-private systems offer promise in countries where political sentiment is shifting toward greater social control of wealth-producing assets.

Land tenure has deep roots in national and ethnic cultures and is reflected in an enormous variety of concepts (with both gross and subtle distinctions) among the nations of the developing world. Solutions that are not sensitive to this variety are unlikely to survive or to ameliorate the problems at which they are aimed. The categories used here are rather rough and frequently uncomfortable attempts to organize an extraordinary range into a useful conceptual framework. When it comes to actual translation into policy, the national or even local context of each project, the institutional milieu in which it will be placed, and the exact nature of the parties interested in its effective execution must have major influence on policy decisions concerning appropriate tenure arrangements. As the German proverb has it, "The Devil is in the details."

25. One long-range strategy worth serious attention is investment in systematic training programs in connection with new tenure systems. Officials in the Republic of Korea made an offer of this type with respect to their system of land readjustment (see William A. Doebele, "Land Readjustment as an Alternative to Taxation for the Recovery of Betterment: The Case of South Korea," in Bahl, 1979).

Toward More Dynamic Concepts of Land Tenure

Urban land reform is of growing importance on the political agenda of many developing countries. But there is no such thing as an optimal set of land tenure institutions. Tenure is a tool that must be adapted to the specific conditions and cultural traditions of each situation. And it is important to recognize that any decision about tenure (such as the initiation of a major project) will have long-term effects and, indeed, will take on a dynamism of its own, as individuals and agencies begin to adjust their behavior to the rules of the game.

Although it is conventional to think of land as being either publicly or privately owned, tenure has in fact been moving, in both developed and developing countries, to more complex forms of shared proprietary interests. Just as most economies today are mixed, so one may seek "the best of both worlds" in shared tenures. Although there is not space to develop this concept in detail here, five categories of unusual interest might be identified.

Government as Assembler, Not Owner

Possibly one of the most interesting of the emerging mixed forms of tenure is public intervention aimed primarily at the large-scale assembly and servicing of land, but not at long-term public ownership of it. The most sophisticated examples of this mix are the land readjustment processes used in the Republic of Korea, Taiwan, and, to some extent, in Japan and the state of Western Australia (see Doebele in Bahl, 1979; Japan, Ministry of Construction, and City Planning Association, 1974, pp. 202-25; and Archer, 1976). Most Swedish municipalities now acquire and hold land, to sell freehold when it is ready for development, and some even limit their intervention to assembling and servicing land just prior to sale for construction. These are highly promising and important approaches with a considerable range of applicability (see chapter 5).

Advance Acquisition of Development Rights

In spite of the obvious administrative problems, there are appealing arguments for the proposition that development values are largely socially created and therefore should have some degree of public owner-ship.[26] In most countries, however, development values are so completely

26. The rather different argument that land can be taxed without distorting effects is also relevant and is discussed in chapter 4.

intermingled with market values that attempts to move development rights into the public domain would be both costly and bitterly resisted, not only by the wealthy, but also by most middle-income and even lower-income persons—in short, by all who have personal stakes in the ownership of real estate and its appreciation in value. For instance, surveys of three *barrios piratas* (pirate subdivisions) in Bogotá showed that even relatively low-income families see real estate appreciation as an investment opportunity (Doebele, 1977).

One solution to this problem might be to acquire, not existing development rights, but only those relating to a future date, say, seven to ten years after the moment of transition. As with all other goods, values in land are discounted over time. For many development rights the discount rate is fairly high, since the owner finds it hard to foresee what changes (including government intervention) will occur in future years. With such uncertainties, plus the high interest rates prevailing in most developing countries, a profit to be reaped a decade ahead will tend to have a very small present value. Thus the cost of acquisition of development rights at this future date might be quite low. However, governments in developing countries might themselves have quite high discount rates for rights which will have value only in the future, particularly because of the fiscally weak institutions involved.

One, almost certainly self-financing, way to reduce the attractiveness of land as a speculative investment and permit greater control through the allocation of development rights would be for a national government to establish a fund (based on its own borrowing rate at the time) from which municipalities could draw to acquire future development rights in areas known to have intensive development potential or for which there are long-term development plans. Initial investment in such a policy need not be large, although it will require national support because of the extremely limited municipal budgets in most developing countries. Such a process would demand a degree of long-range planning to identify areas of major growth potential in the time frame selected. As developing countries move toward putting major urban infrastructure investments in their medium-term economic plans, such identification becomes increasingly necessary in any case—even in the absence of any strategy to acquire development rights.

In many countries, the constitution or legislation governing expropriation (even of development rights) requires the agency to have a specific public use in mind for the property taken. This might mean that a fairly specific master plan, for at least the seven- to ten-year period involved, would have to be officially adopted. Such planning is extremely difficult and leads to costly rigidities. Alternatively, the legislation controlling expropriation might be modified to permit the taking of development rights without such specific planning, although this brings its own problems.

The major disadvantages of acquiring future development rights are the same as for any type of public ownership: administrative skills and integrity may be insufficient to manage assets of this value. This has been demonstrated often where a municipality has, through some historical accident, owned a strategically important area. In most cases, such land has simply been disposed of in the most convenient (or politically expedient) manner, with little attempt to use its potential to achieve the objectives outlined above. Thus, any proposal that contemplates enlarging public landownership must face the question of administrative capacity, which, if not present, can easily make the exercise counterproductive. Although this particular proposal requires early identification of probable critical areas, there would be a lengthy period before actual allocations begin, during which training programs and other administrative "tooling-up" might occur. The approach may thus have advantages over plunging directly into land banking, a step some developing nations are discussing.

The gradual acquisition of development rights over a more extended period is obviously less traumatic, particularly if one assumes a general expansion of administrative capability. It does have the serious disadvantage, already discussed above, that any form of split ownership is an unfamiliar concept, and it requires two calculations of the value of land in conditions where even simple unitary market value might be difficult to establish.[27]

The idea is no panacea, but under certain circumstances, in certain countries, it may have advantages over alternatives now in more common currency. Further study would be helpful to analyze what has actually occurred in cases where municipalities have had the opportunity to acquire future development rights; to assess more carefully the likely savings in doing so as opposed to acquiring land outright for the same purpose (U.S. experience with development rights in areas with high development potential shows them to be virtually equal to full market value of the land); and to define the specific administrative capacity required. If this could be done, experimental applications might be valuable in suitable local contexts.

27. There is some confusion in the law of expropriation as to whether compensation should be paid on the basis of what the owner loses or what the public agency gains. Where real estate is irreplaceable and peculiarly valuable to the owner, but not of such special value to the government, the owner is sometimes granted extra damages beyond its worth to the public agency. It is difficult, however, to imagine the opposite occurring.

Tenure in Improvements

The separation of ownership of structures from ownership of the underlying land is an important feature of the tenure system widely used in the socialist countries of eastern Europe and recently adopted, in principle at least, by Zambia. The system has obvious advantages in that it probably maximizes incentives for private investment in structures, while giving public agencies the rights to the increments attributable to land values and allowing them to change land use as demand requires, subject to payment for the value of any structures lost in the process. Under certain circumstances, such a mixed approach might have distinct merits for site-and-service projects (particularly ones of large scale in which transfers of houses are almost impossible to police), and in legitimizing and upgrading existing squatter settlements.

Neighborhood Ownership

Although very little is known about neighborhood ownership, it appears to be growing in popularity and needs to be reckoned with in tenure policy in developing countries. It may not always be an unmixed blessing to the government in power, but it does possess great vitality for constructive programs at very low public cost and can assist complex and equitable decisions concerning tenure, in ways that would be very difficult for any bureaucracy to match.

New Australian, Indian, and British Proposals

More generally, the national reviews of tenure and land development policies undertaken by the Australian Commission of Inquiry into Land Tenures (1973), the British Community Land Act (1975), and the Indian Urban Land (Ceiling and Regulation) Act (1976) suggest approaches that allow public intervention in existing systems of tenure, some of which deserve close study.

More Specific Proposals

Some specific proposals can be made that would help provide a more suitable tenure framework for future urban growth and improve current allocation of resources.

The Law of Expropriation

In many developing countries, badly outdated legislation makes expropriation so costly and time-consuming that it is, for many purposes, almost useless. Without reasonably efficient expropriation procedures, most of the tenure reforms discussed above are impractical. Even when most public acquisitions are in fact negotiated, an effective expropriation law is necessary as a backup to prevent owners from demanding excessive prices.

Central to effective expropriation procedures is a provision for "quick taking," that is, for giving the government access to the real estate concerned at once, while negotiations and possibly litigation continue as to its fair price. Model legislation for this purpose is now well developed in the United States and most European countries. In many developing countries the difficulty lies in persuading the government of the importance of this item in the planning of legislative reforms and in securing the necessary political support.

Determining adequate compensation also poses problems, especially in large-scale projects. The elimination of small businesses, for example, may involve greater losses than simply the value of physical assets. Similarly, the elderly and minority ethnic groups may have special costs of relocation. For the poor, increasing the journey to work can be critical. Dividing compensation between lessees and lessors also poses difficult issues of equity. These matters have been dealt with effectively in many more developed countries. The problem is that most developing countries do not have the facilities to seek out legislation most appropriate to their own needs.

Cadastral Surveys and Recording Systems

Many developing countries lack adequate basic surveys of property boundaries. This may seem a problem of low priority, yet the absence of a reasonably accurate cadastral system makes all forms of urban land use control extremely difficult. Moreover, any effective system of land taxation and tenure policy is dependent on its existence. Sometimes, for instance, countries have been forced to tax only buildings because landownership is so uncertain. This has been the case in Ghana and in parts of Nigeria and Liberia. The general trend, however, is away from this system as soon as the recording process permits. For an excellent general review, see Lent (1974, pp. 45, 51-52, and 72).

Recent developments in aerial photogrammetry and computer storage of both numerical and graphic data have enormously facilitated the survey process and added to the techniques available for dealing with this problem (see Porter, McMains, and Doebele, 1973). The lack of government willingness to commit resources and trained personnel, however, still leads to serious bottlenecks.

Closely related to accurate information about ownership boundaries is the capability to record the ownership of parcels quickly and accurately. In many developing countries the recording systems, particularly in rapidly growing urban areas, are totally inadequate to meet modern demands. In some parts of the world, particularly in Africa, this condition has resulted from the traditional concept that land belongs to whomever wishes to work it or is subject to the informal decisions of the village council or chief.[28] Elsewhere, such as in parts of Latin America, recording systems exist, but are geared to a more leisurely pace and have been completely unable to keep up with the tempo of contemporary urban change. In still other places, the culture or religion has established many claims by custom, which have never been written down.

The question of clouded titles has been greatly aggravated by large-scale squatting, and the question of the acquisition of rights has been aggravated by "adverse possession." As time passes, not only do the original squatters gain additional legitimacy according to the law in many countries, but they also engage in numerous informal sales, leases, and occupancy agreements which become increasingly impossible to unscramble. Procedures for the rapid and equitable clearing of clouded titles are thus a precondition of any project involving a large amount of urban

---

28. The results of this situation in some parts of Africa are vividly described by the Lloyd Commission on the Registration of Title to Land in Western Nigeria, *Report to the Western Region Legislature,* Sessional Paper no. 2 (1962), para. 2, quoted by Okpala (1977), pp. 42–43:

The problems which arise from the uncertainty of title to land in the Region are too well known to need lengthy exposition. A man who wishes to purchase or lease cannot find out who are the right people to convey it to him; many men buy their land twice from rival claimants, or from two sections of a family. Having acquired the land, a man is reluctant to develop it, being unsure of his rights to it. When he does take the plunge and build an imposing house or plant permanent crops, he finds that his lack of a secure title prevents him from readily selling the property or from mortgaging it to raise credit for further expansion of his business. Well known is the unscrupulous debtor who has cited his house as a security for a loan and who immediately defaults, claiming successfully that the building is on family land, and cannot therefore be attached for his debts. Once caught out, creditors are extremely reluctant to advance money to build a house on what seems likely to be family land as security. Creditors presume therefore that all land within the traditional built-up areas of a town is family land until the contrary is shown. Another serious aspect of the problem is that valuable land lies unused because it is not clear, by customary law, who are the persons empowered to dispose of it.

land or the development of large-scale tourist facilities.[29] One method, suggested by Haar (1976, pp. 155-57) is the use of title insurance, which would assign title to the most probable owners but provide insurance should any other claimants later appear. According to Haar, such a system is already in use in Singapore. Of particular importance is the development of mechanisms that permit projects to move ahead quickly, without waiting for disputes among claimants to title to be settled.

Transfer Taxes

Some developing countries apply heavy taxes at the moment that real property is transferred. These taxes can be seriously inequitable to the poor, who normally have great difficulty in raising the necessary down payment and cannot afford a second burden when their financial capacities are already stretched to the utmost. As a result, they are forced out of a segment of the market to which they would otherwise have access, or else they engage in illegal and unrecorded transfers. Both would appear to be undesirable results of this form of taxation.

In Mexico BANOBRAS organizes its housing projects in the form of trusts (*fideicomisos*), to which occupants are given certificates of participation. This device circumvents the transfer tax, which would otherwise approximately double the down payment necessary (but see chapter 5).

Regularization of Titles in Established Squatter Settlements

Increasing emphasis on regularization and upgrading of existing squatter settlements raises the question of the effect of legitimizing titles in areas that were illegally occupied. The usual argument against such policy is that it encourages further invasions. However, one of the few careful studies of this process (made by Thomasz Sudra in Mexico City) indicates that low-income squatters themselves may not want regularization of tenure. Not only does it expose them to the added expense of property taxation, but, possibly more seriously, it also invites investment in the area by middle-income families, who were unwilling to invest earlier when titles were uncertain (Sudra, 1976).

---

29. A recent example is Zihuatanejo, Mexico, in which FIBAZI (Fiedeicomiso Bahia de Zihuatanejo) spent two years converting the three major *ejidos* from collective agricultural ownership into tenure suitable for the expected wave of touristic building. (William Doebele interviews with Arq. Javier Solorsano and Ing. Juan Bonilla, Zihuatanejo, September 9, 1976, and Ing. Anastasei Perez and Ing. Asoldo Hernandez, Lazaro Cardenas, September 10, 1976.)

Reduced Term Restrictions in Site-and-Service Projects

Many site-and-service projects prohibit the rental of rooms in the houses constructed, particularly those in which participants are given less than freehold interests. This provision, normally insisted upon to prevent the "commercialization" of the project, decreases the total number of habitation units on the market and eliminates an important source of income to the participant. Moreover, it is probable that most of such units house new migrants. Studies in Bogotá indicate that some 76 percent of new migration was accommodated outside the center of the city, much of it presumably in rooms in the low-income barrios piratas. About one-third of the families in such barrios rented out rooms, receiving about one-fifth of their income from this source (Vernaz, 1973, p. 104). There are obvious tradeoffs between numbers housed and standards, which require more careful examination.

Restrictions on transfer of freehold or leasehold titles are also common in these projects. The purpose of such restrictions is to keep the subsidy in the hands of those to be benefited, who are normally chosen for the project only after an elaborate selection process. The policy may, however, lower the productive use of land, even in social terms, by inhibiting its transfer to those who can use it more efficiently, and by preventing the realization of its money value for use in other activities that may have greater economic or social value. Stated another way, public policy is that subsidies are given in a specific form and should not be translated into another. Little is known about this aspect of land tenure as it relates to the probable expenditure patterns of lower-income persons. Studies indicate that the poor are usually rational in their economic behavior. In Hong Kong housing projects, for example, it has long been known that a great deal of technically illegal activity takes place, but the consequences for total economic activity or redistribution of wealth have not been traced. Similarly, in the so-called Citizens' Apartments program in the Republic of Korea it is well established that the original grantees were quickly bought out by middle-class families in need of housing, but how the grantees then used their new capital is unknown.

Conclusions

It is apparent from the above analysis that all systems of land tenure involve tradeoffs, and that none is either ideal or likely to be universally most advantageous. It is probably safe to predict, however, that as the magnitude of urban problems attracts the attention of governments, there will be a political willingness to engage in urban land reform, probably by means of greater public intervention. This can most readily occur at moments of transition, and it is therefore on these that operational interest should be concentrated.

Given the desperate scarcity of serviced lots and housing in all major cities in developing countries, participants are normally ready to accept almost any form of tenure offered as being better than their current situation. This condition tends to conceal the need to confront the issue of which tenure forms are in fact best suited to policy objectives and which are counterproductive.

One particularly important problem is to obtain the information necessary to evaluate changes in policy. In many areas information and documented experience are rare or nonexistent. If current large-scale urban projects and related changes in tenure were to be monitored, however, the resultant analysis together with more general research could contribute greatly to an understanding of the effectiveness of different tenure forms. The cost of such data collection and analysis would be relatively low and the potential benefit to developing countries would be considerable.

4

The Rationale for Government Intervention

Christine M. E. Whitehead

THIS CHAPTER EXAMINES THE REASONS governments might intervene in the urban land market, the techniques they might employ to achieve a better allocation of both land uses and the income from that land, and the problems they are likely to encounter in implementing such urban policies.

The market mechanism is unlikely, on its own, to produce an efficient allocation of land uses. Moreover, the ownership of land is generally unevenly distributed among members of the community so that the market is not likely to allocate the income from land in the way the community would wish. For these reasons all governments intervene in urban land markets, although to widely differing degrees; at the limit, administrative procedures completely replace the market mechanism. Intervention takes many forms, including a regulatory framework, taxation, subsidies to particular activities, and direct ownership and participation in urban investment and the provision of services. By these means the operation of the market is modified or superseded in pursuance of community objectives.

Such intervention in a market-based economy is supported by the belief that the government can implement these policies in a way that reduces inefficiency and makes the resultant distribution of benefits more equitable. Yet many immediate goals may conflict with one another, and governments face problems of obtaining adequate information, of defining suitable techniques, and of fully implementing policies once they are introduced. As a result, the benefits of intervention may be far less than expected. The costs of intervention must therefore be counted as well as the benefits before deciding how to intervene, or indeed whether to intervene at all.

In setting out the main factors to be taken into account, this chapter does not break new ground. Rather, it presents the basic analysis necessary to evaluate the particular techniques of intervention discussed in the later chapters. First, the causes of market failure are examined and thus the prima facie case for intervention in urban land markets. Next the techniques are specified that could in principle be used for a better allocation of land and its benefits, and finally the problems inherent in the interventionary process are analyzed.

The Prima Facie Case for Intervention

It is possible to argue that left to itself the free market would tend to allocate land to its most desirable use and that therefore government intervention is at best unnecessary and at worst counterproductive. This is undoubtedly true, given both a perfect market and an equitable distribution of income. The prerequisites for these conditions, however, are extremely stringent and cover all aspects of utilities, goods, and markets (see, for example, De Graaff, 1957; Arrow and Hahn, 1971; and Varian, 1978). Both market failure and the maldistribution of income are thought to be particularly prevalent with respect to urban land and services because land, being locationally specific, is inherently heterogeneous.[1] If the optimal conditions do not exist, there is a prima facie case for intervention to modify the allocation of land that would arise from market pressures.

The main problems in urban land markets arise from:

- The need to provide certain land with public goods, which cannot be effectively produced through the private market
- The existence of significant locational externalities, both good and bad, which private decisionmakers would not take into account
- Imperfect information on which to base individual decisions and the general costs of using the market
- Unequal division of market power among economic agents, particularly in the case of monopolistic supply
- Differences between how individuals and the community value future and current benefits

1. The belief that markets are so imperfect as to require intervention is not universal even within developing countries. See, for instance, Bauer and Yamey (1968) for a skeptical view; and Mills (1974), who discusses the case specifically in relation to urban structure.

- Differences between individual and community attitudes to risk
- Possible interdependence in utility arising from "merit goods," the consumption of which by an individual benefits other members of the community—a situation not readily reflected in individual decisions
- Differences between the actual and desired distribution of income.[2]

Public Goods

In any market economy in which private decisions generally operate effectively to allocate resources, the traditional reason for government intervention is the provision of public goods (see, for example, Musgrave and Musgrave, 1980). These are goods from which the community derives net benefits but which the private market does not supply—at least not in the desired quantities. The two main attributes of a public good are, first, that consumers cannot be excluded from using it and therefore have no incentive to pay or to reveal their preferences, and second, that one person's consumption does not reduce its availability to others. In these conditions the efficient price is zero. Thus private suppliers will either not produce the good at all or will underproduce and inefficiently charge those prepared to pay. The classic example is national security, and, indeed, the need for its public provision is often regarded as a major reason for the formation of the modern state. Few goods are "pure" public goods, but many urban services—particularly local administration, police services, open space, uncongested roads, and street lighting—contain at least some elements of "publicness." For instance, the cost of an additional person's use of a street light is almost always zero, so it would be inefficient to charge him. Further, although it would be technically possible to set up a metering system, it would be too costly to be worthwhile.

The problem is that although the cost of an additional consumer's use of the goods is negligible, the cost of producing the goods is not. In these circumstances the public sector frequently finds it best to step in and provide the goods itself. It is then faced with financing the supply, and since the benefits are local, this finance must usually come from local sources. Not surprisingly, especially in low-income, rapidly growing urban areas, there is a chronic shortage of funds for these urban services, even though their benefits to the community are clearly greater than their

2. Many different taxonomies can be adopted when analyzing market failure. See, for example, Frankena and Schleffman (1980) for a slightly different approach, specifically applied to land markets.

costs. Thus government intervention in the urban economy, and indeed public provision of services, is explained by the desirability of supplying these nonmarketable goods. But because of their nature, how to provide and finance the desired level of service is likely to remain a continuing problem, in both developing and developed nations.

Externalities

Problems of efficient production and allocation and of equity arise whenever the benefits or costs of decisions are borne by those not directly involved in making the decision to consume or produce. In these conditions, market signals will not reflect the full benefits and costs to the community. Instead, only private costs and benefits will be taken into account and welfare will be reduced. External costs and benefits are thought to be particularly prevalent in the urban economy because many activities have spillover effects on nearby property. Traditional land and building regulations have tried to take this type of externality into account; for example, building requirements are specified to reduce the risk of spreading fire, and sanitation standards are set to limit the problems of contagious disease. Controls such as zoning and planning regulations take account of broader urban externalities, for example, by reducing the costs of production through agglomeration and by avoiding road congestion. In addition, many urban authorities take account of externalities through the public provision of such services as water and sewerage.

Interarea and more macro-based externalities, for example, those arising in rural areas because of large-scale migration to the towns, are also regarded by some as a major cause of inefficiency. These cannot readily be dealt with at the urban level, however, and are best left to national or regional governments to account for them in development plans.

Arguably many externalities, particularly those affecting only a few individuals located near one another, can be dealt with via private contractual arrangements because everyone can gain if they are incorporated into the decisionmaking (see Buchanan and Stubblebine, 1962; Cheung, 1973; and Baumol and Oates, 1979). However, if large numbers of people are involved, or information is not readily available, or there is the possibility of contractual incompleteness, private arrangements are unlikely to be effective. For example, there may be a good case for an urban redevelopment scheme from which all owners will benefit. However, because some of the benefits to each individual will arise from what is done by neighbors, and some of the benefits from the individual's own work will go, to others, all appear to gain from underspending.[3] A solution to the problem might be short-term government ownership or involvement, as in some land readjustment schemes (see chapters 3 and 5). More generally, a wide range of urban land decisions is likely to generate significant spillovers, such as pollution, congestion, or unsuitable urban forms, which suggest an important case for government intervention.

Information

If decisionmakers cannot readily obtain adequate information or have to bear unnecessarily heavy transaction costs when making decisions, inefficiencies are likely to be introduced.[4] At the local level, information and foresight are necessary to achieve economies of scale in the production of urban services and from the interaction of activities. Without knowledge of the future structure of the city, it is extremely unlikely that private decisionmakers will choose the socially most efficient scale or location. This is a problem in all markets, but the costs of incorrect decisions in the land market are often far higher than elsewhere because of their long-term nature. The initial decision cannot be rapidly adjusted if it proves incorrect, and many other decisions that interact with the first will be adversely affected. If government intervention is to be of value, the public sector must be able to obtain, transmit, or evaluate information more effectively than the private sector. Where there is an overall planning mechanism, and particularly where government is directly involved in large urban projects, publicly produced information is likely to be cheaper and more accurate. Given this, policymakers may choose to inform and modify private decision, for instance, by providing detailed urban plans and forecasts, or they may take the decisions into their own hands. The more long-term the decisions and the more they affect overall urban structure, perhaps the more likely is the second approach.

Many policies to improve information and to reduce transaction costs are likely to be more effective if they are applied nationally. These include, for example, improvements in the legal framework related to the land market, the clarification of tenure and ownership rights, and the development of new markets, such as mortgage markets, to meet expanding requirements. Some such policies are specifically aimed at defining property rights and helping the market work more effectively; others, however, supersede the market mechanism.

3. This problem is analyzed in Davis and Whinston (1961). For a discussion of the evaluation of broader housing externalities, see Burns and Grebler (1977).
4. For a discussion of the problems of information and market failure, see for instance, Demsetz (1969) and Williamson (1975).

Market Power

The problems that arise where economic agents can exert significant control over price or output in a market are likely to be particularly prevalent in developing urban areas. Landownership may be concentrated in a few hands; there are significant economies of scale in the provision of urban services and few suppliers (indeed, many can be regarded as natural monopolies); the development, construction, and finance markets are often oligopolistic; the supply of many urban services cannot be expanded quickly enough to meet increased demand, thus existing suppliers gain market power; and there are often continuing shortages of raw materials, skilled labor, finance, and other factors of production in a rapidly growing urban economy.

However, many policies to control relative power, such as rent and other price controls, and taxation of land holdings and land speculation, may themselves generate significant adverse allocative effects (see chapter 5). They are also difficult to implement. Governments therefore often choose more direct forms of intervention, especially where economies of scale are large in relation to the size of market. Yet in these conditions government itself has inherent power, which may be all too readily misused. For instance, if land is brought into government ownership, permission to develop may be limited to increase profits rather than to allocate land efficiently.

Intertemporal Distortions

Private decisionmakers decide whether to invest by looking at their own costs and benefits, including the specific rate of interest they face. But prevailing interest rates and prices may incorrectly reflect society's intertemporal welfare, particularly because individuals are likely to give a low value to benefits and costs beyond their own lifetime, especially the cost to future generations of the present use of resources.[5] In the main, this is likely to lead to underinvestment in future benefits and overconsumption of nonrenewable resources. A good example is the lack of interest in energy conservation. Such incorrect decisions are of particular importance in the urban context because structures and forms are so long-lasting. In these circumstances, the government may choose to subsidize or control interest rates to help induce private investment, or it may modify the price of nonrenewable resources to reduce consumption. Alternatively, it may intervene more directly. Mortgage market inter-

5. See Kay (1972) and Dasgupta (1978), for discussions of social preference and the social discount rate.

vention is a particularly prevalent form of the first approach, while many government-sponsored urban projects are rationalized on the basis of the welfare of future generations.

Uncertainty

Similarly, private individuals may be more risk averse than the community as a whole, because they are unable to pool risks effectively. This again leads to underinvestment, particularly perhaps in newer and relatively untried technology and in large-scale projects. Both of these may be important in rapidly expanding urban areas where the structure is being determined for many years ahead. Since, arguably, only the government can effectively spread large-scale risks, the case for intervention is strong.[6]

Utility Interdependence

It is sometimes argued that the community benefits from individuals' consumption of so-called merit goods.[7] For instance, society as a whole may suffer if people live in poor quality housing. If this is the case, minimum standards may therefore be specified, not because the low-income individuals are prepared to pay for such high standards, but because society feels greater satisfaction if everyone lives at or above a minimum level; that is, there is joint consumption of the minimum quality of housing by the individual and by society as a group.

Minimum levels of many urban services are regarded in some communities, particularly in industrialized countries, as social necessities. Problems often arise, however, because it is easier for the community to decide that certain merit goods should be provided—for example, by specifying building standards—than it is to find the finance or other means to make sure the individuals receive these goods—for example, minimum quality housing. In other words, as so often happens, aspirations outstrip capacity. In addition, it may be all too easy to misspecify standards so as to distort the policy's effect. For instance, standards may be set too high in order to benefit a privileged group at the expense of the rest of the community. But if utility interdependencies do exist, they can be realized only through community decisions. Government intervention is therefore necessary.

6. See Arrow and Lind (1970) and Hirshleifer (1965 and 1966) for discussions of the many approaches to these problems.

7. See Musgrave and Musgrave (1980) and Culyer (1971) for more formal discussions of the nature of merit goods.

Redistribution

Finally, intervention may be aimed at the more equitable distribution of available resources both horizontally (among members of the community who are in similar circumstances) and vertically (from rich to poor). Massive inequalities of both types are prevalent in most rapidly growing cities in developing countries. The case against redistribution in kind in a market system (the way most readily open to urban governments) is strong because one dollar that a household can spend as it chooses is likely to be worth more to it than one dollar's worth of a particular good, and exchange is usually difficult. However, market imperfections may make redistribution in kind more effective—for example, extra cash may simply increase prices, and additional supply can be made available publicly more readily than privately, or redistribution may be politically easier to accomplish via particular goods. Most redistributional policies are probably best undertaken nationally. At the urban level, it may often be far more important to make sure that policies with other objectives do not have adverse distributional effects.

All the factors discussed above help explain why markets fail to allocate both efficiently and equitably. Yet even while concentrating on the case for intervention, it has been impossible to avoid mentioning some of the problems that may arise if governments do in fact intervene. It is not therefore a clear-cut argument: there is market failure, therefore government must do something about it. Rather, it is necessary in each case to examine the measures available to government and assess whether they are capable of improving the position. This involves analyzing, in relation to clearly specified objectives, not only the costs of using the market but also the relative costs and benefits of the best available administrative process. Thus, whether it will be worthwhile to intervene depends on the relative net benefits in each instance.[8] To make a judgment, it is necessary to specify how intervention can best be undertaken and assess its potential effects on resource allocation and distribution.

Choice of Techniques

The majority of economic discussions on the techniques of intervention most likely to realize the highest level of social welfare have concentrated on the possible ways of adjusting private to socially desir-

8. This is a general conclusion when second-best conditions prevail; for a discussion of how second-best rules may be applied, see Rees (1976) and Atkinson and Stiglitz (1980).

able decisions in the presence of externalities. Here it can readily be shown that under strict assumptions there is a formal efficiency equivalence between taxation and subsidies and between either of these and direct controls (see Baumol and Oates, 1979, for the conditions for such equivalence).

Thus, if the production of a good results in costs to other firms and households located nearby, the government may impose a tax on the producer which reflects the social costs at each level of output. In this way externalities are internalized and the decisionmakers will modify production in line with the true marginal social cost. Output will be reduced because the externality is taken into account and weighed against the benefits of the firm's output. Equivalently, a subsidy can be given as an incentive not to produce in cases where social costs offset private benefits. In principle, the only difference lies in distributional effects: in the first case the producer of the external cost suffers a reduction in income, while in the second the community rewards him for not causing additional costs to society. Where the externality is costly, taxation is usually regarded as the more equitable approach, unless there are additional objectives of redistribution or the provision of merit goods. Moreover, taxation can provide a useful source of income, although its use may cause further problems of efficient allocation (see Baumol and Bradford, 1970). Subsidies, however, present the same allocation problems and also require financing from somewhere, a major problem for all governments, particularly in developing countries. Perhaps in part for these reasons, subsidies are hardly touched upon in chapter 5, where the value of taxation as an approach to intervention is discussed in detail.

Exactly equivalent efficiency results can be achieved by regulation that forces private suppliers to produce the socially optimal output. For instance, the authorities could estimate the level of noxious emissions that is optimal given the goods produced and legally require that emissions not go above that level. Again, in principle the only difference lies in the distributional consequences (see Baumol and Oates, 1979).

There may, however, be many practical reasons for choosing one technique rather than another in particular circumstances. To encourage energy conservation, some governments have chosen to tax energy-saving investment, others subsidize it, and still others have specified standards. Often a mixture of techniques may be best. The vast majority of measures aimed at urban externalities has, however, been regulatory. Reasons for this include: locational specificity is more easily dealt with through land use planning than through generally nonlocationally specific taxes and subsidies; regulations are probably easier to enforce and monitor; they may be more acceptable because the reasons for regulation, and thus the benefits, are often more obvious than their costs; and the administrative and legal framework required for such regulations is available in many countries as one of the legacies of colonial power (see chapter 6).

Although regulations are often easier to impose and operate, they are not necessarily more effective than other approaches. External costs and benefits are usually specific to particular conditions, yet regulations are usually defined in very general terms. Their imposition may thus introduce further distortions in some cases, while improving the position in others. In addition, many regulations are specified in terms of maximums and minimums. They therefore do not provide the incentive to modify the externality unless it has overreached the specific limit, even though costs or benefits may be incurred within these limits. For instance, most countries set a maximum size and weight for vehicles to reduce road damage and congestion. But such regulations do nothing to reduce the adverse effects of vehicles that just meet the statutory limit. Thus the apparent simplicity of regulation hides the fact that the correct use of this intervention poses problems precisely analogous to those encountered when specifying suitable taxes and subsidies. It is therefore important to take account of the practical strengths and weaknesses of each technique in particular circumstances when choosing between them.

A further difficulty lies in the piecemeal approach usually applied. Most of the analytic material assumes that it is possible to take one externality at a time and adjust the system appropriately, although analyses based on a general equilibrium framework recognize the problems that arise when starting from a nonoptimal base (see particularly Baumol and Bradford, 1970; Baumol and Oates, 1979, and Rees, 1976, also discuss the more general problems of second best). Yet it is in the nature of urban agglomeration that spillover effects will be widespread, interact with one another, and have different effects on different activities. The estimation of the value of externality and the determination of the most suitable form of intervention are therefore fraught with problems. One particularly relevant point, discussed in chapter 2, is that immediate locational externalities are likely to be given more weight than are more widespread effects that may be far more important to the effective growth of the urban economy.[9]

The problems of identification, estimation, specification, monitoring, and enforcement have led many governments to argue that only direct involvement is likely to provide an urban structure in line with commu-

9. The literature on the identification and measurement of citywide urban agglomeration economies is far more limited and diffuse than on more specific externalities. But see, for instance, Myrdal (1957) on their importance and the problems they cause through potential disequilibrium.

nity objectives. Again in principle, an administrative approach is exactly equivalent to the other techniques as a means of achieving allocative efficiency (see Lange and Taylor, 1938, for the classic analysis of the equivalence of market and administrative systems). Externalities are internalized in this case through the public sector's decision process. An additional potential value is that when ownership of resources lies with the government, there is direct control over distribution. Further, the problems of obtaining information may be more readily dealt with within an administrative framework (but see Coase, 1961, and Williamson, 1975, for contrary views).

But an administrative system also presents problems. In particular, those who actually make the decisions may have little incentive to work directly for the public good. Further, the problems of how to finance government participation are often overwhelming, and where the government is directly involved in only part of the economy, interaction between the administered sector and the rest of the economy may be very difficult.

So far this discussion, like most of the urban literature, has concentrated on possible government approaches to the question of externalities. However, the other forms of market failure discussed above may be equally or even more important causes of inefficient and inequitable land use.

Some of these are analogous to the externality problems in that they cause incorrect market signals. Differences between individual and community time preferences and attitudes to risk fall into this category. Inequities in market power arguably present similar problems that can be dealt with by the public provision of goods and services or by the use of taxation, subsidies, or direct controls to affect the markets for them. Redistribution of income can similarly be achieved either through administrative or fiscal means.

In some instances, however, a particular technique may seem inherently or practically the most suitable. For example, the arguments for public provision of public goods follow from the nature of such goods—although how best to finance them is by no means so clear-cut.[10] The consumption of merit goods is more likely to reach the correct level if the goods are provided directly or accompanied by a subsidy because the community then pays directly for the increase in community welfare. Regulatory techniques, such as the specification of minimum building standards, could in principle be used, but since individuals have no incentive to meet them there are problems of monitoring and control.

10. Even in this case private clubs and secondary contractual arrangements have been emphasized by some. See Musgrave and Musgrave (1980) for a discussion of possible approaches.

The efficient production and dissemination of information present slightly different problems that must be solved before any of the other techniques can be effective. Without correct information, no allocative mechanism, whether administrative or market, can operate well. In a mixed economy government must therefore improve market processes by modifying the legal system or other parts of the institutional and administrative framework to help reduce the costs of private information collection and transmission to individuals. The market for information is a particularly imperfect one, however, where contractual arrangements are all too easily circumvented (see Marschak, 1968). Given these problems, government may in fact be a more efficient producer and transmitter of information, more fully able to use economies of scale of production and to monitor the accuracy of its output. This last can be particularly relevant when the information is employed to define other interventionary tools, since privately produced information is often distorted by the vagaries of market power.

There is usually no simple way to determine which interventionary technique—taxation and subsidies, regulation, or public provision—is best or even whether to intervene at all. In a mixed economy a careful comparison of the different approaches is required, and the various advantages and disadvantages of each must be taken into account; the choice of techniques would then be determined by specific circumstances within a carefully defined framework of objectives.[11] In this assessment a major factor is the extent to which any intervention will turn out to have the predicted effects. This topic is discussed in the following section.

Problems of Intervention

Several practical issues have proved particularly problematic when designing suitable means of intervention. These affect the choice of techniques, the extent to which land use is actually improved, and the distributional consequences of such intervention.

First, governments when intervening rarely have a single objective, and their multiple objectives may well conflict. Second, policies often have side effects that reduce their overall value. Moreover, the interaction of policies often makes it difficult to determine their final impact. Third, technical problems of definition and application make it impossible to design optimal techniques. Fourth, once a policy is in operation, those affected are often able to reduce its effectiveness or even pervert it to their own ends. Fifth, administrative capacities impose obvious limitations on

11. The remaining chapters provide a more detailed analysis of the relative strengths and weaknesses of the three approaches in practical conditions.

what is practicable. All these factors together may strictly limit the government's true capacity to intervene effectively.

Multiple Objectives

Many interventionary techniques are introduced with the hope of meeting often incompatible, multiple objectives. For instance, the value of taxation as a means of dealing with externalities and other market failures has already been noted. Yet most taxation is not undertaken directly for this purpose but rather to raise revenue or to help redistribute income. Taxes levied to reduce distortionary effects—for example, effluent fees and taxes to pay for water and sewerage—may be seen as user fees, which if set correctly will assist resource allocation. More general taxes on sales, income, and property, however, tend to introduce additional distortions.

These different objectives imply that any tax should not distort the workings of the market, except positively to modify allocation in line with defined objectives; it should be equitable, treating those in similar circumstances similarly, but capable of being used to redistribute from rich to poor; and it should be a good revenue raiser, easy to collect and difficult to evade. The problems of devising a tax that meets these requirements even in principle are very great. When the practical difficulties of implementation and the government's insatiable need for finance are remembered they appear overwhelming.[12]

The effects of property taxation, the main source of local funds in many developing countries, illustrate the problem.[13] Governments would like the tax to raise as much revenue as possible, without distorting investment decisions and, at the minimum, without being actually regressive. In recent years, academic views on how these last two objectives might be achieved have completely changed.[14] Under the old view the incidence of any property tax levied on land was assumed to be borne by the owners of that land at the time the tax was imposed, because

12. The financing implications of the rapid population growth are discussed in detail in Linn (1979).

13. See R. W. Bahl, "Urban Property Taxation in LDCs," in Bahl (1979), for a discussion of the proportion of revenue raised in this way. Bahl suggests that the tax, as currently implemented, is unable to respond adequately to rising urban incomes and the growing need for public expenditure, although others see it as the best source for the large additional financial resources required. See in particular the article by C. S. Shoup, also in Bahl (1979).

14. For the standard analysis of the new view, see Mieskowski (1972) and Aaron (1975). For an analysis specific to developing countries, see Charles E. McLure, "The Relevance of the New View of the Incidence of the Property Tax in Developing Countries," in Bahl (1979).

land is held to be in inelastic supply. The part of the tax that was levied on improvements was not borne by owners of capital but was shifted forward to consumers of the goods and services produced, because the supply of capital was regarded as infinitely elastic. On this basis a tax levied on land is viewed as progressive, because ownership is normally concentrated in the higher-income groups. Further, it has no adverse allocative effects because supply is completely inelastic. However, a tax on improvements both distorts investment decisions and is regressive because consumption takes a larger part of the budgets of lower-income groups.

These arguments have resulted in pressure either to abolish property taxation altogether, even though it is a well-tried source of revenue, or to shift away from general property taxation to site value taxes (see chapter 5 and Prest, 1981 and 1982*a*). In most circumstances abolishing property taxes seems impossible because of the revenue loss and because other forms of tax are often equally distortionary. The shift to site value taxes causes administrative problems and sometimes significant loss of revenue.

The new view suggests that neither the allocative nor the redistributive effects are as straightforward as the traditional analysis implies. It is based on the hypothesis that the supply of capital is completely inelastic for the country as a whole but that it is fully mobile within the country and between assets.[15] Under these conditions, a single rate national tax will be borne by all owners of capital in proportion to their asset holdings. Since ownership is concentrated among higher-income groups, the tax is progressive and allocatively neutral—although of course that allocation will change with the redistribution of income. However, if different areas or assets are taxed at different rates, investment choices will be distorted and will move away from highly taxed areas and assets to those where lower rates apply. This would be desirable only if the different rates reflected variations between private and social costs, a point which in practice is unlikely even to be considered.

If this new view is accepted it places strong constraints on local powers of taxation. For if tax rates differ between areas, investment will be adversely affected in areas with the higher rates (but see McClure, 1977). Attempts to increase revenue may thus themselves erode the tax base as well as cause allocative inefficiency. Moreover, site value taxation may also have problems if different rates are applied. If, for example, urban land is taxed more highly than rural, as is often the case to help increase revenue, the total amount of urban land will be reduced and urban land

15. Additional problems arise when there is international mobility of capital. See McLure in Bahl (1979).

use patterns will be distorted.[16] The current shift in emphasis toward efficiency has led to considerable reassessment of the suitability of different tax structures to meet the multiple objectives required of them.

This is just one example, although an important one, of the problems that governments face when specifying actual policy instruments. Although in principle it may be possible to devise approaches which allow all objectives to be met, in practice tradeoffs will almost always be necessary. These should involve positive political, economic, and social judgments to determine priorities. All too often, however, the problems and therefore the need to make such choices remain unrecognized, and resources are wasted in an attempt to meet incompatible objectives.

Undesirable Side Effects

The problems do not end here, for many policies turn out not to operate in the way predicted. Even if the government has been able to specify objectives and design policies apparently consistent with their achievement, unwanted side effects may significantly reduce their value.

For example, the case for taxing betterments—increases in land values arising from the process of urbanization—is generally accepted (see chapter 5). If untaxed, betterments simply increase the incomes of landowners who have done nothing directly to earn this additional income. When a tax is levied this benefit can be transferred to the community. If planning permission is required for development or change of use, there will usually be a once and for all increase in the price of the land. Yet the landowner has done nothing to earn this windfall gain. Imposing a lump sum tax will have no effect on the allocation of resources or on the price of goods produced from the land, so distributional aims will be met at no cost. The case for such a tax is therefore strong.

However, the form of the tax and the way it operates may well result in adverse side effects. First, if landowners are able to affect government zoning decisions, a tax will reduce their expected gains and so reduce their incentive to develop. Second, the tax may affect the timing of development, particularly if there are lobbying costs or if the introduction of the tax alters the attitudes of government to zoning. Third, it is difficult to calculate the extent to which increases in value are directly attributable to planning permission. If they arise from other sources of real cost to the owner, a tax levied at close to 100 percent of the apparent increase will reduce developers' incentives to change land use. In this case, inefficiencies will reoccur. Further, the transaction costs of adminis-

---

16. See Lent (1978) for a discussion of trends in taxation design.

tering the tax, in both money and nonmoney terms, may be considerable for all the agents involved. If so, resources will be wasted and development may be reduced significantly, especially if the government attempts to tax all or nearly all the apparent benefits.[17] Thus a tax introduced for desirable reasons of equity may turn out to have heavy and unexpected costs: a reduced supply of land, a slowdown in the process of change toward more desirable land uses, and resources wasted in attempts to avoid the tax.

A second example of adverse side effects occurs where the market is unable to adjust quickly enough to government policies. Projects that are large in relation to currently available resources, such as many infrastructure investments, can often cause rapid increases in prices. This is because the market cannot expand the supplies of skilled labor, particular raw materials, and administrative and management skills fast enough. Shortages therefore arise and cause financing problems, delays, and uncompleted projects—costs that are borne by the community and reduce the overall benefit of the investment. The shortages also cause a redistribution of income toward the monopoly suppliers of these factors. Careful capital budgeting and sequencing of investment projects may limit these problems, as may additional information to private decisionmakers. Experience suggests, however, that significant and costly side effects of this nature are extremely difficult to avoid, especially in rapidly growing urban economies where resources are stretched and many opportunities to exploit such shortages already exist (see chapter 7).

Technical Problems of Definition and Operation

A third problem arises because it is extremely difficult to turn theoretically straightforward interventionary approaches into operational policy instruments. A good example here lies in charging for urban services. Government often supplies infrastructure and other public services—for example, electricity, water, or public transport—which provide mainly private benefits (they of course also confer social benefits, which are relevant to pricing and output decisions). If such services are provided freely, or at a price below social costs, either the quantity needed to satisfy total demand will be too large for efficiency or, as is far more likely in rapidly growing communities, there will be shortages and consumers will bid up the price of serviced land.[18] Then the benefit is, at least in part,

---

17. The debate on this subject is well reflected in a series of articles in *Urban Studies:* Rose (1973 and 1976), Neutze, (1974), and Foster and Glaister (1975).
18. See chapter 2 for a careful discussion of the meaning of "shortage" and chapter 5 for a more detailed analysis of this incidence problem.

shifted from consumers to usually better-off landowners. There may also be longer-term costs if financing is not available to provide the further services necessary to increase social welfare. The private sector may then step in to fill the gap. But the private supplier often cannot fully use available economies of scale and may also have significant market power. As a result, the services may cost more than necessary in real resource terms and cause further redistribution of income to monopoly suppliers. Charging efficiently for the public provision of services would solve these problems, but how is it to be accomplished?

The obvious starting point is to set price equal to marginal costs, but there are objections both in principle and in practice. First, in the system in which these charges must operate, prices for other goods do not generally reflect marginal costs. Charges should take such distortions into account and will thus be very difficult to determine.[19] Second, the overall benefits of provision to the consumer will usually be far greater than this per unit price, so land prices will still be bid up and benefits shifted. Third, the often high fixed costs may not be covered by such a pricing policy, and financing further services will be more difficult. The usual answer is to levy a multipart tariff with a fixed charge that helps cover the fixed costs. Although this solution is much discussed in the literature, full application is difficult because of lack of information and problems of enforcement (see Bird, 1976b and Prest, 1982b). In some cases, it is likely to prove impossible; in many others, a different approach may be more effective. For instance, a betterment levy on the increase in land value arising from the benefit is often seen as a more suitable solution. But this approach is not a full substitute for pricing because, unless consumers are also charged for their marginal use in relation to true social costs, services cannot be provided and allocated efficiently (see World Bank, 1974a). Even so, where charging is impossible in practice or where a financing gap remains, the case for levying some form of betterment tax is very strong.[20] It is in line with the principle that he who benefits, in this case the landowner, pays.

The technical problems of implementation are: how to define a price structure that adequately reflects the true costs of provision when these are not themselves readily determined; how to cover costs that do not vary with output; and how to make sure that these costs fall on the people who actually benefit. Any operational system can expect to reflect consumer-related costs only in broad terms, but as long as the main

19. See Baumol and Bradford (1970) for a discussion of why there must normally be differences between cost and prices.

20. One relatively successful attempt to finance urban services by valorization charges is described in detail in Doebele, Grimes, and Linn (1979).

factors are taken into account correctly this will be far better than nothing for both efficiency and equity.

Similar problems of collecting information, specifying instruments in line with this information, and ensuring that these are operational and enforceable arise when determining land use regulations. Again broad regulations that take account of major imperfections and objectives are likely to be more effective than extremely detailed controls that cannot be adequately responsive to changing circumstances (see chapter 6). But there are enormous technical limitations on what is practicable, and poorly defined regulations can, in the limit, do more harm than good.

Perversion of Instruments to Meet Other Ends

When discussing government intervention it is normally assumed that those who implement the policies will do so to the best of their ability, in line with specified objectives. This is unlikely to be the case in practice. First, administrators' payment, and indeed employment, rarely depends on successful implementation.[21] Instead, there are likely to be strong incentives for administrators to increase their income through side payments. Even where corruption is controlled, they may choose an easy life rather than try their best to meet other people's aims. Second, many agencies, particularly suppliers of urban services, were set up to meet different primary objectives. In São Paulo, for instance, SABESP, the state organization that provides the infrastructure for water and sewerage, sees its role as expanding supply in response to the strength of demand. It regards the integration of these plans for expansion with those of the municipality and other city planning organizations as a secondary objective. Third, the organization that sets the rules is often not the one that implements them. In São Paulo, building regulations are set by CORGEP, which has overall responsibility for city planning, but implemented by SEHAB, which has little knowledge of the original rationale and may well have different objectives in mind when implementing the regulations.

Those adversely affected also have incentives to evade or change policies, and the greater the difference between what is allowed and what could maximize private benefits, the greater is this incentive. For example, one aim of subsidized public housing is usually to redistribute income to those who receive the housing; another to limit the external costs of poor sanitation, fire, risks, and so on. But if the standard of housing is higher than that which individuals would desire, given their income, they have an incentive to sell their rights. In this way they can increase their

---

21. See Williamson (1975) for a discussion of these problems of managerial control within a market economy.

expenditure on other goods and services. Then specific housing benefits are transferred to the new owners, and the original recipients receive additional income. This is often against the spirit of the policy, particularly if it has a merit-good element. Moreover, many low-income recipients have less bargaining power than those who buy the housing services from them. In this case, the price they receive will be low, and many of the benefits will be passed on to other purchasers, whom the government probably had no desire to assist.

In addition, the external benefits of such projects often depend on maintaining standards related to density of occupation and specific urban forms. Yet individuals may gain considerably from increasing densities and from modifying structures. Such modifications are difficult and costly to monitor and control. Again, the expected benefits are unlikely to be fully achieved.

Similar problems often arise when a mortgage subsidy is provided. Usually this subsidy applies only to part of the required finance, and consumers must find the rest elsewhere. But, where the finance market is relatively undeveloped, suppliers are often able to exercise market power. As a result of the subsidy, they are able to charge more for additional finance, so that the benefit is partly shifted to these suppliers. Furthermore, since the ability to pay has not been increased as expected, housing demand and output will not expand as much as was intended.

Other examples arise from land use planning. Private developers will try to avoid zoning and the regulations that reduce their profitability. There will be pressure to modify plans, and evasion will shift some of the benefits back toward the developer, re-externalizing costs and reducing social welfare. Adverse effects include the costs of organizing the system of control and the costs of evasion as well as the subsequent undesirable redistribution of income. Particularly relevant is the example of building regulations, which set norms that are often extremely complicated and considerably increase the costs of both planning and construction. Builders, who wish to take account of only private cost, thus have a major incentive to avoid the regulations. Detailed monitoring is usually practically impossible, and the potential for side payments is large. Evasion is often at the expense of a shorter life of the property and increased expenditure for repair and maintenance. Thus, to the extent that implementation falls short of the correctly specified interventionary aim, the effects of market failure are reimposed.

Urban economies are made up of individuals and firms as well as of government agencies. Each makes separate decisions on the allocation of resources. Each can try to adapt to intervention, shifting the incidence of a tax here, modifying the actual effect of a regulation there. A prerequisite of successful intervention is therefore that it take account of how the members of the community are likely to react to any measures that attempt to modify the economy in which they operate and adversely affect their own position.

The ultimate incidence of the benefits of any government policy, whether local or national, is unlikely to be as clear-cut as policymakers desire and, indeed, often suggest. Moreover, inefficiencies arise both from the costs of administering the system and from the adjustments that take place in response to the policy. The costs of these must be assessed and weighed against the potential benefits of any given instrument even before a decision is made on whether to implement it.

Legal and Administrative Problems

A final set of problems in choosing techniques arises from the limitations of the existing legal and institutional framework. Most countries with a colonial tradition have land use regulations. Legal powers, however, are often narrowly defined and inadequate to ensure that objectives can be met. For instance, most cities attempt to control densities through plot ratio regulations in order to limit congestion and other external costs and provide services on an efficient scale. Yet plot ratios often apply only to new buildings. Modifications of existing buildings then occur within the law but in line with private rather than social demands. Further, the regulations usually apply only to the structure, not to the actual density of occupation, which normally determines the use of services and the extent of congestion. Even where occupancy is controlled, it is likely to come under a completely different agency, which often deals solely with minimum health standards. In many countries even this type of legislation does not exist, and unregulated congestion builds up. Further, there is usually very limited administrative capacity to monitor and enforce what legislation actually exists, and sometimes few penalties for infringement. It is therefore not surprising that much of the original objective of control is lost, while the costs of intervention remain.

When it comes to the more complex approaches of taxation, subsidies, and even government controls, often an effective legal framework simply does not exist, and the difficulties of passing additional legislation to allow such policies to be implemented may be immense. A matter of particular importance is the right to raise taxes. Many countries have a multitiered system of government, each tier with jealously guarded rights of taxation. Usually only the federal government has the right to introduce new tax bases, and states and municipalities are confined to raising money from well-defined sources. In addition, national governments usually hold the power to sanction or provide local authority debt. Policies that involve large expenditures of public money can thus be carried out only as part of a national program. This presents a dilemma: the effectiveness of large-scale intervention, of the type analyzed in chapter 7, depends heavily on the clear perception that a major aim of the policy is to influence urban form. This is likely to be fully understood only at the local level. However, the capacity to implement these large-scale expenditures depends on national governments, which do not put the same emphasis on urban factors when formulating their investment programs.

Another example of administrative constraint in the choice of techniques arises in the use of compulsory purchase legislation. In some countries this is possible only if the land is to be used for a limited range of well-specified purposes. In this case, more general policies for obtaining surplus value, such as land banking and excess condemnation, are automatically excluded, unless new legislation, against tradition, can be enacted. Even where more general powers exist, custom may make it difficult to exercise them. For instance, the Islamic tradition strongly favors private owners having continuing rights over their property. Public opinion is thus likely to be against the use of compulsory powers even where these are legislated. In still other countries, although legislation exists it is ill-defined, and the success of any large-scale compulsory purchase policy would require both additional clarificatory legislation and a suitable administrative mechanism.

A further practical constraint lies in the financial implications of compulsory purchase. Very few countries expropriate without compensation, although they often set prices administratively. For instance, in Tehran the government was enabled to purchase land within the development boundary at existing use value plus 5 percent, together with a payment for buildings, and this type of policy may be found in many other countries. Even this level of compensation, however, will usually rule out large-scale purchases by the local authority because of the lack of finance.

Thus the existence of suitable legislation, the administrative capacity, the will, and where necessary the requisite financing to implement this legislation are important factors to be taken into consideration when determining which techniques are feasible and which are likely to be the most successful. These problems of intervention are not strictly separable from one another but are all aspects of operating within a thoroughly nonoptimal real world. Their relative importance will vary greatly from one country to another, and even from one locality to another in the same country.

Conclusions

It is at least possible to specify a set of questions which should be answered before deciding whether to intervene at all and if so in what way. These questions include:

- Does the legal framework exist?
- Is the information available to specify the policy in line with objectives, or can such information be obtained?
- Is the administrative capacity available to operate the system?
- Can the administration be given the incentive to implement the policy effectively?
- Can the necessary financing be made available without adversely affecting other more valuable policies elsewhere?
- Will those adversely affected be able to modify the policy and so reduce or remove the benefits?
- Will those affected be able to pass on the costs to others and so pervert the original objectives of equity and efficiency?
- Will secondary adverse effects offset apparent gains?

These are all aspects of a more general question: Do the benefits of the policy *as actually implemented* outweigh the costs *actually incurred*? Experience suggests that the new policies likely to be worthwhile are those that introduce clear gains to almost everyone and that establish the organization to make these gains attainable. For instance, minimal fire and health regulations in site-and-service schemes have low costs and obvious benefits to those living in the area. These have been found to be generally both enforceable and beneficial.

Similarly, taxation and charging appear to work when those who have to pay see they are receiving a worthwhile benefit which would not otherwise be available. This has been the experience with valorization charges in Bogotá (see chapter 5; Johannes F. Linn, "Incidence of Urban Property Taxation in Colombia," in Bahl, 1979; and Doebele, Grimes, and Linn, 1979). Other examples are land readjustment policies where government acts simply as an organizing agency and the participants receive the benefit of redevelopment (see chapter 3). Government may also be more effective than the market in organizing large-scale investment projects where there are significant economies of scale, agglomeration economies, and desirable spillover effects. It also has a better chance than the market of integrating decisions to achieve a more desirable urban system through land use regulations and other policies. These scenarios suggest that gross market failures arising from lack of information and coordination are the most readily improved by administrative intervention. Such conditions are common in the rapidly growing cities of the developing world.

Some policies, although providing significant benefits to the community and to individuals, often place such heavy costs on individuals in relation to their ability to pay that they cannot be implemented: the incentive to evade is too great. Examples here are building standards significantly above those currently available, and zoning regulations which limit mixed uses.

Success has proved particularly elusive when the main intention has been redistribution. The relative power of the groups involved is likely to offset much of the redistributive effect, often with accompanying losses in efficiency. This does not imply that such policies should not be attempted, but rather that only partial success should be expected and that they should be made as simple as possible to operate and monitor. Site-and-service schemes, for example, though obviously not meeting all their expected objectives, do in many cases provide services more efficiently than does the market, and some of the benefits do reach the intended recipients. In contrast, high-standard public housing appears to have relatively fewer efficiency benefits and is usually a far more expensive way of redistributing more to fewer people. Mortgage subsidies often have even less redistributive effect, with many of the ultimate benefits falling to landowners and financiers.

Further, success is unlikely if the implementation of the policy requires complex informational and institutional structures. Examples include the use of tax bases that depend on detailed and up-to-date information on ownership and structures, which either does not exist or is so incomplete that the take is limited, evasion easy, and the result grossly inequitable. Another example is the relative lack of success of land banking, which requires highly sophisticated management skills if the land is to be employed in its most efficient use and costs are not to outweigh revenues (see chapter 5).

In conclusion, experience suggests there are many opportunities for government to reduce the costs of providing urban services and to improve land use—sometimes by removing ill-conceived or out-of-date controls (for instance, where building regulations increase costs without concomitant benefits); sometimes by making information more readily available or supplying the organizational capacity that the private market is unable to provide; sometimes by bearing risks too large for individuals. Here all can benefit from well-designed, well-implemented policies.

But other types of policies are far less certain to achieve their aims. In particular, many governments try to distribute the social gains of urbanization more fairly, but success here is rare, in part because of the relative power of the potential losers in the community. In addition, there are often significant losses in efficiency because of unsuccessful implementation.

It should therefore not be regarded as axiomatic that market failure and maldistribution will be corrected by government intervention. The costs of such intervention are very real. Experience does suggest, however, that if developing countries can solve the mundane problems of providing adequate information, management skills, and monitoring and enforcement capacity, there are many policies that can significantly improve conditions both for those now living in the expanding urban areas and for the far larger numbers who will live there in the future.

5

Intervention through Property Taxation and Public Ownership

Donald C. Shoup

THIS CHAPTER EXAMINES TWO FORMS of intervention in the urban land market: property taxation and public ownership. The assessment of any given policy depends on what objectives are to be met, and unobtainable objectives can create their own problems. Three familiar objectives for land policy are adopted here: distributional equity, efficiency of resource allocation, and government revenue. The relationship of betterment to these objectives is discussed first, and then property taxation and government ownership are evaluated with respect to the same objectives.

Betterment

When governments make site-specific public investment, rent increases may shift the public benefits from tenants to landowners. For example, if households value the benefits of new water services at more than their water bills, competition for the serviced land will drive up rents and thus shift some of the benefits of the water services from residents to landowners.

The Bustee Improvement Organisation in Calcutta shows how the benefits of public services can shift from occupant to owner when the site is not owner-occupied. About one-third of Calcutta's population live in bustees (slum housing) with a complicated tenure arrangement: landowners rent sites to housing entrepreneurs called thika tenants, who build huts and in turn rent them to occupants. The government has attempted to upgrade sites by installing public services such as water, electricity, drainage, and sanitary facilities (see Grimes, 1976). Initially the bustee dwellers benefit, but if the improvements lead to increased rents some of the benefits shift first to the thika tenants who own the huts, and in turn to the landowners. The extent of the shift depends on how quickly housing and land rents adjust. The elasticity of supply of huts on the serviced land will limit the size of rent increases, but the supply is inelastic in dense upgrading projects. Rent control would limit the shifting of benefits away from bustee dwellers, but brings problems of its own.

This is not to say that upgrading bustees is unwise, but rather that landownership and tenure determine the final incidence of local public service benefits where the value of these services to the consumer is greater than the direct price charged. The final distributional impact of low service charges is probably very different from the initial impact unless residents own their homes.

Changes in property value are sometimes used to measure net benefits of specific services, and this logically implies that property owners receive all these benefits. If, for example, piped water is supplied to all houses without charge, the residents' consumer surplus from water will be larger than when users pay for water. Therefore user charges tend to reduce the capitalization of project benefits into land values. Without user charges, residents pay for water indirectly through land rents. With user charges, residents pay for water directly, and land rent rises by a lesser amount, imposing a smaller burden on those who use little water. By this reasoning, the incidence of user charges may be very similar to the incidence of betterment levies when the capitalization of consumer surplus in land values is considered.

The ways in which betterment arises and the factors determining who receives the benefit must be taken into account when evaluating property taxation and public ownership as urban land use policies. It is to these topics we now turn.

Property Taxation

"After all the proper subjects of taxation have been exhausted, if the exigencies of the state still continue to require new taxes, they must be imposed on improper ones." —ADAM SMITH

Taxes are not usually seen as significant tools to influence land use because revenue is the objective, but there are exceptions. For example, Taiwan and Chile tax vacant land to stimulate development in certain zones, Jakarta has higher tax rates on land not used in accordance with its zoning, and the Republic of Korea taxes speculative gains in land value.

Even when revenue is the only objective, however, property taxation affects land use, and these effects are often directly contrary to other objectives, such as improving housing.

Most conceivable land tax systems seem to have been tried somewhere. For purposes of comparison, different tax systems can be classified according to their definition of the tax base—the subject of most disagreement over tax policy. The three major contenders for the property tax base are total property value, site value, and betterment.

The two most persistently proposed land tax reforms refer to changes in the tax base. Both stem from the work of Henry George, who, in contrast to Adam Smith, believed that the exigencies of the state had almost exhausted the improper subjects of taxation and that no tax had been imposed on the proper one.

The recommended reforms are, first, that the property tax base should be changed from improved value to land value and, second, that betterment should be taxed. These two proposals raise many of the most important issues of land tax policy, and the following discussion evaluates them according to the three major tax objectives outlined earlier: distributional equity, efficiency of resource allocation, and revenue. The section concludes with a proposal for a new way to pay betterment taxes.

To evaluate any tax one must first estimate (or assume) its incidence. Two approaches are possible. The first is differential incidence, in which government revenue and expenditures are assumed to be fixed; an increase in one tax is matched by a decrease in some other tax, so the problem is really to estimate the incidence of two taxes at once. This approach is most appropriate when evaluating major structural changes in the tax system, and it is used here in discussing the merits of land taxes as opposed to property value taxes. The second approach, which is more appropriate for estimating the effects of a betterment tax, is to assume that the tax revenue will finance a specific expenditure and to examine the results of the tax and expenditure together. The incidence of any tax is rarely unambiguous, however, and even with the long-studied general property tax there are wide differences of opinion.[1] The incidence of the same tax can also be different in different countries because of differences in administration (Roy W. Bahl, "The Practice of Urban Property Taxation in Less Developed Countries," in Bahl, 1979).

1. Charles E. McLure, "The Relevance of the New View of the Incidence of the Property Tax in Developing Countries," in Bahl (1979), surveyed his own views on the incidence of the property tax. In a 1968 study he assumed that in Colombia two-thirds of the property tax was borne in proportion to nonfood expenditures, and one-third was borne by upper-income owners of capital; in another study done in 1972 he assumed that the tax was borne entirely by owners of the taxed property.

Land Value or Total Property Value as the Tax Base?

Land value (also called site value) has long been advocated as an alternative to total property value for the real estate tax base. Theoretical arguments strongly favor taxation of site value, but evidence only weakly confirms the predicted benefits of exempting improvement value from the tax base. The relevant policy choice is whether to shift the tax base from improved value to site value rather than to choose initially between them, and the replacement of one tax base by another raises questions not encountered in the simple comparison of their long-run effects. Therefore, both short-run and long-run effects of shifting toward heavier land taxation are explored below according to the criterion of how well the objectives of equity, efficiency, and revenue are met.

EQUITY. A shift in the property tax base from total property value to land value would reduce some distributional inequities and introduce others. If the land value tax is a levy on pure land rent and therefore unshiftable, the incidence of the tax change is on the owners of land at the time the tax change is announced. In practice, no such change of tax base can ever be announced suddenly; in Jamaica, for example, it was eighteen years between the enactment of legislation introducing site value taxation in 1956 and the completion of assessments in 1974.

Because landowners bear the burden of pure site value taxes, the most important element in evaluating the equity consequences of shifting the tax base toward land value is an ethical judgment about the existing distribution of land. If landownership is highly concentrated in higher-income groups, the redistribution accompanying the tax base change would at least be popular with a large number of taxpayers. Indeed, one of the reasons for introducing site value taxation in Jamaica was the unequal distribution of land (see O. St. Clair Risden, "A History of Jamaica's Experience with Site Value Taxation," in Bahl, 1979). In 1965, 3 percent of all farms were larger than twenty-five acres, yet they accounted for 63 percent of total farm acreage; 80 percent of all farms were smaller than five acres and accounted for only 15 percent of total farm acreage.[2]

---

2. This view corresponds to the findings of Archibald M. Woodruff and L. L. Ecker-Racz, "Property Taxes and Land Use Patterns in Australia and New Zealand" (in Becker, 1979, pp. 185–86): "The fact that a number of Australian and New Zealand communities have been voting to change to unimproved capital value basis for property taxation has less implication for the inherent superiority of that system over others, as it generally reflects taxpayers' desire to minimise tax bills. Communities vote to shift to unimproved capital

(Note continues on following page.)

Landownership is also highly concentrated in Hawaii, which adopted a higher property tax rate on land than on buildings in 1964. In 1960, approximately 84 percent of all privately owned land in Hawaii and 70 percent of all privately owned land in Honolulu was in holdings of 5,000 or more acres (Baker, 1961). By 1962, more than two-thirds of new residential development land in Honolulu was available only with lease-hold tenure, and seventeen landowners accounted for 99.9 percent of all residential leaseholds (Vargha, 1964).

Despite this high concentration of landownership, the property tax change was unpopular with many voters, and in 1980 Hawaii abandoned its higher tax rate on land. Because lessees were typically required to pay the property taxes on their leased land, the graded tax bore heavily on homeowners whose leased homesites were underimproved in compari-son with the market. And because the land leases run for up to ninety-nine years, increases in land taxes could not be passed back to the landowners except in the very long run.

The Hawaiian experience from 1964 to 1980 shows the short-run problems caused by shifting to a tax system that promises long-run advantages. It also emphasizes the importance of tenure arrangements as they influence the distributional consequences of taxes.

If land value taxes reduce land values, those who own the land (or lessees who hold an interest in the land) at the time the tax is imposed bear the burden of the tax. Bird (1976) points out, however, that current landowners continue to bear the burden of a capitalized tax in the politically relevant sense that they would gain if the tax were reduced.

A site value tax captures betterment, although the low effective rates in most countries indicate that this is not yet an important source of revenue. When taxation is based on the market value of land, any increase in land value automatically increases the annual tax liability, regardless of the cause and when or whether the land changes hands. Therefore, a pure site value tax has a broader base than either betterment levies (which generally recoup the cost of public investments) or capital gains taxes (which are generally triggered only at the time land changes hands). Further, if the assessed land value is independent of any activity on the owner's part, a land value tax should not affect the allocation of land. Since the equal-yield tax rate on land value is higher than that on total property value, the land value tax captures a greater proportion of increases in land value than does the general property tax.

---

value when they are on the outskirts of a developing metropolis and a majority of homeowners stand to benefit at the expense of a few. The reverse is true in older, prosperous sections of metropolitan areas where the shift would be in the opposite direction and store and factory owners would benefit at the expense of the more numerous homeowners."

The distributional consequences of raising the tax rate on land must be considered along with the consequences of lowering the tax rate on improvements. Unfortunately, the theory is unsettled, and most developing countries lack the factual basis on which incidence estimates depend (see Bird, 1976, and McLure in Bahl, 1979). For example, there are very few facts about the distribution of urban landownership among income groups.

In this uncertain context, Linn ("Incidence of Urban Property Taxation in Colombia," in Bahl, 1979) examined the differential incidence of a change from general property taxation to site value taxation in Colombia, and found that it would have either an approximately neutral or a somewhat progressive long-run effect. Linn points out that the switch to site value taxation would be more progressive if low-valued properties were exempted from taxation, which happens in many countries.

Progressive rate structures can align land tax burdens crudely with ability to pay. The land value tax rate in Taiwan is graduated from 1.5 to 7.0 percent of assessed value, and in 1974 about 43 percent of all land tax revenue was derived from land assessed at more than the 1.5 percent basic rate (see Lent, 1976). Owner-occupied land is taxed at a preferential rate of 0.7 percent and factory sites at 1.5 percent to promote homeownership and industry. The land tax rate in Jamaica is also graduated, from 1 percent to 4.5 percent of assessed value over J$50,000. Although fewer than 1 percent of all parcels were valued at more than J$50,000, they yielded more than half the total revenue from the land tax (see Risden in Bahl, 1979).

If a site value tax rate is to have exemptions or to be progressive, it seems logical to tax the total value of the landholdings, rather than that of individual parcels.[3] Otherwise, the rate structure encourages subdivision without a change in ownership. In Taiwan the progressive tax rate is levied on the cumulated value of all land held by an owner within each prefect or municipality. This seems reasonable if the objective is to avoid monopoly power in the land market.

A progressive rate structure is not well suited to a general property tax because, at the upper end of the scale, a high tax rate would be a strong disincentive to capital-intensive land uses. By contrast, a high tax rate on land encourages rather than discourages investment in improvements and should deconcentrate landholdings.

Because the imposition of site value taxation amounts to the appropriation of a share of the land's value, some proposals for a movement toward

---

3. This, however, presents problems of avoidance in many countries, since each parcel can be owned by a separate corporation and many people may be owners of each corporation.

site value taxation call for both a phased reduction in building taxes and a phased increase in land taxes. Since the increase in tax liability is deferred, the impact on current landowners is reduced—but whatever benefits may accrue as a result of the reform are also delayed. An increase in taxes is a risk accepted by all landowners, and maintenance of the status quo rewards those who gamble that the tax system will not be changed.

EFFICIENCY. There are two basic efficiency arguments for shifting the property tax base from improvement value to land value. One is that taxation of buildings, or of any capital improvements to land, deters both new construction and maintenance and thus increases the price of housing and other real estate. A property tax on land value alone does not vary with individual decisions to build, and thus people are free to build what they think best.

A second argument for changing the tax base is that there are direct benefits that derive from high taxes on land. Since few taxes are thought to have any advantages other than the revenue they produce, the claim that site value taxation can actually increase the efficiency of the urban land market sets it apart. The argument is that if land is taxed according to its revenue potential there is a stimulus to develop the land to its full capacity. Although a wealth-maximizing landowner in a perfect market already has this incentive, in imperfect markets the cash-flow requirements of a land value tax spurs owners to allocate land to its highest use. Moreover, since the value of land depends on its public services and development capacity, site value taxation pressures owners to develop already serviced land and relieves demands to extend new services to raw land. Since development capacity depends on zoning, taxation according to land value also promotes the use of land for its zoned purposes rather than for some less intensive activity.

Despite these generally accepted theoretical arguments, few empirical studies have shown that land use patterns differ markedly between areas where general property taxation is used and those where site value taxation is used. Richman (1965) found no effect in Pittsburgh where land is taxed more heavily than buildings, and Woodruff and Ecker-Racz (in Becker, 1979) found no differences among suburbs in Australia with different property tax systems. Clark (1974) examined the land use patterns in Auckland, New Zealand, where within one metropolitan area jurisdictions have the local option of using any of three property tax bases: total value of land and buildings, unimproved land value, or annual rental value of the property. Although the three systems were operating side by side, no significant differences were found in either land use or changes in land use. This was so despite the fact that the property tax revenues from each system were comparable to that in most U.S. cities.

Even the theoretical argument that a general property tax reduces investment in improvements has been challenged by the "new view" of property tax incidence in which capital is assumed to be in fixed supply to the nation, so that the effect of the tax is to reduce the rate of return to suppliers of capital, but not to reduce capital formation. If so, and if the property tax rate is uniform on all property in the country, there would be no inefficiency introduced by the tax.[4]

It seems clear on theoretical grounds that higher land taxes will reduce the market value of land (see Walters' discussion of appropriation ratios in chapter 2), and there is some empirical verification for this effect. The effect of a site value tax on the rate of appreciation of land values must, however, be analyzed somewhat differently. As developed in chapter 2, the rate of return to landowners is the sum of the rate of return of the land in current use plus the rate of price appreciation of land. For vacant fringe land awaiting development, the return in current use may be zero or negative; if so, the rate of appreciation must cover both the supply price of capital (the interest rate) and the land tax. Therefore, to provide the same after-tax rate of return as that on other assets, land prices must increase faster in the presence of an annual land value tax. Although a site value tax would be expected to lower the general level of land prices, it should not be expected to reduce the rate of appreciation of these prices. For example, Grimes (1974) found that land taxes did not reduce the rate of increase of land prices in the countries he studied.

To discourage speculation and encourage development of land that is already provided with infrastructure, vacant or underutilized land can be taxed at a uniform rate or a rate that escalates with the length of the period in which the land is held idle. An important argument for a tax on vacant land is that it can stimulate the economies of agglomeration that compact, contiguous development can bring. This will be beneficial if government is better informed than private decisionmakers. In general, however, it is not desirable to encourage the immediate development of all urban land. Many sites need to be held for later expansion of facilities or for denser development not yet justified. The definition of what is or is not "development" of a vacant site may also be a difficult issue. If the definition is too loose, premature buildings will be constructed merely to

---

4. Johannes F. Linn ("Incidence of Urban Property Taxation in Colombia," in Bahl, 1979) has further challenged the old view of the property tax. He points out that the assumption that the supply of urban land is perfectly inelastic can be questioned on the grounds that the quantity of urbanized land in most cities does expand over time. If the supply of urban land is price elastic, then a local tax on land value may be shifted. Whether this is true depends on how the tax is imposed, and in particular on whether fringe landowners have some say in whether their land will be included in the urban tax district.

satisfy the tax requirement. If defined at a rigidly high standard, undue hardship for many low-income families will result.

In Taiwan a surtax of between 200 and 500 percent of the regular land tax is levied on private land that has been designated as a building site but that remains vacant. All sites on which the value of improvements is less than 10 percent of the land value are considered vacant (Lent, 1976). The tax is levied only in selected areas, which in 1974 included less than 1 percent of all land subject to the conventional land value tax. It has been estimated, however, that between 1968 and 1973 the vacant land tax led about half the owners subject to the tax to construct improvements on their land.

Finally, the macroeconomic effects of property taxes on resource allocation can be important. Feldstein (1977) has argued that if a land tax reduces land value, one result is that a larger amount of desired wealth must be accumulated in the form of produced capital. Because land and capital are substitutes in investors' portfolios, a tax that reduces land value would increase the equilibrium capital stock. This could be an important stimulus in countries where land value is a large part of total wealth.

REVENUE. The revenue effects of a change toward site value taxation depend in part on the ratio of land value to total property value. There are few estimates of this, and there is general agreement that existing assessed values for tax purposes are poor indicators of true values.

The revenue performance of land value taxes in developing countries that employ them has not been impressive. For instance, Jamaica in 1974 completed an eighteen-year process of changing from a general property tax to a site value tax system, yet collected only 5 percent of its total tax revenue from land taxes in 1975–76 (Risden in Bahl, 1979). In Taiwan, where there is a long-standing commitment to the principles of land value taxation, the revenue from urban land value taxes was 1.5 percent of total tax revenue, and rural land taxes contributed another 2.2 percent, compared with 3 percent contributed by the "house tax" assessed on the value of improvements (Lent, 1976).

At the subnational level, land taxes are a more important source of revenue; for instance, they contributed between 10 and 20 percent of provincial tax collections in Taiwan between 1967 and 1974 (Grimes, 1974). Nevertheless, the general experience is that real estate taxes produce less revenue when land alone is taxed than when total property value is taxed.

With regard to the relative costs of assessing taxes, Brown (1965) found that in New Zealand the cost was $NZ0.60 per assessment for unimproved land values, and $NZ4.00 per assessment for land and improvement value. This suggests that a pure site value tax will be cheaper to administer than a general property tax.[5] In developed areas a general property tax gives a greater opportunity to check the accuracy of assessment by reference to sale values recorded in transactions, but this is less important at the urban fringe where there are more transactions of vacant land to give evidence of current values.

Betterment as a Tax Base?

Annual property taxes on capital value capture only a small share of betterment because most tax rates are low and assessed values lag far behind market prices. However, betterment can be taxed separately, and two types of betterment taxes are discussed below.

First, when the goal is to finance site-specific public investment, special assessments can be imposed on the betterment caused by investment. If the property is assessed before the project is undertaken, the tax base is the increase in land or total property value expected to occur as a result of the expenditure. Because betterment is difficult to measure, project costs are usually apportioned according to a simpler tax base, such as frontage or land area, that can serve as the measure of special benefit received. Special assessments are an alternative to financing services by user fees, especially when it is technically or politically difficult to charge for services directly.

Doebele, Grimes, and Linn (1979) have analyzed betterment levies that recover public investment costs in Bogotá, while Macon and Merino Mañon (1975) surveyed betterment levies throughout Latin America. Both studies provide excellent discussions of the important problems of determining the area benefited by the public expenditure, determining the total betterment to be recovered, and dividing the levy among benefited properties.

Second, land value increases can be taxed at the time property owner-ship is transferred, either as a special capital gains tax on land or simply as part of the general system of capital gains taxation. The tax is based on what has already happened to land values, and the revenue is generally not earmarked for any specific property-related use. This sort of tax is more commonly administered by a national rather than a local govern-ment.

A third type of betterment tax is on the gain in value associated with a land use change. Because of its intimate relationship to the land use

5. Technical problems in assessing site value for tax purposes are described in William S. Vickery, "Defining Land Value for Taxation Purposes," and Ursula K. Hicks, "Can Land be Assessed for Purposes of Site Value Taxation," both in Holland (1971).

planning process, this type of gains tax is feasible only where there are very strong land use regulations. Even Britain, which has such regulations, has had considerable difficulty in administering development value taxes, and they are not discussed here.

EQUITY. The incidence of betterment levies is not necessarily on those legally obliged to pay them. Neutze (1970, p. 328) takes the position that it is "virtually impossible to devise a tax that will directly reduce in substantial degree, or directly capture a significant part of, the increment in the value of land resulting from its conversion to urban use. Almost any kind of tax will mostly be passed on to the final consumer of the developed land." Archer (1976) cites evidence that the Sydney betterment levy of 30 percent of gains from rezoning was passed on to land users. Many land sale contracts even included an explicit provision that the buyer pay the Sydney levy, and this quickly generated a popular belief that the levy was shifted.

If betterment taxes are not shifted, they would, like the site value tax, fall on those who own the land at the time the tax is introduced. Land prices would be lower, but the subsequent rate of return would be unaffected (Shoup, 1970; Roger S. Smith, "The Effects of Land Taxes on Development Timing and Rates of Change in Land Prices," in Bahl 1979). The exact amount of future betterment is never known with certainty, however, and is especially uncertain when there are many possible locations for future public infrastructure investment. Therefore, even if the average rate of return on landholdings is no greater than on other assets, some owners receive large increases in land value from the public investments while others receive little. A betterment levy would tend to capture these imperfectly anticipated gains from public investment and would thus reduce the variation in owners' after-tax incomes.

Although benefited owners may not oppose a betterment tax if the revenue is used to provide services that cause the betterment, an important equity question should not be neglected. Some lower-income occupants may be unwilling to pay for the benefit of a particular public investment, such as paved road. If the investment makes the neighborhood more attractive, higher-income groups may then bid up rents and land values. Therefore public investment can cause property values to rise by more than the betterment levies, but original owners may wish to move rather than pay the tax out of their current income. This is an "efficient" outcome, because land will be allocated to those who value it most, given that the public investment is going to be made. Some owners might suffer a welfare loss, however, and might prefer no public investment and no betterment tax.

Financing public works by betterment levies is equivalent to requiring owner-occupants to receive a public service and pay for it (through the levy) or else move out, realizing whatever net capital gain remains after payment of the levy. If the government tries to capture all the betterment provided by public facilities, owners must either stay and pay the charge or else move out with no capital gain. Therefore all owners who value the new services at less than the tax would suffer a net loss whether they move or not. Insofar as the poor are less willing to pay for new public services, attempts to capture 100 percent of betterment will reduce the welfare of low-income owner-occupants.

Renters may also move if a new public service causes rents to be bid up in the benefited area. They suffer a welfare loss equal to their full costs of relocation. Even those who stay may value the new service less than the accompanying rent increase and thus would be made worse off. But if the tax is incident on the landowner, it can be, by definition, imposed without harming the renter. It is betterment that dislocates renters, not the betterment levy.

EFFICIENCY. Betterment levies introduce discipline into the demand for public expenditures. When expenditures that benefit specific sites are financed from general revenues, there is political competition for the valuable public decisions that confer land value gains without compensating payment. A tax on the land value gains conferred by public expenditures reduces the incentive to spend resources merely to influence the distribution of public investment.

Another point (discussed in chapter 2) is that in some countries betterment levies may be the only effective way to finance public investment. If the "shortage" of serviced land in developing countries is due in part to an unwillingness or inability to charge a cost-recovery price for public services, an alternative is to finance the service provision by taxation of the land value gain that arises when the services are extended. The tax effectively takes the place of a price for services.

The rate structure of a general land value increment tax can also affect resource allocation. For instance, Taiwan has a progressive tax rate on increases in land value which varies from 20 percent of the gain on increments less than 100 percent up to 80 percent of those over 300 percent. Since the gain is generally larger on land held for longer periods, this rate structure presumably hurts short-term speculators and encourages "straw" transactions to make one large gain appear to be several small gains. Despite this incentive, in 1975 more than 60 percent of the revenue from the land value increment tax came from transactions subject to the 80 percent tax rate (Lent, 1976).

A capital gains tax payable at the time of sale can produce a lock-in effect. There is, however, almost no evidence as to how important this is in the land market. In Taiwan the tax on realized gains is supplemented by a tax on unrealized increases for properties that are not transferred in any ten-year period. This reduces the incentive to delay sale in order to avoid taxes.

REVENUE. Few countries collect much revenue from taxes on increases in land values. For example, in Taiwan the land value increment tax yielded only 2.7 percent of total tax revenue in 1976 (Lent, 1976). Grimes (1974, p. 147) concluded in his survey of social appropriation of betterment:

> In all countries examined . . . receipts from betterment levies and land value increment taxes were low compared with receipts from property taxes and other revenue sources. In some cases, particularly Great Britain and South Korea, this disappointing performance was compounded by expectations when the taxes were introduced that the revenue obtained could not fail to be impressive.

Although national land value increment taxes designed to produce general revenue have been disappointing, the performance of local betterment levies designed to recover the cost of specific projects has been more impressive. In Bogotá, "valorization" charges are used to finance public improvements that benefit specific areas, and the charges are based on the increases in land value caused by the public improvement. In some years the revenue from these valorization charges has exceeded 50 percent of the total revenue collected by the general property tax (Linn, 1976). The revenue potential of land value increment taxes appears to be greatest when the tax is clearly linked to a specific expenditure that will not occur unless the increment tax finances it.

A Suggested Improvement—Deferred Special Assessment

Although betterment taxes score highly on the criteria of both equity and efficiency, a major difficulty in practice is the cash-flow problem for benefited owners, who pay taxes in cash but realize no compensating cash benefits unless they sell their property. Even if the government allows owners to stretch payment of their assessments through installments, the principal and interest payments still present a cash-flow problem for many owners. Because it is costly to use equity in an owner-occupied home to pay taxes, the cash-flow problem alone can make it impractical to use special assessments to finance even public investments, such as for water supply, that increase land values by more than their cost.

One possible way to deal with this cash-flow problem would be to allow owners of benefited property to defer payment of special assessments, with accumulated interest, as long as they own their properties (Shoup, 1980, presents this proposal more fully). The timing of payments entirely at the owner's option thus distinguishes a deferred special assessment from conventional special assessments or betterment levies. The local government would, in effect, offer loans to owners to pay the betterment tax. If owners were charged the market rate of interest on the deferred assessment, the present discounted value of future payments would equal the initial special assessment, so the government would lose nothing by the delay.

Local governments would run little risk of default if the country's land registration and property tax systems were sufficiently integrated to prevent legal transfer of ownership without payment. Even in cities where it is difficult to collect annual property taxes, it may be easy to collect deferred assessments because the seller has the cash from the sale when the assessment is due, and both the seller and the buyer need the government's cooperation to transfer legal title to the property. For instance, land in Colombia cannot be transferred without a certification that all valorization charges have been paid.

Despite its great security of repayment, a deferred assessment could never result in foreclosure for nonpayment because, by definition, it would not be due until a property is sold. This would be an especially important advantage in developing countries where many property owners participate only marginally in the market economy and have no reliable cash income with which to pay taxes. Even though taxation is the only way to finance a greatly desired public investment, many owners would understandably resist any new tax that threatens the loss of a home by foreclosure. The terms of a deferred assessment specifically exclude the possibility that an owner will ever be evicted for nonpayment, and for this reason deferred assessment should be less unpopular than other property taxes.

The benefits of such an approach from the owner's point of view are clear. Desired services are obtained without any cash-flow problem or fear of foreclosure; and since expected public service benefits are capitalized into property values, the owners take the value of these benefits away with them when they sell and leave the neighborhood. The burden of paying the deferred assessments is, however, borne by the original owner because the tax cannot be passed on to anyone else any more than a mortgage can be. Property with deferred assessment debt would sell for no more than similar property without debt, so the tax would be paid only by the seller no matter how large it had grown over time. Further, if a market rate of interest is charged on assessment debt, the sale date does not affect the present discounted value of the deferred assessment payment. Thus, a deferred assessment accumulating at the market rate of interest should have no effect on an owner's decision when to sell or redevelop a property.

Conventional approaches to easing the burden of paying special assessments often misidentify the cash-flow problem as one of low income. In Bogotá, for instance, valorization taxes are normally due within six months, but low-income owners are granted periods of up to five years to pay in yearly installments with no interest charges (Doebele, Grimes, and Linn, 1979). This offer requires a substantial subsidy (one quarter of the capital cost if the cost of capital is 10 percent a year) but does not wholly solve the cash-flow problem. Deferred assessments could solve every owner's cash-flow problem, and yet require no subsidy if the government charges a market interest rate on assessment debt.

Finally, the opportunity to use deferred assessments for neighborhood public investment would be a strong incentive for owners to register their land titles, because deferred assessments depend on an unambiguous system to record land ownership and transfer. Such registration would not only make the urban land market more efficient, but also make annual property taxes more collectible, especially if they too could be deferred at a market interest rate. Postponement of property taxes could also solve the politically difficult cash-flow problem that site value taxation can cause for low-income owners of highly valued land. Therefore, shifting toward site value taxation and simultaneously offering tax deferment might overcome some of the practical objections to exempting improvements from the tax base.

Public Ownership

Public ownership of land is best examined in practical contexts, and two very different forms, land banking and land readjustment, are discussed below. The focus is on intervention in, rather than replacement of, land markets, and most land is assumed to be privately owned.

Land Banking

Land banking usually refers either to advance acquisition of sites for government use or to larger-scale public ownership of undeveloped land planned for future urban use. The first subsection considers banking sites for the government's own use, and the second, public dealings in the land market to influence land uses and prices.

FOR FUTURE GOVERNMENT USE. Increasing population and rising land prices give a strong incentive to buy land before need. The objectives of advance acquisition are mainly to locate future public facilities efficiently and to pay less for the sites. Shoup and Mack (1968) found that the chief benefit of advance acquisition was to preserve the sites best suited for future public purposes from premature commitment to private use. Land value appreciation alone justified the advance acquisition, but the greater benefit was to keep the land available. For example, one government bought sites for school expansion before they were needed, so as to prevent private construction on them.

Although the "captured" appreciation is a transfer from the previous owners to the government, it is a net gain in efficiency to prevent premature private construction which must then be demolished to make way for future public use. For some future facilities that need large or specific sites, advance acquisition is almost essential, because earlier private development can easily make later public use too expensive.

Insofar as the government possesses information concerning its own future actions, advance acquisition for future facilities has potential for capturing the betterment they create. But to be successful, the government has to act before the information becomes public knowledge, and land acquisition is often a slow process. If the government's land-buying intentions are kept "secret," there is great opportunity for private trading with inside knowledge. Government purchases would signal its intentions in any case, and land values would tend to rise in response, even without any public announcement. Further, any comprehensive land use plan indicates roughly where services will be provided, and expectations will affect land values long in advance.

Land banked for future public use can be put to an interim use that yields revenue or some other public benefits, but governments can have a hard time evicting interim users (perhaps squatters) when the time comes to build. Temporary tenants sometimes construct permanent improvements to solidify their claim to land, and this magnifies the apparent injustice of reclaiming it from them. This difficulty often requires that banked land be kept idle or that interim users be "incorporated" into the later public use.

Banking sites for future use has costs that are not always easy to measure. The government has to finance the bank, and interest costs can exceed the appreciation captured. A low government borrowing cost can make advance acquisition appear profitable, but in practice the shadow interest rate on public investment funds is usually much higher.

There is also the chance of buying land that later turns out to be inappropriate for an intended public use. If a site acquired in advance is used instead of one that is more suitable at the time of need, the full value of the appreciation is not a true net gain to the government. But in some cases only the inventory of publicly owned sites is considered, and the benefit of having captured appreciation may be far outweighed by the poor location of the completed facility. Shoup and Mack (1968) found that only one-fourth of U.S. cities that acquired land in advance made any attempt to calculate the subsequent market value or carrying costs of the sites they bought.

A land bank of future public sites requires management, and this cost may be considerable if complicated safeguards are necessary to ensure disinterested behavior by the managers. The scarcity of expert land managers, willing to work only on the public behalf, may in many circumstances be the greatest impediment to a successful program of advance acquisition.

TO INFLUENCE LAND USES AND PRICES. Quite aside from advance acquisition for future public use, large-scale land banking has been recommended as a way of providing public infrastructure and capturing the betterment it creates. The argument runs that if the government could purchase all land to be converted from rural to urban use and pay compensation at agricultural value, planners would be better able to direct urban growth and the government could collect the betterment created. If the government were the only buyer of raw land for conversion, its offer price, backed by the power of compulsory purchase at agricultural value, would set a ceiling price for private transactions. The bank could service the raw land, then sell the building sites, or lease them if the serviced land is to stay in permanent public ownership.

Government monopoly of the land-conversion process is most closely approached in Sweden and the Netherlands (Neutze, 1973). However, the institutional framework and administrative resources in these countries are completely different from those in most rapidly urbanizing nations, and it is doubtful if the process could succeed without them. Doebele's (1974) analysis showed that the favorable results in Sweden resulted not only from the use of large-scale public ownership, but also from an "intricate complex of interlocking and mutually self-supporting institutions all focussed on common objectives." In particular, the important role of secrecy in the operations of the public land acquisition agency places a premium on the incorruptibility of the civil servants involved.

The introduction of a land bank operation to buy raw land at its opportunity cost in nonurban uses would involve reducing the value of all raw land to its current use value. It would also greatly increase the rewards to illegal subdivision of unserviced land, already a severe problem in many countries. Thus, success of the land bank in capturing betterment would require strict enforcement against illegal subdivision. But, in practice, the price of illegally subdivided land can approach that of legally subdivided land, especially if the government pursues a policy of subsequently upgrading the illegal settlements by providing clear titles and public services. One example of the incentives provided by legalizing squatter settlements is a 1967 program in Seoul, Korea, to give subsidies and legal permits to owners of squatter houses to which specified improvements had been made. In one area 1,000 new houses were noted within one month of the announcement of the program.[6]

Although local government purchase of land before the provision of urban public services has the potential to capture the rural-to-urban betterment and to provide a controlled supply of building sites, the potential is very unlikely to be realized in most cities with a rapidly growing low-income population. Government control over both squatting and illegal subdivision is likely to be weak or, if effective, must involve harsh controls. If the land bank is not a monopsonist and instead buys land at market prices, its potential for capturing betterment or influencing land prices is greatly reduced. If the holdings of private land speculators are not simultaneously reduced, the government's entry into the market as a buyer of undeveloped land would presumably raise the demand for land and thus raise rather than lower its price. Carr and Smith (1975) argue that a land bank will reduce land prices only if speculators reduce their holdings by more than the size of the land bank itself. The government cannot sell land to reduce prices without first having bought it, and if a secular rise in land prices is the problem, countercyclical buying and selling would have little impact.

Land banking operations in the raw land market can affect the supply of building sites by assembling land and reselling it with restrictions on the type and timing of the uses to which the land may be put. If, for instance, land is sold with the requirement that construction of specified improvements be completed within a given period, the government has greater control over the market, but the reluctance to use strong control measures short of government purchase may imply a lack of political will or consensus necessary for extensive land banking to work. Further, many observers feel that existing land use controls hinder more than help the low-income population. By setting inappropriately high standards for permitted construction, density, and services, governments in developing nations have, it is argued, reduced the alternatives open to those who cannot afford housing of such high standard (Turner, 1976). Any

6. William A. Doebele, "Land Readjustment as an Alternative to Taxation for the Recovery of Betterment: The Case of South Korea," in Bahl (1979).

policy that strengthens the government's control over land development may actually work a greater hardship on those who now obtain their housing outside formal channels. Thus, a land bank must be realistically considered in the light of the uses which government officials will make of it. One obvious temptation is to use banked land for public use when another location would actually be better, and this has allegedly been a problem with some site-and-service projects.

Managers of a land bank intended to influence the pattern of urban development obviously have to make economic and political decisions about the desirability of future development. Dishonest practices in both the acquisition and disposition of land are difficult to control, especially if social objectives justify deviating from market prices in purchase or sale, or if there is secrecy. This is an inevitable problem of land bankers, but an alternative form of public ownership, discussed next, reduces this problem to a minimum.

Land Readjustment

Land readjustment is a temporary form of public ownership that is simple in principle and sophisticated in practice. It appears particularly promising because of its demonstrated success in the Republic of Korea, Japan, Taiwan, and elsewhere. Doebele (in Bahl, 1979) describes the process in Korea, where it has been used to convert small and irregular agricultural parcels into replotted building sites with full public services for over one quarter of Seoul (see also the discussion in chapter 3).

Either the government or a petition from 80 percent of the landowners can start the readjustment process to convert fringe land from rural to urban use. The readjustment authority then prepares a site plan for the entire area, replots the land for private building sites and public uses, and installs all the expensive urban infrastructure, such as paved roads, sewers, and electricity. The market value of the new building sites is estimated, and just enough sites are retained by the government for auction to repay the cost of public planning and infrastructure. The original owners then get back the remaining sites in proportion to their initial contributions—usually from their original holding. Owners farm their land right up to the time infrastructure is installed, so that fringe land is not idle during the conversion to urban use.

The number of sites that must be auctioned to finance the project cost depends on the prices they bring. Korean public authorities keep project land prices high by making sure that the supply of lots they make available does not exceed demand at any time (Doebele in Bahl, 1979). An alternative policy would be to readjust more land every year to push down the price of serviced land. The government would have to auction more of the now less valuable sites to recoup its cost, so the readjusted landowners would receive less betterment. But more rural landowners could participate, and urban land prices would be lower.

Land readjustment is the process of bartering raw land for serviced land, and is therefore suited to countries where governments find it difficult to finance public infrastructure investment. Landowners cannot escape paying project costs even if taxes are hard to collect, because their contributions are decided in kind before the project begins. Landowners also pay all the holding costs while the project is under way, so the readjustment authority has only to finance the infrastructure investment, and that only until sites are auctioned. In effect, those who buy the auctioned "cost recovery" land pay for the infrastructure.

One problem, however, is that many owners receive several building sites in exchange for their raw land contributions, and this delays use of serviced land. Because the lack of mortgage money compounds the mismatch between owners and would-be buyers, strengthening the mortgage market could improve the effectiveness of the readjustment process. If development does not occur promptly, the large infrastructure investment yields little or no return.

Another way to accelerate building on serviced sites would be to return fewer building sites to large landowners, auction the rest, and divide the proceeds, net of government planning and infrastructure costs, among participating landowners in proportion to their initial land contributions. Although this is a departure from the basic barter principles of readjustment, it would assure that initial landowners have sufficient cash to begin construction on their own sites, and that no owners have more land than they could themselves use. The auction process could be further modified by antispeculation requirements in the sale agreement, or by a tax on vacant land.

Although most readjusted sites are bartered, the auctioned sites demonstrate market values. If sites bring high prices and go only to high-income families, they are clearly too large or too well serviced for low-income families to afford, and more but smaller sites might bring a higher total value. The auction therefore not only recovers the government's cost of planning and infrastructure but also gives a market survey of the results.

Conclusions

Rather than recapitulate, it is perhaps more useful to end with some specific recommendations that emerge from this chapter.

Where there are shortages of serviced land, higher rents and capital values shift some of the benefits of public services to landowners. At the same time, governments often cannot extend basic services to raw land because they cannot finance the public expenditures. Given these factors, a lack of serviced land may be partly attributed to the failure to tax the betterment caused by public services. Although betterment levies have often proved disappointing, there is evidence of success when they are perceived as a price that owners must pay to receive public services. This introduces some discipline into the political process of allocating public expenditures and permits a more extensive program of servicing raw land for urban uses.

User charges are an alternative to betterment levies for some public services. Because service benefits net of user charges raise rents and land values, the burden of user charges should shift from users to landowners. Thus, the ultimate distributional consequences of user charges and betterment levies may be quite similar. Since rate structures for user charges can be made progressive, their well-known efficiency as rationing devices would suggest greater reliance on them to cover at least marginal cost. To the extent that user charges affect land values, they should also not be neglected as a device to recapture betterment.

There are compelling grounds for not attempting to tax 100 percent of betterment. In particular, the normal assessment errors in estimating land values may be greatly magnified when assessing the difference between land values before and after betterment. Given the well-known problems of administering tax systems that are conceptually much simpler, it seems prudent to begin modestly.

Finally, two promising ways to increase urban public investment are deferred assessment and land readjustment. Because realized increases in land value are the ultimate source of repayment for public investments financed by deferred assessment and land readjustment, both methods offer great security to lenders without unduly burdening the current income of borrowers. Therefore, both deferred assessment and land readjustment offer excellent opportunities for increased domestic and international lending to finance local public investment.

6

Intervention through Land Use Regulation

John M. Courtney

GOVERNMENTS IN ALL COUNTRIES have perceived the need to regulate the use of urban land in the general interest of the community. The immediate reason for intervention is usually the need for land for roads, utilities, and other public services or because of spillover effects, the tendency for the use of land for one purpose to result in costs or benefits to users elsewhere. In an uncontrolled land market, individual owners and users have little incentive to take account of the costs (or benefits) they impose on others. So governments may provide financial incentives in the form of taxes or subsidies. Where the spillover effects are locationally specific, governments may impose direct controls that require individuals to use land in ways which benefit the community as a whole, or at the least create no serious harm. Within planned economies spillover effects will, in principle, be included in the direct estimates of costs and benefits of possible uses and so be taken into account when determining the most suitable urban structure for the community.

The Objectives and Problems of Land Use Regulation

Regulating land use in the community interest involves more than the recognition of spillover effects on contiguous land. One objective is to provide public amenities, such as open space, which would be unlikely to be privately produced. Another is to increase efficiency: for example, by guiding development and redevelopment of land to more desirable purposes, limiting urban sprawl and unnecessary encroachment on agricultural land, and achieving economies of scale and least-cost production of public services. Finally, there are distributional aims such as making land available to all groups in the community and ensuring that the benefits of development go to the community as a whole. Accomplishing these goals may entail a wide range of policies:

- To free land from unmarketable titles and remove jurisdictional barriers obstructing rational development
- To release urban land from constraints such as excessive zoning restrictions or concentrated ownership, and thus reduce land price increases
- To provide more efficiently the land needed for public or for publicly desired private development
- To enable the community to capture land value increments so that land development contributes to public revenues
- To provide essential housing, for instance for new migrants and the urban poor, and stimulate individual homeownership and self-help development
- To stimulate cooperative private self-help or public building and construction enterprises
- To stabilize real estate and mortgage values through the formation or expansion of lending institutions as well as other measures to ensure site improvements at affordable prices.

In general, the techniques used fall into three basic categories: incentives which utilize government power and financial resources to organize land uses more effectively; restrictions utilizing government power to restrain or otherwise direct private land use and development activities; and management improvements which remove barriers to the effective use of these incentives and restrictions on market forces. Incentives include the provision of infrastructure and services to facilitate development, as well as direct financing of development of the site itself. They may also include direct involvement in the purchase, compulsory acquisition, or nationalization of land for development. Restrictions include zoning, subdivision, and building controls and the prohibition or relocation of development, such as slums and squatter settlements. Management improvements may include the clearance of titles, training in the administration of code enforcement and zoning procedures, efficiencies in record keeping and in processing applications, improved surveys and mapping, and procedures for intra- and intergovernmental coordination of decisions affecting land use. In many countries, elements of all groups of techniques are combined to implement some form of overall planning. This chapter, however, focuses mainly on the second group and discusses the nature and value of restrictive controls, used alone or as part of the planning process.

Depending on the way in which they are enacted and implemented, restrictive land use controls can be either helpful or detrimental in meeting community objectives. To benefit the community the regulatory framework must be linked to the economic and social objectives and be capable of implementation. Adequate information is required to define the framework, to modify it in the light of changing circumstances, and particularly to adjust it to take account of the effects of rapid urban growth. Effective control mechanisms and the will to monitor and enforce the regulations must also be present.

Land use regulations in less developed countries often fail to achieve greater efficiency and equity in the use of urban land for many reasons:

- Their static nature puts the public sector in a position of reaction and constraint rather than initiation and promotion.
- The inappropriateness of the standards chosen often increases costs above those necessary to meet minimum health and safety requirements.
- Implementing the regulations is costly in terms of both the time and money used for administration and their effect on prices.
- The inflexibility of controls makes orderly adjustment to rapid change extremely difficult.
- The high value of favorable decisions to landowners and users generates a climate of corruption.
- The conflict of interest between different groups means that regulatory measures are often drafted to protect special interests and to serve existing owners, at the expense of new development and the more equitable distribution of benefits.
- Speculation, which arises from the weak enforcement and possible modification of regulations, can lead to the rapid escalation of land prices, the exclusion of low-income households, and increases in the costs of services.
- The traditional approaches to regulation and development of land are inadequately taken into account in the drafting and administration of regulatory measures.

As a result, plans often bear little relation to people's needs and wishes, and they are in any case distorted by limited implementation. These problems are exacerbated, particularly in the face of rapid change, by the lack of a consistent overall policy framework and of mechanisms for resolving conflicts between different objectives. To ensure a higher level of success, the measures must be tailored to specific cultural and budgetary resources and to the real development needs of the community for which they are designed.

Despite the high incidence of failure of present land use policies in the developing world, governments must establish some degree of control

over the use of land in order to create the minimum order required to
make cities workable. The controls must positively allow for complementary activities and at the same time act as brakes on negative
interactions. Inasmuch as controls do have this valuable role, developing
countries should recognize and make use of opportunities for the reform
of land use regulatory instruments. This requires an appreciation of the
nature and past shortcomings of specific instruments of control as well as
recognition of the costs, benefits, and implementability of planned
reforms. In the next section the main regulatory instruments available to
governments within the framework defined above are therefore briefly
discussed and evaluated.

The problem in defining new regulatory instruments is to enhance the
virtues of controls (so that they are intrinsically direct, readily monitored,
and so on) while obviating their difficulties (ineffective definition and
implementation, contrary results). One reason for failure has been the
lack of accompanying measures to provide serviced land in adequate
quantities. If this can be dealt with, the benefits of suitable allocation of
use will become more obvious and the pressures on nonimplementation
will lessen. Another reason has been inflexible and unsuitable standards.
It must be recognized that different regulatory frameworks are necessary
for different conditions; for instance, measures suitable for control of the
central business district may be entirely inappropriate for regulating
peripheral development. In addition, performance standards provide
greater flexibility and capacity to allow for local conditions than do
traditional approaches.

There is a need both for restrictions on land use and for the incentives
of direct government involvement in land use and investment. The two
approaches must be made to work together. This will require packages of
regulatory controls and of incentive measures to obtain the best results.
But all such approaches need to be kept simple and easy to administer if
they are to be effective in developing countries. Too much regulation
may well be as harmful as too little, but the incentive to add more
controls is often difficult to resist in the face of obvious urban problems.

Review and Evaluation of Land Use
Control Mechanisms

The five most common forms of land use regulation and control are:
zoning, subdivision regulations, building regulations, approval by government agencies, and urban planning. The first three provide a hierarchy
of regulatory techniques covering different sizes of land area and levels of
detail. The first applies to the general structure of the whole city and is

usually the least detailed. The second covers the immediate relationships between contiguous plots in greater detail. The third is the most detailed and controls the nature of the structure permitted on each plot, sometimes including the allowable uses. These three instruments are normally used in conjunction and, indeed, often include elements of one another. They are, however, by no means always determined by the same group of decisionmakers.

Agency approval is the usual method of implementing the regulations specified under the first three controls. However, the approval procedure merits separate consideration since in many cases it is operated by one or more organizations completely unrelated to the planning bodies determining the regulations. The urban plan also requires individual treatment. Although it usually employs the techniques already discussed, it is a far more comprehensive tool, involving the more positive government powers of investment, acquisition, taxation and subsidy, and other direct involvement in urban development. For each form of control I examine its objectives and main characteristics and then evaluate its potential to improve the urban structure.

Zoning

Zoning is the demarcation of a city by ordinances and the establishment of regulations to govern the use of the zoned land. It also includes general rules about location, bulk, height, and thus plot ratios, shape, use, and coverage of structures within each zone. It is an attempt to organize and systematize the growth of urban areas by setting up categories, classes, or districts of land in the community, prescribing the uses to which buildings and land may be put, and applying uniform restrictions on the shape and placement of buildings. The main objectives of such regulations are to improve efficiency (which includes restricting uses to particular areas to limit adverse spillover effects), to promote agglomeration benefits, to specify minimum health and safety requirements, and to provide land for public goods and services. Zoning is also used to affect the distribution of benefits, especially the protection of the rights of existing owners, although it can be used more positively to release land for redistributional purposes such as low-income housing.

Zoning is the control most frequently employed to regulate the use of land. In its most traditional form its purpose is to ensure a proper amount of land for all the activities that must be performed in a contemporary community, to fix the best location for each, and to avoid the encroachment of incompatible uses. To meet these aims cities and municipalities may regulate the use of land and buildings by restricting areas to industrial, commercial, residential, agricultural, and other purposes.

Such uses may be broken down into further subclassifications, such as single and multifamily districts for the residential areas and more specific types of use for the commercial and manufacturing zones. Zones are often mixed, taking into account both complementarity and adverse interrelationships.

Early zoning ordinances were based on a scale of intensity ranging from single-family residential (least intense) to heavy industrial use (most intense). Designation of distinct areas for residential, commercial, and industrial uses for every community soon proved impractical. Modern use zoning has therefore become a more flexible and ad hoc device.

A second type of zoning ordinance is that of "bulk control" applied to both residential and commercial buildings. It has three purposes: control of the density of population, production, and traffic; provision of adequate daylight and air; and provision of sufficient privacy and open space. Older zoning ordinances regulated the shape, volume, and placement of buildings by height limitations, setback requirements (that buildings be set back from the street a certain distance for each additional unit of height), and requirements for open space surrounding buildings and courtyards. They were applied to all buildings in the relevant zone. This form of control was criticized for both its rigidity and the often unnecessary cost imposed upon the builder or developer.

More modern controls use volume or floor area ratios based on the relationship between the floor space needed in the building and the area of the lot. Spacing between buildings to admit daylight is also defined. The greater flexibility allows more freedom to develop better and more interesting buildings.

In recent years a more comprehensive but flexible approach to zoning has been introduced in many countries. The new techniques emphasize comprehensive development of large-scale projects to produce critical masses of compatible and self-reinforcing land uses as well as flexibility and adjustment to changing circumstances within the delineated area. The techniques include zoning for mixed-use development, transit impact, and cluster and planned-unit development.

Mixed-use zoning may be applied to very intense, large-scale estate developments made up of several well-planned and mutually supporting projects. It permits significant physical and functional integration of project components, and development in conformity with a coherent plan that stipulates the type and scale of uses, permitted densities, and related items. Transit impact zoning is a similar approach for rezoning land around a public transport station to permit planned mixed-use development and higher densities appropriate to the greater accessibility of the area.

Planned-unit development zoning may be applied to parcels of land containing a residential housing cluster of prescribed density and the appropriate commercial and institutional facilities to serve the residents. By clustering houses and consolidating open space, substantial areas can be left in a natural state. Less land is used for streets, utility runs are more efficient, drainage is better, and less grading and site preparation are required. It can therefore produce a better residential environment at lower cost and higher profit to the developer. Some of these approaches have so far been limited to developed countries. However, all are suggestions that may be of considerable value in developing countries.

Even these types of zoning may prove difficult to modify, especially if the request is not initiated by the landowner. Further techniques, such as floating and conditional zoning, give even more flexibility to the administering government.

With floating zoning a district is described in the zoning ordinances but is not located on the zoning map until the need arises. The ordinance simply describes what can be done in the floating district, such as building apartment houses, and lists the circumstances under which the city's governing body will consider zoning property for this use. As such, it might more accurately be described as a development performance standard, but one which allows a more flexible approach to new demands.

Conditional, or contract, zoning enables the municipality to bargain with developers for certain concessions and thus helps the community retain some of the benefits. A city, for example, may agree to rezone land in a residential district for a hospital but require the developer to surround the hospital with trees and blend it into the neighborhood.

Finally, there are instruments such as interim and phased zoning to alleviate problems in the timing of development and in plan modification. Under interim zoning a moratorium on building, clearing trees, or tearing down historical landmarks is imposed while the city considers whether to purchase the area or to rezone it. With phased zoning a special permit is required before actual development can occur. For example, land already designated for residential use cannot be subdivided for development until the landowner obtains this permit. It is granted only if he can show that adequate public services such as sewers, drainage, park sites, and roads are available. Thus, development in the restricted area is phased to the city's willingness and ability to extend public services. Other aspects of development, such as provision of open space by the developer, construction of low-income housing, and conformity to design standards, may be incorporated as criteria. In this way the city can encourage the particular type of development it desires.

In practice, zoning often encounters two distinct types of difficulty: incorrect definition of the framework by which social objectives are to be met, and costly and limited implementability often leading to results different from those planned. In relation to the first, traditional zoning regulations are oriented to the development of one lot at a time within a general framework, and to traditional blocks intersected by the usual gridiron pattern of streets. They make very little sense when rigidly applied to large-scale projects. The newer forms of regulations give more latitude to the builders in their design and have produced greater returns to the developer, as well as to the community, from cost savings and agglomeration benefits.

With respect to the second, to be of value, zoning must be a legal instrument. As such it is a potentially strong and powerful tool in preventing blight, eliminating conflicting land use, and ensuring the orderly implementation of development. As a legal instrument, however, zoning is difficult to modify and acts mainly as a restrictive force in relation to a static framework rather than as a positive incentive and guideline to development.

Land and building costs may be increased by zoning restrictions on the uses to which land may be put or on the nature of the improvements required. To some extent this is necessary to bring development into line with social objectives, but standards and controls often prove inappropriate, increasing costs unnecessarily.

Zoning may have undesirable distributional effects—for instance, in the case of overzoning (the designation of an excessive amount of land for a particular category of use) to protect existing owners' land values, or when zoning is used to exclude certain minorities from particular neighborhoods. If its implementation is sporadic and piecemeal it further upsets the workings of the land market and may intensify the maldistribution of "surplus value."

Zoning functions best when it is one of several tools employed in the planning process. Although its purpose of efficiently and equitably locating activities in relation to one another is clearly necessary, zoning operating alone is easily defeated. It cannot effectively outlaw existing uses, is resisted by owners, and often limits desirable changes in land use. It may, if improperly specified, retard valuable investment or force builders to find less suitable sites where restrictions are less onerous. In developing countries where the supply of urbanized land is increasing more slowly than the growth of urban population, it may readily lead to illegal development.

Subdivision Regulations

Subdivision regulations govern the development of raw land for residential or other purposes. They prescribe standards for lot sizes and layout, street improvements, procedures for dedicating private land to public purposes, and other requirements in far more detail than in the zoning plan. They also include procedures for filing maps and for receiving the approval of the public departments that grant permission. In the main, the objective of such detailed controls is to ensure that developments take account of the community's need for public goods and services, of minimum standard requirements, and of immediate locational spillovers of costs and benefits.

The subdivision of land prior to development is one of the most important determinants of neighborhood patterns. Once the size and shape of lots have been defined, the essential character of land uses, street patterns, and public utilities is determined. Lot size and shape also strongly affect the type, size, and quality of structures and the density of population.

The nature of intervention varies greatly from country to country. In some countries, such as India, there is very little formal control outside city limits and often little actually within the cities. Development may take place without services or any attempt to organize an efficient spatial structure. In other cases developers are required to conform to a regulatory framework, and possibly a detailed master plan. Some cities exercise considerable additional control over developers by requiring conditions to be met before they will provide streets, lighting, water, and other services.

The regulation and planning of subdivision on the outskirts of cities are widely accepted as essential to development. Proper and timely planning of expansion can preserve the sound structure of cities in the long term. An important element is the dedication of land for public purposes. In Israel, for instance, planning authorities may take as much as 40 to 50 percent of a private developer's land for open spaces and other public uses. In some cities of Latin America, property owners contribute considerable land for street widening and parks. In Mexico City, for example, 15 percent of subdivided property must be given for parks, while in Bogotá, Colombia, as much as 35 percent of the land has, until recently, been given to the city for streets, avenues, and other public facilities.

Many developing countries use this approach to the regulation of private development and to the specification of public involvement. In the Philippines, the Human Settlements Commission has prepared subdivision regulations for all urban areas, defining minimum standards of design and requirements for street layouts, subdivision of lots, easements, and utilities similar in character to the U.S. subdivision ordinances. In the Middle East (Iran, Jordan, Saudi Arabia, and Lebanon), subdivision controls, usually administered by the municipalities, determine the essential character of a neighborhood for a long time in the future. The original subdivision of rural land, the arrangement of the streets, the dimensions and shapes of the block lots, and the provision of urban spaces and public buildings must conform to national regulations.

A different approach to that of public control over private subdivision has been taken by many countries that are planning suburbs on publicly owned lands. Examples include the garden suburbs around Haifa and Tel Aviv in Israel and the housing development projects in Singapore.

One major problem in the Middle East is that, although controls exist over land within old municipal boundaries, there is little or no control over existing villages or new developments outside these boundaries. Without additional regulations suitable for these areas, unsanitary substandard buildings or unplanned narrow streets evolve. These built-up areas lack essential community facilities. Their development creates health, aesthetic, financial, and administrative problems of substantial magnitude for the municipality under whose jurisdiction they ultimately fall. In countries where cities are growing rapidly and there are shortages of public utilities, these problems are likely to continue, either because controls do not exist or, perhaps more important, because they cannot readily be implemented. The rapid growth of squatter settlements, typical of most developing countries' cities, compounds these problems.

In the main, subdivision regulation can be effectively applied only to areas being urbanized for the first time, and even then there are difficulties of enforcement. Hence the growing interest in a method of urban development widely and successfully practiced in Japan and the Republic of Korea, that of land readjustment (see chapters 3 and 5). This is a sophisticated form of land subdivision with a major element of participation on the part of the public sector. In Japan, land readjustment has already been executed or is being carried out on 27 percent of the country's total urban land area. In some cities such as Osaka and Yokohama, land readjustment has played a major part in urban development. In the Republic of Korea about 60 percent of habitable land within a 10 to 15 kilometer belt around Seoul has been developed or redeveloped through such land readjustment projects.

One major problem is that most subdivision regulations in developing countries have been based on experience in the developed countries. Subdivision regulation has proven a powerful tool in assisting and controlling suburbanization in the United States, for instance, and in France where public control over detailed plans has existed for fifty years. But the needs and conditions of developing countries require a significantly different set of standards—more flexible, more able to take account of rapid changes, more clearly related to local conditions and standards of living, and more easily implemented. Current standards are often too high, too detailed and inflexible, unrelated to local conditions and often even to the planning objectives of the community. Moreover, the control of subdivision is usually in local political hands and may well be manipulated to protect the vested interests of the few rather than to foster the interests of the many.

Building Regulations

Building regulations limit or define the way new structures are to be built and the materials to be used. They may also be applied to the maintenance and improvement of existing buildings. They may prohibit the erection of any structure whatever or restrict the style of architecture, the cost of the structure, the materials, the position of the building on the lot, or its distance from the street, its height or depth. More recently, building regulations have included requirements for parks, parking, and other amenities as a condition for approval of a subdivision or street pattern. They may also include controls over the use to which the building may be put—for example, for residential purposes only or for specified types of enterprise—as well as minimum conditions which dwellings must meet to be regarded as fit for human habitation. They may be in the form of building and housing codes legislated at the national or, more usually, the local level, or they may be written into deeds or other instruments as part of the contractual arrangement.

Their main objective is that of securing socially acceptable minimum standards. Originally there were three main reasons for such regulation: fire protection, structural safety, and sanitation. Today, codes include not only a far wider range of protection but often aesthetic considerations as well. In addition, they are seen as an important device for preventing the deterioration of the housing stock.

Building regulations are one of the oldest and most common methods of controlling land development. These are defined for a specific local, regional, or national area, depending on the size of the country, the political structure, the variations in climate, the local materials used, local standards, and other factors. In the United States, for instance, they are made by cities, while in Japan they operate at a national level.

Some codes go into great detail; some are more general. Detailed codes have little flexibility of choice and tend to lead to standardized design. More general specifications state the results to be achieved and a standard of performance for each structural member. This broadens the area for originality in design, although it also allows a great deal of discretion to the supervising official. Because of technological advance, regulations now often also specify the strength of materials and of structural parts, as well as standards for plumbing, electricity, elevators, heating, and ventilation. Commercial, industrial, and public buildings as well as residential buildings are all generally subject to codes. In developing countries, however, although in principle all buildings are usually subject to codes, in practice an informal sector is likely to arise in which neither building nor use regulations are operative. The problem of enforcement is even greater when regulations relate to existing units.

Although building regulations are essential, particularly in areas where private building dominates, their limitations should be understood if they are to be useful. Current problems include overrigidity of design, manipulation by vested interests, forced use of certain materials, and a tendency for codes to run behind technology. Although the preparation of a good code requires not only local experience but also constant experimentation and testing, there is a tendency for one jurisdiction to adopt the regulations of another without modification or appropriate evaluation. Turkey, for example, adopted a code used in Germany, which was abused, ignored, and eventually proved useless, in the main because of its unsuitability. Similarly, the uniform application of regulations in all sections of a country, irrespective of climate and cultural differences, can lead to inappropriate development or disregard of the regulations.

The imposition of building regulations, while necessary if minimum standards are to be adhered to, has often raised building costs and widened the gulf between what the consumer must pay for rent and what he can afford. This problem is exacerbated by inefficient controls, such as those that exclude the use of cheap local building materials or of unskilled labor. Every regulation that raises cost, unless compensated by a rise in real income or by subsidies, removes another segment of the population from the group which can afford a legally acceptable home.

Because of rising building costs there has been a notable tendency in many parts of the world either to lower standards by reducing lot sizes and eliminating amenities, often below a tolerable minimum, or to accept that standards will not be met. Structures in squatter settlements, for instance, usually fall below the standards formally established in these countries. International involvement, particularly with respect to slum upgrading, raises some very serious questions about the relationship between current standards and existing building conditions, and about the extent to which the disparity between the two can in some way be reconciled.

This disparity also raises important problems of implementability. In the administration of building regulations, the abuse of authority by inspectors encourages illegal construction and bribery. In several African countries, for instance, buildings are supposed to be inspected before occupancy, but because of inadequacies in the inspection process, a large number are incorrectly certified as meeting standards. There is no easy solution to this problem in countries where corrupt administrative practices are common throughout the public service system. But even where there is considerable incentive to operate the codes, they are likely to prove unenforceable, at least in part, so long as standards are set significantly higher than those consumers can afford. When incomes are low even the most basic regulations cannot always be implemented. For instance, in South and Southeast Asia minimum standards of house construction to reduce fire hazards have generally been found to be unenforceable in low-income areas.

In many circumstances the capacity to implement regulations may be increased by reducing general standards, while maintaining minimum standards for health and safety, perhaps with the assistance of a subsidy. Site-and-service schemes have been designed in this way in the Philippines, Korea, Kenya, and Jamaica, to mention a few examples. They point the way to a more positive definition of building regulations as a series of performance standards rather than as inflexible input requirements and constraints. Clear statements of what will satisfy each regulation allow producers to take local physical conditions into account. In determining output standards of this type, what consumers can afford to pay, including what government or international agencies are prepared to subsidize, must be kept in mind. Initially, they should be designed to deal only with the most immediate social needs, but over time, as standards of living rise, they can be adjusted upward to take account of other factors.

Approval by Government Agencies

Approval by government agencies is the main way in which controls over development rights, subdivision, and building are enforced. Generally, building permits are required to ensure compliance with the local bylaws and in some cases with the general city plan. A building permit is usually granted tentatively on the basis of schematic designs of the proposed building or group of buildings prepared in line with zoning, subdivision, and building regulations. The designs are finally approved when the full set of contract documents is available. These documents are stamped, filed, and recorded so that the development is designated as conforming to requirements.

Government agencies also have the power to deny permission to build, and this is perhaps their most important control—although a refusal to issue a permanent permit may sometimes be challenged if it is thought to be unreasonable. Most governments of developing countries empower building or zoning inspectors to deny permission for development which is incompatible with public regulations. In most cases this power is exercised only sporadically. Where it is used it may have other purposes than to bring about compliance with regulations. For instance, some countries use the denial technique to force minorities or nationals of other countries into joint ventures with local businessmen, as well as to prevent urban sprawl. The power often extends to the right to demolish buildings which do not comply with the regulations or to fine owners of nonconforming units. The most usual use of this power is in relation to the destruction of squatter settlements, but it may also be applied to buildings within the formal sector, whether residential, commercial, or (less usually) industrial.

A major difficulty is the proliferation of agencies involved in any particular development and the lack of interaction between those that enforce the ordinances and those that operate them. Moreover, there is no necessary relationship between the capacity to obtain one set of permissions and another. This problem is by no means confined to the developing countries. In a major U.S. city, for example, the process may include several reviews with local and federal fine arts commissions, many separate meetings with the building department and with the zoning commission, and several meetings with the general council's office of the local government. To overcome effectively each of these hurdles requires a sound knowledge of local government regulations, procedures, and building and zoning codes on the part of a team of architects, planners, lawyers, and a political expediter. This tedious process does not necessarily ensure that better buildings are produced and is a prime example of the regulatory web that Western countries have woven. It adds substantial costs in professional expertise, and in the time and resources necessary to complete the project. Developing countries cannot afford the luxury of such a process of checks and balances in their building procedures.

Urban Planning

In the broadest sense, planning is the allocation of scarce resources to achieve certain goals, and it therefore includes most functions of government. The common use of the term, however, refers to the process of making decisions about the physical environment and evaluating how changes in this environment affect people and the economy in relation to some specified objective. The plan is then put into operation with the use of the regulatory instruments discussed above.

The most commonly used planning processes are: comprehensive general planning, master planning, strategic planning, and structure planning. Comprehensive and master planning tend to assume a static or slow-growing urban situation, quite manageable in terms of public investment decisions, and the long-range planning of major infrastructure projects. This assumption is usually close to reality in developed countries, where a prime objective of planning is to maintain the established order. Developing countries, however, are characterized by rapid growth, a major backlog of demand for infrastructure investment, and heavy competition for the limited financial resources. The pressing urgency of change with limited resources requires a more dynamic planning process. Traditional planning of this type thus tends to become in reality an isolated activity with little impact on continuous decision-making. In addition, it often lacks effective tools for implementation; zoning and police powers, normally the only tools implied by master plans, are usually inadequate.

A process which lends itself more readily to the demand of developing countries is that of strategic or structure planning. Action planning has many similar attributes. This approach highlights the critical issues, identifies the priority investments for infrastructure, and thereby establishes the areas in which growth and change should occur. It is applied not only to the expansion of the city, but also to the renewal, upgrading, or densification of older areas. Such planning does not require elaborate data gathering and can readily become an ongoing process involving selective action in key areas. It does require that priorities be established and that planning and decisionmaking be responsive to them. When the planning process is used to guide key investment decisions, it becomes an important positive tool in controlling and influencing the pattern of development and thereby encouraging efficiencies in public resource allocation over time and space.

The approach evolved in the United Kingdom as a response to the problems of the traditional British planning techniques. These techniques are often still applied in Commonwealth countries. The structure plan provides a framework for decisionmaking, both in map form and in a written statement of the policies and main proposals for change. These policies, programs, and priorities for action are related to a set of desired objectives and include the arrangement and character of services, spaces, and structures which may have an important bearing on the city or the general pattern of change and renewal. Most significantly, a structure plan specifies the practical actions necessary to influence events toward these defined objectives. Finally, it involves local decisionmaking and public participation. Although there are many problems in this planning process, its level of action and dynamics is more appropriate for the situation in developing countries than other more traditional approaches.

In many parts of the developing world, urban planning is still viewed primarily as physical planning of an essentially static nature, lacking both investment priorities and effective land use control policies. Only limited attention is paid to ensuring a feasible means of implementation, to anticipating the reaction of market forces, and to assessing the cost of various government agencies and the economic effects on different income groups.

In light of the experience of existing systems, it would appear that for an urban plan to be effective it must have a number of clearly defined elements. In particular, it must be based on well-defined social, economic, and environmental aims, be easily understood, and be as simple as possible. Further, it must allow for speedy plan preparation and decision-making as well as ready adaptation to changing circumstances. This means that it should be based on information which can be collected reasonably and cheaply. It must concentrate on those elements that are most important for the community and that offer the most obvious benefits of planning. For the developing countries this is likely to mean establishing a framework for ordering public investment priorities, focusing on programs to meet specific basic needs, and encouraging the guidance rather than the restrictive function of planning. It should avoid overcentralization, separate as far as possible statewide, regional, and local issues, and provide for public involvement. Finally, it must be implementable with the manpower resources that can be made available, and must be seen to be so implemented. Such a list of requirements is unlikely to be met in full, but what should be attempted is reasonably clear.

Conclusions

There is a wide range of experience, good and bad, with land use controls in both the developed and developing countries. The controls discussed in this chapter are largely restrictive, but they have not usually been designed and tailored for the urban conditions in developing countries, such as the shortage of skilled administrative personnel. This may be an important reason for the greater success of more direct incentive measures in developing countries. In particular, their effectiveness may be attributed to their higher visibility and the ease with which they can be linked to current project-oriented approaches. On balance, past experience may indicate only that little attention has yet been paid to identifying goals and simplifying administrative procedures when designing regulations. In the absence of substantially better alternatives, the regulatory approach is bound to remain significant. The lessons of past experience should therefore be used to improve existing controls, rather than to abolish them.

Moreover, changes occurring in the sociopolitical context are likely to increase the acceptability of such controls. Indications of these changes can be seen throughout the developing world (see, for instance, U.N. Department of Economic and Social Affairs, 1971 and 1975). Not only are regulations limiting landowners' powers, such as zoning and building codes, becoming more generally accepted as a government responsibility, but many governments are getting far more involved in controlling the ownership and use of land. In particular, they are attempting to limit excessive concentration of land on the one hand and to assist the assembly of land for development on the other.

Further, governments are expanding their direct involvement into urban land development and particularly housing operations. This involves not only more drastic use of existing controls but also the institution of new types of regulation on land use, ranging from greater restrictions on buildings and rents to nationalization of land. In addition, governments increasingly attempt to curb land shortages and price rises both by direct controls and taxation and by regulations to vary the supply of land.

Finally, the definition of public use is widening to encompass not only roads, parks, schools, and bridges but also housing, parking, airports, other transport, and even industrial facilities.

Given a political commitment to change, a number of basic improvements should be made to render land use controls more effective. First, where existing land use regulations are unworkable—hampered by obsolescence, inconsistencies, poor information, and lack of skilled manpower—immediate improvements may be possible, such as updating local ordinances and increasing the supply and skills of available manpower to administer the control system. Second, more efficient controls, such as the newer zoning categories, particularly if operated in conjunction with a strategic development plan linked to specified goals, can help make sure development meets the desired social objectives of efficiency and equity.

To obtain these benefits, a nationwide reform of the full range of land use controls and related policies is likely to be necessary. This should include inquiry into the larger context of land practices: law, administration, available skills, plans, projects, allocation and alignment of political power, land interests, public investment priorities, and so on. Without these investigations, it may be difficult to design and tailor the regulatory measures to provide for the full range of requirements at affordable and replicable standards.

In addition, it is necessary to examine the extent and form of regulations, their strengths and weaknesses, the agencies responsible, the extent of overlap and conflict of authority, the discretion vested in their operation, in law and in fact, and the degree of centralization of authority.

One subject of particular interest is the possibility of a land register. If based on cadastral land mapping that describes each site and shows lot size, land value, and ownership, this can form a basis for both use controls and planning. In addition, if these land valuations are based on transaction prices and land use legislation, they would help greatly to improve the tax base.

To achieve these improvements any set of land use regulations must meet these minimal criteria:

- Their enforcement must be feasible at the level of administrative capability that can be reasonably expected.
- The cost of their administration must be reasonable in the light of other demands on public funds.
- They must permit the kind of development that is desired by the target groups at costs they can afford.
- They must be designed to minimize the potential for arbitrary manipulation.
- The set of all policies affecting land use must be consistent with the overall framework and approach to development.

Through such a program of changes it should be possible to devise a system, or set of systems, of land regulations appropriate to the differing conditions of developing countries, which retain some of the best qualities of conventional land use control while avoiding the adverse effects currently experienced.

7

Intervention through Direct Participation

Malcolm D. Rivkin

IN ANY URBANIZING AREA government policy, programs, and actions affect the pattern of urban development. Many other factors also help shape this pattern, including market demand for the range of urban activities, tenure arrangements, and, at any point in time, the existing structure of man-made physical facilities which new growth must accommodate.

Although the role of government differs widely, public policy to regulate and control the pattern of urban development is of considerable significance in all parts of the developing world. Many serious problems of urban land use in developing countries are probably capable of mitigation only through some form of government intervention. Continued in-migration produces intense demand for land that cannot be satisfied by available sites. Extremely high densities of use and people are found on inadequately serviced land. Low-income workers are relegated to housing far from places of potential employment. Extreme traffic congestion and inadequate sanitation produce dangers to public health. In addition, the free market mechanism is not noted for its altruism: in rapidly growing cities in developing countries the market is therefore likely to be a poor vehicle for achieving equity in the pattern of physical development.

This chapter discusses how government might work to produce greater efficiency and equity in the allocation of urban land use and services. It suggests that the principal tools may not be formal land use regulation and control such as master planning and the various instruments of zoning, building codes, and subdivision. Instead, the primary control devices may be rarely perceived as affecting urban structure, namely, devices associated with direct public capital investment and finance. In this context, the regulatory controls are valuable supplementary techniques.

Rationale for Land Use Regulation and Control

The concept of regulation and control of land use implies a rule-setting function on the part of the government. If the starting point is that of a free-market economy, it is appropriate to ask first why government should undertake to establish rules relating to how land is used. One view is that the marketplace cannot be trusted to produce a rational, efficient land use system; in particular, it is unsuitable as a mechanism to accommodate all legitimate demands for space at a given time and simultaneously to allow for long-term growth in that demand. Land is a scarce resource requiring stewardship by public bodies that can balance short-term against long-term benefits and balance the claims of one interest group against another.

A United Nations study of land use regulation and control throughout the world underscored this aspect:

> The demand for urban land is growing, yet the supply is both genuinely and artificially limited. The situation radically increases land costs and in turn consumes scarce investment capital better used elsewhere. It also irrationally distorts patterns of urban growth and development . . . [and] as the urban infrastructure becomes more costly and inefficient and institutions and facilities fail to provide adequate services to their populations, urban, social and economic imbalances and injustices are intensified . . . the quality of the total urban environment erodes (U.N. Department of Economic and Social Affairs, 1975, p. iv).

In this context even the more capitalistic, free enterprise–oriented societies have increasingly imposed some measure of public control over the use of urban land. Government policy has become more important everywhere, although the nature and degree of intervention varies from country to country and from city to city, depending on political, economic, and social traditions.

The starting assumption in this chapter is, therefore, that governments should intervene in some way to guide the allocative and distributive effects of urban land use. Specific objectives that a government might pursue include the following.

Efficiency. Land controls may be instituted to ensure that the city "works": that sufficient land is available at its resource cost for all urban activities (housing, industry, services, recreation, and the like) and for the public facilities (such as roads, sewers, and hospitals) to support them; that these activities and facilities are appropriately accessible to each other; and that service capacity is sufficient for these demands.

Health, safety, and welfare. The protective function of government is to safeguard health, safety, and welfare. In the area of land use, this function includes setting rules to limit overcrowding on land, defining standards for the adequate design and capacity of utilities, establishing construction regulations to ensure the safety of buildings, determining the allowable level of noxious air and water emissions, and a host of other measures that affect the quality of urban life. Again the underlying objective is to use land in a way that increases net social welfare as much as possible.

Equity. Regulations to increase equity are of two kinds: those ensuring that certain activities or people which increase social welfare are not denied land within the urban area or adequate access to other activities (such as employment) and services (such as transportation and water); and those protecting the rights of owners or users of land against arbitrary seizure, intrusion, or classification by government or private parties, especially where such actions would diminish the effective use of the land.

Adaptability. Regulations and controls should ensure that the urban pattern can readily adapt to new patterns of population growth and economic activity. For example, activities and services should be able to expand, where their value exceeds resource cost, as demand for them increases; and areas or facilities should be able to be converted to other uses as their value to society changes.

Conflict resolution. A control system must also be capable of resolving conflicts between competing objectives and competing uses.

These aims are not discrete. For instance, "adaptability" can be considered an aspect of "efficiency," and "health, safety, and welfare" contains components of both "efficiency" and "equity." They do, however, cover a range of objectives which a government could pursue if it wished to foster a land use pattern able to meet legitimate needs of urban society.

If urban governments do accept these objectives and proceed to establish and enforce rules for the use of land that take them into account, these controls will significantly affect land values in three ways: (1) directly on the value of land itself; (2) through the costs of site development, building construction, and operation; and (3) through government revenues from real property taxation.

First, although many other factors influence land values—the supply of sites of different types and the demand for such land, the physical characteristics of the land, its accessiblity, and so on—the designation of use and density is a powerful instrument in the hands of government, if the marketplace regards the regulatory actions as serious. By way of example, take two pieces of vacant land of equal size, equally accessible to transportation and utilities, and equally suitable for a wide range of construction. If a planning agency or a zoning authority designates parcel A as a site for multistory office buildings and makes parcel B available only for individual, one-story houses on large plots, there would be a rush of value to parcel A because of its greater potential yield. Replicated many times in a planning and zoning process, this allocation of uses and densities can indeed become a major force in establishing the pattern of land values within an urban area.

Second, prescribing standards affects the costs of development and construction. For instance, by requiring certain materials (concrete rather than wood) or minimum internal space per occupant, building regulations establish construction costs that will be different from and often higher than those private enterprise, left to its own devices, would incur. Land development regulations which define on-site installation of utilities, minimum open space on a lot per dwelling unit, requirements for parking space, and the like have a similar effect on costs. Thus, although much of the cost of improvements depends on the type of facility and on the cost of labor and material, regulations can—if enforced—add to these costs and affect both the value and use of land.

Third, in most countries where property taxes serve as a form of municipal or national revenue, some computation of the value of land and improvements forms a basis for tax levies. To the degree that government land use regulation affects the value of the land and the costs of construction, it is also likely to affect the valuation of the property for tax purposes and thus the revenues derived from property taxes.

Constraints on Land Use Regulation and Control

Although evidence is limited and research almost nonexistent, formal government rule-setting in developing countries appears to have been largely ineffective in achieving efficiency and equity in the allocation and regulation of land use. Numerous reasons for this may be advanced. Governments may give such rule-setting little priority; they may have too little information to determine these rules; and they often lack the skills to implement them, while the private gains from avoiding constraints are great. Finally, rapid growth exacerbates the problems of both planning and implementation.

Few urban governments (or national administrations, for that matter) have accepted land use control as a top priority. Without this priority specific policies toward land use have not been defined, nor explicit objectives established. Instead, numerous planning activities have been commissioned to establish a physical form or design of an urban area, but without clear regard to questions of efficiency, equity, and adaptability. Unsuitable codes, ordinances, and other instruments have been adopted—often derived from developed countries where circumstances are totally different. Both planning and codes thus become unenforceable.

Even the most unsophisticated and rudimentary effort to establish positive controls requires information. At the very minimum it is necessary to have records of existing land use, development density, and ownership, along with accurate information on soil characteristics, the location and capacity of existing utilities and services, and so on. For planning purposes, information on economic and social characteristics of the population and its activities is essential. The information base in many developing cities is improving, especially data on physical attributes compiled with the aid of aerial photography. But, by and large, cities still lack accurate and up-to-date data on many of the above items. This must inhibit the application if not the formulation of comprehensive regulatory techniques.

Improvization in the face of inadequate data is possible, but it takes skilled people to establish and interpret substitutes. Moreover, the most sensitive control system in the world has little value for long-range planning and development if unsupported by skilled personnel with the ability to enforce the system.

Developing countries are hampered by having few trained professionals to prepare plans, formulate development regulations, or administer these controls. Even in Commonwealth countries, where appraisal represents a traditional skill for which training is sometimes available, municipal evaluators and inspectors are in very short supply. Often, as in some Latin American countries, they are administratively removed from the process of planning and formulating ordinances. Moreover, when permit systems do exist they are often subject to graft and corruption.

The enormous significance of land as an economic good in the developing world increases resistance to government attempts at regulation and control. In many developing countries land is a principal choice for individual investment. There may be few options, either as to type of investment (stock markets, banks, industrial operations) or as to security or yield. As a result, land speculation is rampant. As one high urban official said to me, "How do you expect us to adopt control measures over land use and land speculation when we, the officials, are speculators ourselves?"

Many urban areas are growing so rapidly that they outstrip even the more realistic control procedures. When population grows at rates of 6 percent, 10 percent, and even 20 percent a year, few efforts at rule-setting yet devised can effectively direct the consequences for land use. Witness for instance the long-term plan for Ankara carefully drawn during the 1920s to guide development of the new capital through this century. The 1980 population target was exceeded by 1950, and no regulatory devices instituted since then have been able to channel effectively the explosion of population and economic activity.

A corollary to the impact of rapid growth is the inability of plans and ordinances to change over time. Once any control system is established, there are vested interests in its maintenance. Despite nostrums in the literature of urban development, few plans are updated, few ordinances are amended.

As a result of these factors, although the potential effect of government land use policies is great, efforts to set rules may have relatively little effect on the use and therefore on the value of land, or may even be counterproductive.

Some Examples of Interplay and Impact

Government policies directed at other objectives often have major unintended influence on spatial development and the use of land. Such policies, interacting with techniques of land use control, affect the pattern of urban development and could thus, implicitly, help meet the objectives discussed above.

Throughout, this analysis is hampered by the fact that land use is underresearched. Very little systematic investigation deals directly with land use controls in developing countries. Very little empirical evidence has been assembled as a basis for measuring the impact of various government policies or actions on urban land. Perhaps the most comprehensive effort is the United Nations report (U.N. Department of Economic and Social Affairs, 1971 and 1975). This seven-volume study goes far toward identifying the array of measures employed by many developing countries, but sorely lacks documented assessments of effectiveness, impact, or failure.

Without definitive investigations, a more impressionistic course is to cite examples of how government actions have interplayed with market and pricing mechanisms and with physical constraints to shape urban development in specific settings. Through these examples, the leverage potential of direct public investment and finance may be seen, along with the more limited but supporting role of formal planning and regulations.

These examples come from both the developed and the developing world. Illustrations from North America have been selected because they have been exhaustively researched, not because the public intervention techniques employed are necessarily applicable to the developing world. Illustrations from developing countries come from personal observations which suggest linkages between public action and land use patterns, although systematic documentation of cause and effect is rarely available.

Effects of National Policy

National investment policies and programs frequently shape the pattern of urbanizing land and affect the location and densities of urban activities within individual communities. But often they are strictly sectoral in nature and are conducted without regard to their impact on land use. Illustrations of two such situations follow.

SUBURBAN GROWTH IN THE UNITED STATES. One of the most extensive and documented examples of a national program working in concert with private market forces was the conversion of suburban land in the United States between 1945 and 1970.[1] During this period the growth of central cities slowed or stopped, and large areas of the countryside were converted into low-density suburban communities. By 1970 the majority of America's urban population lived in the suburbs, and most new employment activities were also there. Some very powerful market factors had been at work. A serious housing shortage existed after World War II. High birth rates and generally higher incomes spurred the desire for privacy and space. Heavy migration to central cities by the poor and minority groups helped push middle-class families out. A demand existed. But it was able to be met and land patterns were established because of two federal programs formulated without explicit land use objectives.

The first was the mortgage-insuring activities of the Federal Housing Administration and the Veterans Administration. Their provision of low-cost, long-term financing allowed large quantities of inexpensive housing to be constructed on the relatively cheap land available in undeveloped suburbs. These new residential areas attracted commercial services and supporting public facilities, which created new networks of communities and led to further suburban development.

The second was the Interstate Highway Program of the U.S. Department of Transportation, launched in 1953, which provided fast, convenient intercity expressways. These highways made vast areas of undevel-

1. The extensive literature depicting the character and causes of suburban development in the United States includes Clawson and Hall (1973), McKelvey (1968), Massachusetts Institute of Technology (1958), and De Leon and Enns (1973).

oped countryside readily accessible to the central city and to each other and extended the potential commuting radius to central city jobs by many miles. They also enabled new and existing industries and warehousing to obtain ample low-cost suburban sites accessible to their markets and labor supply. Thus new suburban employment centers grew up adjacent to the expressways. This pattern is observable across the country. And although zoning, subdivision, and other land use controls helped shape specific characteristics of development, the basic patterns were not planned but arose from the credit and transport investment programs interacting with market demand.

HIGHWAYS AND URBANIZATION IN TURKEY. A parallel to the U.S. example may be the role of highway construction in the development of Turkish cities from 1950 to 1960 (see Rivkin, 1965). After independence in 1923, the government encouraged urban growth in the interior of the country through public capital investment, together with constraints on growth in the main cities of Istanbul and Izmir. Railroad lines were extended and state-owned industries were located in interior cities. In 1927 the country had five cities with populations of more than 50,000; in 1950 there were twelve.

After World War II transportation investment was switched to roads. In 1950 a powerful semi-autonomous highway agency was created with two primary goals: national defense and agricultural improvement. Urban development was not an explicit objective. During the 1950s Turkey's all-weather, hard-surfaced road network more than doubled. Many highways paralleled the railroads constructed earlier and provided interior communities with additional accessibility. The decade also saw the beginning of an unanticipated and continuing wave of rural-urban migration. Population in cities of more than 50,000 more than doubled. Although much of the increase went to Istanbul and Izmir, their share of population in cities of more than 50,000 actually dropped from 61 to 49 percent. The number of cities of this size rose from twelve to twenty-seven, many in eastern, southern, and interior regions. All were served by links in the new highway network. Many had access to the railroad as well, and most were also sites of decentralized state-owned industrial investment. But the common characteristic was the highway connection.

In this case, massive public investment in highways had a major influence on the distribution of urbanization across the country. It helped establish a pattern of growth centers, in which demands for housing, utilities, and sites for contemporary industrial and commercial establishments have subsequently been felt. (Most recent estimates indicate that Turkey in the mid-1970s had twenty cities of more than 100,000, many of which began their growth spurts during the highway-building decade of the 1950s.) There is, however, no indication in the literature that these impacts on land use patterns had been foreseen as part of the highway program or were planned in advance.

Policy at the Local Level

The effects of public investment decisions can be most readily traced within a specific urban area. Sometimes the decisions to influence the pattern of urban development are made consciously, together with the decisions to provide particular facilities. Sometimes the decisions are accompanied by various kinds of control techniques which channel the impacts in line with explicit objectives. Often, however, investments occur without thought of their effect on urban structure, which intensifies problems related to the use of land.

THE TORONTO SUBWAY. Land development associated with the Toronto, Canada, subway system is an excellent example of the interplay between market demand and public activity at the city level (Rivkin Associates, Inc., 1976a). The various government investment and regulatory initiatives were coordinated, and the shaping of land use was an objective.

Toronto is a metropolitan area of about 3.5 million people, which has doubled in size since 1953 and the opening of the first element of its extensive subway system. The first line ran through the center of the old city where there was considerable pent-up demand but little vacant land for new development. The subway intensified this demand by making the core area readily accessible to large numbers of people.

In the course of construction, the subway agencies acquired more land at the station entrances than was required for the stations themselves. Planning policy for the city and region called for intense, multistory, mixed use in the core and near the subway facilities. Zoning regulations were adjusted to encourage greater density of development near the subway stations. The subway agency leased surplus land to private developers who submitted projects compatible with area planning policy. Numerous developers were interested both in acquiring use of the surplus land and in assembling contiguous parcels at their own expense.

The result has been a new, compact, downtown business and financial core with more than 200 complex, highly intensive, private projects clustered around the subway entrances. Moreover, revenues from the leases alone are expected to repay the cost of acquisition for the entire subway system by the mid-1980s. The land remains in municipal ownership, and improvements revert to the municipality after the lease term of up to fifty-five years. Land rent is set at market value, and property and improvements are fully taxed.

A commercial center has thus been created with little overspill beyond easy walking distances of the subway. Formal land use regulations certainly played some part in this process, but mainly by adding incentives to concentration and the restriction of overspill. The subway investment and the favorable leasing arrangements appeared to play the most important roles in determining the structure of development.

JAKARTA HIGHWAY AND ISTANBUL BRIDGE. The insertion of a major road can also have substantial impact. Indeed, in cities where modern highway transportation has not existed, the first insertion can become the primary shaper of urban form. Jakarta is an excellent example, as yet undocumented by research into cause and effect. During the past decade a wide highway several kilometers long was constructed from north to south through low-rise, high-density residential areas. The purpose was to connect suburban Kebayoran with the capital and government office buildings. The road has subsequently become a generator of linear development. Most high-rise, high-density commercial and hotel structures in Jakarta are arrayed along its edge, at and between intersections, strung out over comparatively long distances in a very narrow band along the roadway. Immediately abutting the individual structures are the older residential areas.

The highway appears to have been a principal force in shaping this development pattern, and it presents the city with serious problems. On the one hand, the high-rise, high-value facilities with ready access to the road represent a benefit to the city. On the other hand, significant problems of land use arise from the lack of compactness, the congestion, the difficulty of maintaining residential property because of the intensity of development, and from the prospects for change of use which increase speculation. Although Jakarta may now be formulating plans to deal with these issues, there is clear evidence that the highway was not considered as a development-shaping tool when it was initially planned.

A similar set of issues emerged in Istanbul as a result of the construction of the Bosphorous bridge. Until its opening, the only means of crossing between the European and Asiatic sides of the city was the ferry service. At the Cabotage, in the congested core of the old center, trucks would line up for twenty-four hours to obtain passage. After many years of planning, a toll bridge was built across the Bosphorous several kilometers north of the city, but well within the metropolitan Istanbul area. Traffic and revenues have, reportedly, far exceeded the original estimates.

To the best of my knowledge, little direct consideration of the effects on land use was given in choosing the site and planning the bridge, even though on both sides of the Bosphorous were large areas of undeveloped land in private ownership. The bridge and its access roads have pulled commercial and residential development from elsewhere in the region, and speculative activity in the approach areas has apparently been considerable. Because only the transportation functions, not the land use, were considered, the road has "solved" a transportation problem, but haphazard growth has compounded the difficulties of land use distribution.

These examples suggest that direct investment, especially in transport and infrastructure facilities, is likely to have far-reaching effects on local patterns of land use. With the assistance of land use regulation, this investment could be used to structure cities in line with defined land use objectives. But all too often the implications for land use are not taken into account at the planning stage, and land use problems are often exacerbated rather than alleviated. But the potential for more effective urban development exists.

WORKER HOUSING IN CURITIBA NEW TOWN. The government did sense the development-shaping potential of major infrastructure investment in some cases in Brazil. The National Housing Bank of Brazil (BNH) concluded in the early 1970s that the lack of utilities and services in many areas impeded its support of housing production. The BNH expanded its activities (originally restricted to financing housing units) to include financing roads, sewer and water systems, schools, and even shopping centers. One of the projects the BNH agreed to finance was an industrial new town outside the city of Curitiba. It would provide infrastructure for a complete industrial, residential, and commercial community on land assembled by private industrial corporations. The sponsors, however, had not provided for workers' housing in the community, and land prices were too high for its provision through the market. The BNH bargained with the project sponsors for large areas of land for low-income housing in close proximity to employment. Industry subsidized the land costs while the BNH financed the housing units. Here a government body used its financial leverage to intervene in land use on behalf of equity considerations.

THE SINGAPORE MODEL. Very few examples exist where government investment and regulatory policy have worked both consciously and effectively with the market to shape urban land use on a major scale. Singapore is one such example, although again these comments are based on observation, not documentation. Singapore has a master plan, administered by a planning agency, which controls the location, scale, and density of development. The national government provides infrastructure, social housing, and so-called new towns within the central city. These are carefully planned extensions of the developed center into the few remaining rural areas. Of special significance is government policy to locate workers' housing close to places of employment, even when this makes use of high-value land.

In Singapore land use policy is closely linked with the basic capital investment and administrative activities of government. Government takes an activist's role in shaping land use. One of the most striking examples has been the recent ban on certain kinds of automobile traffic in the once-congested central business district during rush hour. Singapore has dared to do what no other government has done. Enforcement so far appears to have been successful in reducing congestion and automobile use (Watson and Holland, 1978).

Singapore has effectively directed and controlled land development through comprehensive planning related to well-specified objectives, although it is not clear whether the planning occurred after the determination of basic investment and density policy or whether it guided policy formation. Singapore's capacity to implement its plans would appear to be powerfully affected by the scarcity of land. For Singapore cannot afford waste. It is an island with intense population pressure and no land to use beyond its well-defined geographic boundaries. This real scarcity of land is readily perceivable by entrepreneur and bureaucrat alike and forces the husbanding of resources. Government intervention to control land use is thus readily accepted by power groups within the society.

Most rapidly growing cities of the developing world lack this obvious scarcity of land. Growth can always occur, although the patterns may be inefficient and the spread of squatter housing, the dispersion of industry, and the lack of utilities present real problems. The question of land scarcity is a far more subtle one elsewhere and involves concepts of efficiency and equity rather than the sheer physical survival of a metropolis. Thus far in few urban societies has the government found these concepts compelling enough to warrant as activistic and comprehensive a role as in Singapore.

The cases cited above illustrate that considerable control over development can be wielded with conscious attention and the allocation of sufficient human and financial resources. In conditions of rapid growth, however, with its attendant economic and social difficulties, such devices as plans, codes, and ordinances are likely to be inadequate by themselves. If a nation wants to create order in its urban patterns it should look elsewhere, and particularly to large investments, for the appropriate leverage.

The Array of Techniques

This section identifies in more detail three groups of techniques which can be applied in various combinations by government to pursue consciously the process of land use formation and control. The first two include techniques that have been applied, in one form or another, within rapidly growing cities of the developing world. The third includes promising new approaches that, to my knowledge, have not yet been significantly attempted in a developing country.

In the first group of measures government is an actual actor in the land development process by virtue of its powers to make and orchestrate investments. The techniques include provision of infrastructure, land acquisition, government action as developer and financier, instruments for mixed public and private development, and surgical action. In the second group government sets the parameters for land development within this framework. Private parties and public agencies play the land use "game" while government enforces the rules and monitors activity. The measures include planning, codes, and ordinances, withholding of permission, value freezing, and taxation. New measures now being tested in developed countries, which combine rule-setting with direct public investment, make up the third group. They are: infrastructure impact planning, guide planning for critical areas, and capital budgeting.

Direct Intervention

INFRASTRUCTURE PROVISION. Adequate infrastructure is critical to the formation and survival of many complex urban activities. If the supply is restricted and demand for these activities is growing, government should act to provide additional facilities in accord with overall objectives of land use. Otherwise the existing stock in key areas will be stretched beyond capacity, and the character and quality of stable land uses will be eroded by continued growth.

Government normally provides roads, sewer and water lines and treatment facilities, electricity, and other basic facilities. Levels of responsibility differ. In some situations it builds only the major roads and utilities. In others it is also responsible for minor facilities, down to the neighborhood level. These facilities are the bones of the urban body around which land development agglomerates and the most intensive speculative activities and land price rises occur.

Government may also provide secondary or support infrastructure for a community: schools, health centers and hospitals, recreation areas, community buildings. These facilities rarely stimulate new growth, although there are exceptions. They do, however, contribute to the welfare of the community and can stabilize land use patterns in accord with overall public objectives.

This provision of infrastructure is the single most powerful technique for shaping land use at government's disposal, short of actually acquiring and developing the land. Yet it is usually undertaken to solve particular physical problems (such as to increase capacity in an existing system or to open up new areas for development) without allied measures for planning and control or attention to overall objectives.

Probably the bulk of public capital expenditures in an urban area is for infrastructure, except when government itself enters into production of housing and industry. Financing techniques vary with the kind of facility involved and its regional or local importance. Funds can come from general revenues, special appropriations to a sectoral agency at the national or local level, issuance of bonds, or through betterment levies on adjacent properties. The size of the investment may present financing difficulties, but it is precisely because of its size that one wonders why governments so rarely consider the secondary impact which often transforms the use and value of adjacent land. One reason is that of organization. The responsible agencies are often strictly sectoral or functional, with authority limited to their facility-building responsibilities. Broadening their responsibilities to include considerations of land use would normally require changing legislation, as well as expanding the scarce supply of planning personnel and skills.

LAND ACQUISITION. Direct land acquisition by the government is often the only firm guarantee that land will be available for public purposes (see also chapters 3 and 5). Most commonly, the government acquires sites for utilities, schools, hospitals, other public facilities, and park and recreation space. If land is acquired in advance of need, prices may be low since its value depends in part on the provision of infrastructure. Often, however, acquisition takes place well after the identification of need, when land costs have been driven up in expectation of the value of future uses, as well as by speculative pressures. Despite high costs, many governments have also acquired land for housing and industry to compensate for the inability or unwillingness of private enterprise to assemble land for these purposes.

Three basic approaches may be considered: acquisition for specific facilities, excess acquisition for specific or general development, and land banking. Acquisition for specific facilities is the most common (see the extensive bibliography in Rivkin Associates, Inc., 1976a). It can occur when a need is felt and capital for construction programmed, or in advance, as a kind of banking operation (as in many European nations and to some degree in the United States). This approach does not allow control over nearby land unless regulatory procedures are available or are established in conjunction with the acquisition.

Excess acquisition occurs when the agency expands its ownership into surrounding lands. This can be a significant means of controlling development attracted to an area by the presence of infrastructure or other public investment. It can be used, for example, to further particular projects or to acquire for the community the additional value arising from the social investment and so help meet the objectives of land use planning. The effectiveness of excess acquisition often depends on the quality of the planning that determined the size and nature of the surplus parcels acquired. In many countries, there are often serious political and legal constraints on the use of this technique.

Land banking is an approach whereby a government acquires substantial areas of land well in advance of need and ultimately releases them for development in line with planning objectives. The concept covers a variety of approaches and has significant implications for land tenure and land value, which are dealt with in chapters 3 and 5. It is undoubtedly one of the most powerful control techniques. By purchasing land reserves, especially at the fringes of metropolitan expansion, government bodies can determine the character, location, density, and timing of land uses as a city expands. Using some form of plan as a guide, public policy can directly control development without relying on the private marketplace as an intermediary. Land banking activities have ranged from the acquisition of sites for new towns outside the main city (as in Singapore and Malaysia) to the purchase of the majority of sites with good potential for housing (Saskatoon, Saskatchewan). The technique has been successfully applied in many European countries and is now being taken up by developing countries such as India, Chile, and Turkey, although its implementation is often hindered by lack of finance (Rivkin, 1976, pp. 33–34). Creation of such land development authorities has been a matter of particular interest to international technical assistance agencies.

Although of significant promise, the mere creation of a land-purchasing authority is no guarantee of control. Land purchases on a large scale are expensive. Resources must be available to support the effort but are frequently not forthcoming. Even when acquisition is possible, control is not certain, nor is there automatic assurance that the ultimate development will be efficient or equitable.

First, the lands must be managed prior to their ultimate development. Without effective control, the land may be illegally occupied by squatters, who are likely to be politically difficult to remove. Many of the squatter settlements in Asia and Latin America, for instance, have been on government-owned land.

Second, government ownership is no indication that wise or publicly oriented use is contemplated, especially since such decisions involve a wide variety of government bodies, whose main concern is not with efficient land use. Indeed, government agencies sometimes act as land speculators, withholding sites in key areas from development, with vague or no plans for their ultimate use.

Third, if the purpose of land banking is the ultimate development of an area in accordance with some public objectives, these objectives need to be articulated, plans for their fulfillment are essential, and the timing of implementation needs to be determined. Without such advance planning, land assembly operations merely transfer ownership and may encourage speculation and retard transformation for urban purposes.

GOVERNMENT AS DEVELOPER AND FINANCIER. The most direct role of government is to stimulate the creation of projects and facilities by acting as primary builder (through housing authorities, industrial development agencies, new town mechanisms, and the like) or as financing agent (through credit mechanisms). The extent of involvement varies. In rare cases such as Brasília, the government takes responsibility for building a whole new city. More frequently, there are smaller-scale projects or partial government involvement as in Turkey, where the government acquired land and constructed factories, housing, and services in small cities of the interior. Many individual public enterprises, however, operate independently from one another, outside the local regulatory framework, and out of line with planning objectives. In contrast, the program of Brazil's BNH concentrates all housing as well as infrastructure assistance in one agency, avoiding problems by rationalizing and coordinating all project activities within each community.

Site-and-service programs for low-income housing, now adopted in many developing countries, are examples of this activist role. Supported by international agencies such as the World Bank, they have profound significance for land use patterns. Normally these projects involve the acquisition of land, installation of utilities and services, and leasing or sale of plots to low-income families who construct their own dwellings with financial or technical help, or receive core units or partial houses constructed by the sponsoring agency. One example is in Zambia, where a major portion of the expansion of Lusaka is occurring through government sponsorship of site-and-service projects.

Perhaps the most comprehensive multipurpose development agency is Malaysia's Urban Development Authority (UDA), a national agency empowered to work in all urban areas. It has the traditional powers to acquire and bank land and to build public housing, but to increase the participation of Malays in the economy it can also finance and participate in industrial, commercial, and residential investment to build or purchase anything from individual units to new towns. The objective is to facilitate economic development and cultural change, but the Malaysian government ment explicitly recognizes the land use implications and considers the UDA control of urban land a major mission. Although direct development ment intervention is the principal approach, financial and regulatory instruments have also been used and ample funds have been made available. Experience with this approach is limited, the UDA having been in operation only since the early 1970s. Its effectiveness as a tool for development and land use control should be an important subject for empirical research.

One limitation is that substantial sums of money are needed to start a multipurpose development corporation. As with land acquisition, inade quate funding can cripple its operation. From a managerial standpoint, a multipurpose corporation could provide training in a wide range of urban planning and development skills (in finance, planning, engineering, project management). But it needs those skills at the outset, before it can effectively assume its responsibilities, and it can be impotent without a trained and diversified core staff.

INSTRUMENTS FOR MIXED PUBLIC AND PRIVATE DEVELOPMENT. Another approach is that of mixed public and private involvement geared to developing land in locations the government deems appropriate for new subdivision (see also chapter 3). The key instruments are control of infrastructure, the power to determine the nature of new building, and the power of condemnation. The UDA is one example of a public corporation with significant private participation. Land readjustment, as practiced in the Republic of Korea and Japan, is another. It involves condemnation of properties within a stipulated area on the urban fringe or in nearby rural districts. The land is then replotted in accordance with a government-developed subdivision plan, infrastructure installed, and the property redistributed to the original owners in proportion to their original holdings, with portions withheld to compensate the government for its costs (see chapter 5). In a third approach, created by the BNH in Brazil, a municipal government earmarks a specific area for future development, normally on the fringe of the existing city. A detailed plan is prepared, and BNH agrees to finance construction of all the utilities and services required. Revenue for this construction is obtained by levying a betterment tax on the properties within the area at a rate considerably higher than that paid on undeveloped land. Owners are thus given the incentive to develop productive uses in accordance with the plan or to sell to someone who will.

These approaches involve obvious problems of implementation. Most particularly full agreement between participants is necessary. As with many of the regulatory techniques, effective operation requires the availability of government personnel skilled enough to monitor and coordinate the joint efforts. And sources of capital must also be available for both public and private participants.

SURGICAL ACTION: SLUM OR SQUATTER REMOVAL. In addition to creating or stimulating new development, many governments have done just the reverse and removed existing development—usually inadequate housing or derelict industrial units and warehousing. They have also removed squatter settlements from public lands. Frequently these actions are combined with resettlement schemes and the preparation of the sites for new uses. Often, as in the repeated Turkish attempts to raze *gecekondus* in Istanbul and Ankara and resettle the population, considerable resistance to relocation occurs. In Kuala Lumpur and Singapore, however, the governments have rebuilt public housing on the cleared sites. Alternatively, as in Jakarta, they have substituted improvement schemes for clearance. Such programs accept the existence of the settlements and proceed to bring streets, water, and sewage disposal into the neighborhoods, selectively removing structures from land required for the utilities. Considerable resident cooperation and contribution of labor has been forthcoming. As a result, the existing urban pattern remains, but its internal operations are made more efficient and healthy.

The managerial and financial aspects of surgical action are complex and closely related to its explosive political character. Relocation is an extremely difficult process, requiring a measure of human sensitivity not normally applied. Relocation can be very costly, which may account for the poor, often inaccessible locations frequently chosen for new settlements in the past. Plans are necessary for the reuse of cleared sites, so they do not lie fallow but contribute to meeting urban needs. The whole process requires careful planning and execution.

This wide range of techniques for direct government investments offers the best chance of modifying land development to improve efficiency and distribution. As has been seen, however, although these techniques provide the opportunity, it is not always easy to implement schemes in line with the specified objectives. Financial, managerial, and planning skills are necessary, as well as the political will.

Planning and Controls

Although much of a government's direct investment and financial support takes place without the explicit objective of land use control, most countries establish regulations that direct the location and construction of physical facilities by private enterprise and government agencies (see chapter 6). While the rule-setting function is of potential importance, its effects are generally subsidiary to those of direct investment.

PLANNING. Land use planning is the traditional and most explicit means of establishing a framework to guide land use decisions, usually at the city level. Planning takes place with various degrees of sophistication and detail. One approach, derived from the British system and generally used throughout the former colonies, is to prepare extremely detailed plans for land use, transportation, and density which give official status to the pattern to be achieved. A similar approach is taken in other countries, such as Turkey. In Latin America, land use planning is similarly detailed but even more influenced by architectural design concepts. These approaches risk failure in implementation if public investment decisions are not linked to the plan prescriptions, and if insufficient or inadequately trained personnel operate the system. The rigidity of such approaches contributes to the gap between plan and performance.

There are certainly areas where financial resources and political commitment have been sufficient to implement such plans. Brasília is the prime example, but a rare one. But Brasília, Ankara, Rawalpindi, and other showplaces were new cities that were planned from the start, and rapid population and economic growth did not have to be fitted into an existing fabric.

In Commonwealth countries with strong planning traditions, plans have perhaps been more effective than in countries which lack a tradition as a guide to investment. In Singapore, for example, the master plan is a significant control mechanism over the type, scale, and timing of development. Planning in Malaysia and Kenya has similar structural integration and is backed with enough funds to maintain land use planning on a continuing basis.

A less detailed approach has been applied in other countries. Brazil's national planning agency uses "guide planning" in smaller towns. With limited technical assistance, it identifies gross areas as suitable for various land uses and locates roads, schools, and other public improvements to support the development. It is a highly flexible approach, well suited to situations where information is sparse and change rapid (Rivkin, 1976).

Another flexible approach is a form of "comprehensive planning," now generally fostered by international technical assistance agencies. It contains more sophisticated goal setting and analysis than does guide planning, but avoids the pitfalls of detailed site-by-site prescriptions. It consists of a statement of objectives for land use and facilities; forecasts of population and economic growth and assessment of physical needs; preparation of general land use and transportation guides; identification of the location and capacity of open space, schools, health facilities, road , water, sewer, and other utilities; some definition of staging, timing, and linkages of investments; and an implementation program involving legislation, government, and private action (Rivkin, 1976, pp. 29-30).

The precise character of the planning process is a matter to be worked out in the context of the particular country and city. An example of a plan for a metropolitan region is the one sponsored by the World Bank and the United Nations for Greater Karachi; one for a small and essentially new city is Malaysia's plan for Kuantan.

Clearly the quality and comprehensiveness of plans have a great bearing on their effectiveness and rest heavily on the skills of the people who prepare them. Of central importance, however, is whether the plan is linked to government policies for capital investment and credit. Often it is not. The planning agency is frequently remote from the central decisionmaking authorities in developed as well as developing countries, and planning thus becomes an academic exercise.

CODES AND ORDINANCES. Codes and ordinances which regulate the placement of facilities on land, determine allowable densities, and set standards for utilities, services, and structures are basic to the management of most cities. Generally, four techniques are used singly or in combination:

- Zoning divides a community into an array of districts designated by their predominant use and defines, in more or less detail, the nature of the development allowed.
- Subdivision controls deal with the actual treatment of the development site, prescribing lot size, shape, and width; the character, capacity, and location of utilities; the requirements for open space; standards for internal road systems; and so on.
- Building codes deal with the structural nature and adequacy of a building, sometimes specifying minimum room sizes and even the number of persons who may occupy a given amount of floor space.
- Withholding of permission denies the right to develop.

These codes and ordinances are normally preventative rather than creative, although they can be considered as positive ways of enforcing minimum land use and building standards. In most communities implementation is through permits, which must be received prior to actual construction or occupancy. Often, as in Turkey and the Commonwealth countries, these regulations are a component of the master plan. In Latin American countries they tend to be separate instruments, enforced by a local building department. Even if they are not enforced the codes may serve as benchmarks to influence local development practice. Their content and administration present serious problems, however, which in many situations make them relatively useless.

Since the developing world often borrows regulations from dissimilar countries with little adaptation, its cities then lack instruments responsive to their own construction conditions and land use patterns. This may result in the use of inappropriate and costly materials, streets too wide or too narrow for local traffic, site requirements that waste land, and so on. And because of their unsuitability, rules may often be ignored or circumvented.

Another limitation derives from the high standards often employed. What may be minimal standards in Western countries can be beyond the present capability of many cities in the developing world, particularly in the case of housing for the poorest classes. To some degree this explains the high costs and unacceptable living arrangements (to the residents) of numerous publicly sponsored housing estates in developing countries. National pride often makes reducing or relaxing these standards politically infeasible.

A third limitation is the extent of administration required. Even when codes are part of a master plan, administration of them is often delegated to municipal agencies with few qualified people and little incentive to implement them. Linked to this is the problem of corruption. Code enforcement requires issuance of permits. Since the development industry has much to gain from obtaining them, permits tend to be marketable commodities. Although a master plan may set laudable goals, the susceptibility to corruption associated throughout the world with urban construction can thwart these goals project by project. Thus code enforcement requires significant financial resources and technical and managerial skills of a high quality, unlikely to be readily available in rapidly developing cities.

Although zoning and subdivision regulations can be deterrents to undesirable development, the ultimate barrier is the denial of permission to build. Most city administrations have a department empowered to deny permission to development incompatible with public policies. Malaysia, for instance, frequently uses the denial technique to prevent such development or to persuade landowners to enter into joint ventures with Malay businessmen. In Turkey and Brazil, however, the power is available but is rarely used.

VALUE-FREEZING. When government agencies lack resources to acquire land for public works or housing within a reasonable time after a site has been identified, value-freezing may be used as a control technique. Otherwise public knowledge of the plan or the intent to purchase may increase land values and make acquisition prohibitive. Turkey has authority to freeze site values for a four-year period, within which acquisition can presumably occur. Malaysia also uses the technique, and each state can set the length of time for control, normally up to one year. The approach is a variant of preemption, the authority exercised frequently in Europe and Japan by which the government purchases designated land, usually at the urban fringe, for a fixed price at any time the owner decides to sell. Preemption offers the means to control urban expansion without tying up large amounts of public capital, but it has been rarely employed.

TAXATION. Governments can, in principle, levy taxes on land held out of development for speculative purposes and on proceeds of land sales that show profits arising from planning benefits (see chapter 5). In practice, few developing country governments have exercised this power. There are exceptions. Singapore has a land value increment tax; the Republic of Korea has tried a real property speculation tax; and Taiwan has instituted a land value increment tax as well as a penalty tax on properties not developed or planned within a certain time. In the early 1970s Malaysia instituted a heavy penalty on speculative profits for both urban and rural land. These taxes may, however, have contributed more to revenue raising than to the modification of land use (Rivkin, 1976, p. 39).

Differential tax rates can also be used as an incentive to certain forms and locations of development. Several countries (including Turkey, Israel, and India) use tax incentives as a means of stimulating growth in intermediate cities and development regions. During the 1960s, for example, India offered such tax incentives for certain industries while denying them permits to locate in Bombay and Calcutta, but with little success. Thus far the technique has been applied only to areas outside the major cities. Taxation could be used as an incentive for differential location within a metropolitan area, but no examples of this use are known.

Thus, although the potential exists for defining a regulatory framework in line with overall planning objectives, including the redistribution of the public benefits of development, in practice the techniques employed have often been unsuitable and implementation problematic. It is difficult to believe, given rapid growth and the shortage of skilled administrators, that the problems can be fully overcome. These techniques, though important, are likely always to have a role subsidiary to that of direct investment in determining urban structure. Some of the most promising approaches recognize these difficulties and also the benefits of an integrated approach.

Some Promising Additional Approaches

Techniques alone do not hold the answer to land use control. Far more important factors are the quality of personnel in whatever formal governmental intervention may exist, the government's commitment to incorporate land use concerns into its basic development policy, and the financial resources devoted to both investment and administrative measures on a priority basis. Nevertheless, there are some techniques, which have rarely, if ever, been applied in the developing world, that hold promise for improving the process of land use control. The three discussed below—infrastructure impact planning, guide planning for critical areas, and capital budgeting—have been employed only in the more developed countries and there only recently.

These approaches rely as much on common sense as on high-level expertise, although training in their application is clearly desirable. They are not high-technology solutions, but have emerged in recognition that, even in more economically advanced nations, simpler approaches to land use have to be found. Their greatest virtue lies in flexibility and adaptability to changing situations. They are thus relevant to developing countries. Each involves a form of land use planning, but with far less detail and over a far shorter time than is usual. Each combines land use planning with investment activity of the government. Each can be used in combination with, or as a substitute for, many of the instruments cited above. Other techniques used in developed countries, such as development rights transfer, are not suggested because they involve modeling, which requires an extensive information base or complicated monitoring. Each of the three suggested techniques requires that the land use planners be an integral part of the agency making the capital investment decisions. With priority given to questions of land use control and adequate staffing, this integration should be possible.

INFRASTRUCTURE IMPACT PLANNING. Impact planning provides a framework for assessing and organizing the secondary effects of specific large infrastructure investments, such as a highway, a water system, or a sewer system. Such planning could also be applied to major productive investments that have land use impacts, such as steel mills or petroleum refineries. It adds a new dimension to the traditional form of planning for these activities; namely, priority attention to their implications for land use.

Impact planning first involves an analytic exercise. During the course of basic site selection, the area in which environmental, social, and economic effects may be felt is delineated. These effects are then identified, and the dimensions of and changes in land use are estimated and quantified to the degree possible. If comparable data exist, this analytic task is fairly straightforward. If, as in many developing countries, data are hard to come by, the exercise must be based on judgment. But judgment is far preferable to no advance consideration of secondary effects, which is generally the norm today. And this analytic effort can itself affect the precise location and scope of the investment, especially if the government wishes to use the facility as a development-shaping tool.

Once these designs are made, planning for a desirable pattern of land use in the impact area can take place. It can be supplemented by a battery of tools at the disposal of government: excess condemnation to assemble sites for publicly supported uses in the impact area, zoning provisions to prevent undesirable development and provide sanction for growth in accordance with the plan, financial incentives in the form of credit availability, lease arrangements for approved uses and densities, creation of public development corporations to help form the desired patterns, and so on. These tools are applied within the specific context of the major public facility investment.

In recent years, impact planning has become a widely adopted approach in the United States. Environmental Impact Statements, dealing with land use and economic as well as environmental matters, are now required for sewer support grants by the U.S. Environmental Protection Agency (see, for example, New Jersey, Department of Community Affairs, 1975). I do not know of instances where it has been applied in developing world cities, but such analytic procedures could well be formulated there on an ad hoc basis for particular circumstances. It is the thought process, not the data, that is important.

Infrastructure impact planning falls far short of comprehensive, urban-wide analysis. It recognizes, however, both a need for pragmatism (by having, for instance, limited objectives) and the powerful change-inducing effects of basic public services.

GUIDE PLANNING FOR CRITICAL AREAS. Guide planning was referred to earlier as a technique employed in smaller cities of Brazil. It provides some conceptual framework for the distribution of land use and densities and the location of major utilities. It is performed rapidly and is meant to last until more detailed measures can be adopted. A variant applicable to larger, more complex metropolitan regions would be to divide the land into three broad categories—critical, preservation, and stable—and then to concentrate mainly on the critical areas, namely, those sections of the metropolis that are undergoing, or most likely to undergo, development pressure. Analytic effort would then determine what array of measures could be rapidly introduced to guide their growth. Preservation areas could receive some attention to determine whether special measures should be taken to retard their transformation. Stable areas would effectively be left out of consideration in the short run. Planning activity would thus be focused, not diffused.

The designation of critical areas for special planning and investment treatment has become of increasing concern in the United States, especially in environmentally sensitive regions such as coastal areas. One study in New Jersey defined guidelines to delineate the region into these three types of zone, based on a rapid review of key environmental and land use characteristics (Rivkin Associates, 1976b). For each zone, a series of rudimentary principles was established to take account of the land uses and densities most likely to occur and the land and water features affected. These guidelines serve as a basis for state government review of permits, and they are being applied to every request for a project permit. They are buttressed by other state and local regulatory systems and will hold until a more comprehensive plan is prepared. Delineation of critical areas within an urban region and rapid formulation of guidelines for their control and development fall far short of comprehensive urban planning. But is such comprehensiveness suitable, or even practicable, in developing countries?

CAPITAL BUDGETING. The capital budget is a mechanism that can combine both infrastructure impact planning and guidelines for critical areas. It identifies all the major government programs and investment priorities affecting an urban area in the short term, brings them together, and reviews their impact prior to authorization. In developing nations, the lack of coordination among different agencies responsible for infrastructure and other investment projects is legendary. By relating these projects on a map and reviewing their costs, timing, and impacts, it is possible to specify the areas affected by infrastructure investment. It is also possible to identify the corrective measures, additional commitments, and supplementary controls that may be necessary for their selective implementation. The capital budget process can also generate information that may cause shifts in priorities or timing, especially in regard to complementary public investments. It is a process normally conducted in developed countries by a municipal planning agency and could become a planning function in developing cities as well. The Karachi master plan, cited earlier, goes so far as to establish complementary short-run investment priorities among the most critical urban services and is one of the first such efforts at capital budgeting in the developing world.

Toward a More Effective Policy of Land Use Control

In preceding sections I have reviewed the rationale for government intervention to control land use, the objectives that intervention could pursue, the constraints that impede effective regulatory efforts, some examples of actual situations where government action has influenced land use patterns, and the array of instruments available for the exercise of government policy. I have attempted to demonstrate the immense variety of development problems and policies to be addressed. It is suggested, however, that certain general principles can be established to guide future thinking on land control issues in rapidly growing cities in developing countries. (In new cities such as Brasília or centers where growth is modest, the principles may also be relevant, but the problems have different dimensions.)

A nation or an urban government must establish explicit priorities for the control of urban land. Without definition of priorities by the institutions and individuals who guide economic growth and direct capital investment in cities, any planning or regulatory efforts are academic. The human, economic, and physical factors that impede the application of land use guidance are too strong for any but the utmost attention to influence.

Once a priority is established and objectives for land control made explicit, follow-through should be limited in scope and tailored to the capability of likely human and financial resources. So-called comprehensive solutions are to be eschewed. Under conditions of rapid growth it is not possible to work effectively on all aspects of urban development in all areas of a city simultaneously and expect results. Certainly guiding principles can and should be established and some form of overall growth and development targets set. But the formulation of urban-wide plans and ordinances should not be allowed to paralyze pragmatic attempts to handle critical issues, which cannot wait for comprehensive schemes.

Direct investment activities (such as utilities construction, land acquisition, and the establishment of development credit) are often likely to have much greater effects on the use and value of land than indirect rule-setting or control devices. National investment policy has profound influence, at the macro level, on the distribution of urban development and the growth of urban areas. Local investment policy affects land values and the development potential for growth within a given urban area. Regulations and controls to achieve land use objectives such as efficiency, adaptability, or equity should be linked with these investment activities, if a government is serious in its desire to direct the course of urban growth.

No one set of measures or combination of regulatory devices and investment techniques can be prescribed for all cities of the developing world. An array of techniques is available, all of which have potential significance and validity, but the choice for a particular community must be made within the special economic, social, and physical context of that community and must be both relevant and feasible. Indeed, special local circumstances may suggest still other applicable instruments. This conclusion gives little comfort to purist approaches. But the fact remains that every city and every land use context is different, and any effort to formulate and apply techniques must be sensitive to these particular local conditions.

Bibliography

Aaron, Henry J. 1975. *Who Pays the Property Tax? A New View*. Washington, D.C.: Brookings Institution.

Archer, R. W. 1974. The Leasehold System of Urban Development: Land Tenure, Decision-Making and the Land Market in Urban Development and Land Use. *Regional Studies*. 8: 225–38.

———. 1976. *Land Pooling for Planned Urban Development in Perth, Western Australia*. Canberra: Metropolitan Research Trust.

Arrow, Kenneth J., and Frank H. Hahn. 1971. *General Competitive Analysis*. Edinburgh: Oliver and Boyd.

Arrow, Kenneth J., and Robert C. Lind. 1970. Uncertainty and the Evaluation of Public Expenditure Devices. *American Economic Review* 60(3).

Atkinson, Anthony B., and Joseph E. Stiglitz. 1980. *Lectures on Public Economics*. New York: McGraw-Hill.

Australian Commission of Inquiry into Land Tenures. 1973. *First Report*. Canberra: Australian Government Publicity Service.

Bahl, Roy W. 1977. *Comparing and Evaluating the Use of Urban Property Taxes in Less Developed Countries*. Metropolitan Studies Program, Occasional Paper no. 32. Syracuse, N.Y.: Maxwell School, Syracuse University.

———, ed. 1979. *The Taxation of Urban Property in Less Developed Countries*. Committee on Taxation, Resources and Economic Development. Madison: University of Wisconsin Press.

Bahl, Roy W., S. S. Coelen, and Jeremy J. Warford. 1973. *Estimation of the Economic Benefits of Water Supply and Sewerage Projects*. Syracuse, N.Y.: Metropolitan and Regional Research Center, Syracuse University.

Baker, Harold L. 1961. *The Land Situation in the State of Hawaii*. Land Study Bureau Circular no. 13. Honolulu: University of Hawaii.

BANOBRAS (Banco Nacional de Obras y Servicios Públicos). 1969. *Programa Buena Vivienda*. Mexico City.

Bauer, Peter T., and Basil S. Yamey. 1968. *Markets, Marketing Controls and Market Reform*. London: Weidenfeld and Nicolson.

Baumol, William J., and David F. Bradford. 1970. Optimal Departures from Marginal Cost Pricing. *American Economic Review* 60(3).

Baumol, William J., and William E. Oates. 1979. *The Theory of Environmental Policy*. Englewood Cliffs, N. J.: Prentice-Hall.

Becker, Arthur P., ed. 1969. *Land and Building Taxes: Their Effect in Economic Development*. Madison: University of Wisconsin Press.

Beier, George, Anthony Churchill, Michael Cohen, and Bertrand Renaud. 1975. *The Task Ahead for the Cities of the Developing Countries*. World Bank Staff Working Paper no. 209. Washington, D.C.

Bird, Richard M. 1976a. The Incidence of the Property Tax: Old Wine in New Bottles? Paper presented to the Symposium on Property Taxation sponsored by the Ministry of State for Urban Affairs, Toronto.

————. 1976b. *Charging for Public Services: A New Look at an Old Idea*. Toronto: Canadian Tax Foundation.

Bosselman, Frederick, David Collies, and John Banta. 1973. *The Taking Issue*. Washington, D.C.: U.S. Government Printing Office.

Bresciani-Turroni, Constantino. 1937. *The Economics of Inflation*. Trans. Millicent E. Sayers. London: Allen and Unwin.

Brown, J. Bruce. 1968. The Incidence of Property Taxes under Three Alternative Systems in Urban Areas in New Zealand. *National Tax Journal* (September).

Buchanan, James M., and W. G. Stubblebine. 1962. Externality. *Economica* 29(116), November.

Burns, Leland S., and Leo Grebler. 1977. *The Housing of Nations*. London: Macmillan Press.

Carr, Jack, and L. B. Smith. 1975. Public Land Banking and the Price of Land. *Land Economics* (November).

Cheung, Steven N. S. 1973. The Fable of the Bees. *Journal of Law and Economics* 16(1), April.

————. 1974. The Theory of Price Control. *Journal of Law and Economics* 17(1), April.

————. 1979. Rent Control and Housing Reconstruction: The Post-war Experience of Pre-war Premises in Hong Kong. *Journal of Law and Economics* 22(1), April.

Clark, W. A. 1974. *The Impact of Property Taxation on Urban Spatial Development*. Report no. 187. Los Angeles: Institute of Government and Public Affairs, University of California.

Clawson, Marion, and Peter Hall. 1973. *Planning and Urban Growth: An Anglo-American Comparison*. Baltimore, Md.: Johns Hopkins University Press.

Coase, Ronald H. 1961. The Problem of Social Costs. *Journal of Law and Economics* 3, October.

Collier, David. 1976. *Squatters and Oligarchs: Authoritarian Rule and Policy Change in Peru*. Baltimore, Md.: Johns Hopkins University Press.

Conn, Stephen. 1969. *The Squatters' Rights of Favelados*. CIDOC Cuaderno no. 32. Cuernavaca, Mexico: Centro Intercultural de Documentación.

Culyer, Anthony J. 1971. Merit Goods and the Welfare Economics of Coercion. *Public Finance* 26(4).

Darin-Drabkin, Haim. 1976. *Land Policy and Urban Growth*. Oxford: Pergamon.

Dasgupta, Partha S. 1978. Fairness between Generations and the Social Discount Rate. *Resources Policy* 4(3).

Davis, Otto A., and Andrew B. Whinston. 1961. The Economics of Urban Renewal. *Journal of Law and Contemporary Problems* 26(1), Winter.

De Graaff, Johannes. 1957. *Theoretical Welfare Economics*. New York: Cambridge University Press.

De Leon, Peter, and John Enns. 1973. *The Impact of Highways upon Metropolitan Dispersion*. St. Louis, Mo.: Rand Corporation.

Demsetz, Harold. 1969. Information and Efficiency: Another Viewpoint. *Journal of Law and Economics* 12(1), April.

Doebele, William A. 1969. Legal Issues in Regional Development. In L. Rodwin and Associates. *Planning Urban Growth and Regional Development*. Cambridge, Mass.: M.I.T. Press.

———. 1974. A Commentary on Urban Land Policy in Sweden. Washington, D.C.: World Bank. Restricted circulation.

———. 1977. The Private Market and Low Income Urbanisation in Developing Countries: The Pirate Subdivisions of Bogotá. *American Journal of Corporation Law* 25 (3), Summer.

Doebele, William A., and Orville F. Grimes, Jr. 1977. *Valorization Charges as a Method for Financing Urban Public Works: The Example of Bogotá, Colombia*. World Bank Staff Working Paper no. 254. Washington, D.C.

Doebele, William A., Orville F. Grimes, and Johannes F. Linn. 1979. Participation of Beneficiaries in Financing Urban Services: Valorization Charges in Bogotá, Colombia. *Land Economics* 55, February.

Doxiades, C. A. 1973. *The Great Urban Crimes We Permit by Law*. Athens: Lycabuttus Press.

Evers, Hans-Dieter. 1975. Urban Expansion and Landownership in Underdeveloped Societies. *Urban Affairs Quarterly* 11(1), September.

Feldstein, Martin. 1977. The Surprising Incidence of a Tax on Pure Rent: A New Answer to an Old Question. *Journal of Political Economy* 85 (2), April.

Foster, Christopher D., and Stephen Glaister. 1975. The Anatomy of the Development Value Tax. *Urban Studies* 12 (2), June.

Frankena, Mark W., and David T. Schleffman. 1980. *Economic Analysis of Provincial Land Use Policy in Ontario*. Ontario Economic Council Research Study no. 18. Ottawa.

Grimes, Orville F., Jr. 1974. *Urban Land and Public Policy: Social Appropriation of Betterment*. World Bank Staff Working Paper no. 179. Washington, D.C. Also in P. Downing, ed. *Local Service Pricing and Urban Spatial Structure*. Vancouver: University of British Columbia Press, 1977.

———. 1976. *Housing for Low-Income Families*. Baltimore, Md.: Johns Hopkins University Press.

Haar, Charles M. 1976. A Program for Land Registration and Land Transfer in Indonesia. *Ekistics* 41 (244), March.

Hall, Peter, and others. 1973. *The Containment of Urban England*. London: Allen and Unwin.

Hirshleifer, Jack. 1965. Investment Decisions under Uncertainty: Choice Theoretic Approaches. *Quarterly Journal of Economics* (November).

———. 1966. Investment Decisions under Uncertainty: Applications of the State Preference Approach. *Quarterly Journal of Economics* (May).

Holland, Daniel M. 1971. *The Assessment of Land Value*. Madison: University of Wisconsin Press.

Japan, Ministry of Construction, and City Planning Association. 1974. *City Planning in Japan*. Tokyo: Ministry of Construction.

Karst, Kenneth, Murray L. Schwartz, and Audrey J. Schwartz. 1973. *The Evolution of Law in the Barrios of Caracas*. Los Angeles: University of California Press.

Kay, John A. 1972. Social Discount Rates. *Journal of Public Economics* 1 (3/4).

Kehoe, Dalton, David Morley, Stuart B. Proudfoot, and Neal A. Roberts, eds. 1976. *Public Land Ownership: Framework for Evaluation*. Lexington, Mass.: D. C. Heath.

Lange, Oskar, and Frederick M. Taylor. 1938. *On the Economic Theory of Socialism*. Minneapolis: University of Minnesota Press.

Lent, George E. 1974. The Urban Property Tax in Developing Countries. *Finanzarchiv*, 33 (1).

———. 1976. *Taiwan's Land Tax Policy*. Working Paper FAD/76/2. Washington, D.C.: International Monetary Fund, Fiscal Affairs Department.

———. 1978. Experience with Urban Land Value Tax in Developing Countries. *Bulletin for International Fiscal Documentation* 32(12), February.

Linn, Johannes F. 1979. The Costs of Urbanisation. Urban and Regional Report no. 76-16. Washington, D.C.: World Bank.

———. 1982. *Cities in the Developing World: Policies for Their Equitable and Efficient Growth*. New York: Oxford University Press.

Little, I. M. D., and J. A. Mirrlees. 1974. *Project Appraisal and Planning for Developing Countries*. London: Heinemann Educational Press.

Macon, Jorge, and José Merino Mañon. 1975. *Betterment Levies in Latin America: Nature, Experience and Recommendations for their Adaptation in the Financing of Public Works Projects*. Washington, D.C.: Inter-American Development Bank, Economic and Social Development Department, General Studies Division.

Marschak, James. 1968. Economics of Inquiring, Communicating, Deciding. *American Economic Review* 58(2), May.

Magaven, James L., John Thomas, and Myra Stewart. 1975. Law, Urban Development and the Urban Poor in Developing Countries. *Washington University Law Quarterly*, no. 1, pp. 45–111.

Massachusetts Institute of Technology. 1958. *Economic Impact Study of Massachusetts Route 128.* Cambridge, Mass.

McClure, Charles E. 1977. The New View of the Property Tax: A Caveat. *National Tax Journal* 30(1), March.

McKelvey, Blake. 1968. *The Emergence of Metropolitan America, 1915–1966.* New Brunswick, N.J.: Rutgers University Press.

Mieskowski, Peter. 1972. The Property Tax: An Excise Tax or a Profits Tax? *Journal of Public Economics* 1 (1).

Mills, Edward S. 1974. Do Market Economics Distort City Sizes? In H. Swain and R. D. MacKinnon, eds. *Issues in the Management of Urban Systems.* Papers and Proceedings from an International Institute for Applied Systems Analysis Conference on National Settlement Systems and Strategies, Schloss Laxemburg, Austria.

Musgrave, Richard A., and Peggy Musgrave. 1980. *Public Finance in Theory and Practice.* New York: McGraw-Hill.

Muth, R. F. 1969. *Cities and Housing.* Chicago, Ill.: University of Chicago Press.

Myrdal, Gunnar. 1957. *Economic Theory and Underdeveloped Regions.* London: Duckworth.

National Association of Home Builders. 1968. *Community Builders Handbook.* Washington, D.C.: Urban Land Institute.

Nelson, Joan. 1969. *Migrants, Urban Poverty and Instability in Developing Nations.* Occasional Papers in International Affairs no. 22. Cambridge, Mass.: Harvard University Center for International Affairs.

Neutze, G. Max. 1970. The Price of Land for Urban Development. *Economic Record* 46 (115).

———. 1973. *The Price of Land and Land Use Planning: Policy Instruments in the Urban Land Market.* Paris: OECD.

———. 1974. The Development Value Tax: A Comment. *Urban Studies* 11 (1), February.

New Jersey, Department of Community Affairs. 1975. *Guidelines for Evaluating Secondary Impacts of Regional Service Systems.* Trenton, N. J.

Norwood, H. C. 1972. Ndirande: A Squatter Colony in Malawi. *Town Planning Review* 43(2), April.

Okpala, Donatus C. I. 1977. The Potentials and Perils of Public Urban Land Ownership and Management: A Case Study of the Lagos Executive Development Board (Nigeria), 1928–1972. Ph.D. dissertation. Massachusetts Institute of Technology.

Pakistan, Government of. 1974. *The Karachi Development Plan 1974–85: Final Report.* National Pilot Project no. 3. Assisted by UNDP Project PAK/681/540.

Perlman, Janice E. 1976. *The Myth of Marginality.* Berkeley and Los Angeles: University of California Press.

Porter, William, Wren McMains, and William A. Doebele. 1973. Land Information Systems for the Housing Organisation, Iran. Unpublished report on U.N. mission. IRA/73/023.

Prest, Alan R. 1981. *The Taxation of Urban Land.* Manchester: Manchester University Press.

—————. 1982*a*. Land Taxation and Urban Finances in Less-Developed Countries. In Matthew Cullen and Sharon Woolery, eds. *Proceedings of the World Congress on Land Policy, 1980.* Lexington, Mass.: D.C. Heath.

—————. 1982*b*. On Charging for Local Government Services. *Three Banks Review* (133), March.

Rees, Ray. 1976. *Public Enterprise Economics.* London: Weidenfeld and Nicolson.

Reiner, Thomas, and Robert H. Wilson. 1978. Planning and Decision-Making in the Soviet City: Rent, Land and Urban Form Considerations. In Ian Hamilton and Tony French, eds. *The Socialist City,* Chichester: Wiley.

Richman, Raymond L. 1965. The Theory and Practice of Site-value Taxation in Pittsburgh. *Proceedings of the Fifty-Seventh Annual Conference on Taxation.* Harrisburg, Penn.: National Tax Association.

Rivas, Diego Robles. 1972. Development Alternatives for the Peruvian Barriada. In Guillermo Geisee and Jorge Hardoy, eds. *Regional and Urban Development Policies: A Latin American Perspective.* Latin American Urban Research, vol. 2. Beverly Hills, Calif.: Sage.

Rivkin, Malcolm D. 1965. *Area Development for National Growth: The Turkish Precedent.* New York: Praeger.

—————. 1976. *Land Use and the Intermediate Size City in Developing Countries, with Case Studies of Turkey, Brazil and Malaysia.* New York: Praeger.

Rivkin Associates, Inc. 1976*a*. *Acquisition of Land for Joint Highway and Community Development.* Pt. I, Conceptual Framework. Pt. II, Case Studies and Evaluation. Washington, D.C.: U.S. Dept. of Transportation.

—————. 1976*b*. *Interim Land Use and Density Guidelines for the Coastal Area of New Jersey.* Trenton: New Jersey Department of Environmental Protection.

Roberts, Neal A. 1977. *The Government as Land Developer.* Lexington, Mass.: D. C. Heath.

Rose, Louis A. 1973. The Development Value Tax. *Urban Studies* 10 (2), June.

—————. 1976. The Development Value Tax. A Reply. *Urban Studies* 13(1), February.

Sarin, Madhu. 1976. Growth and Vitality of Nonplanned Services in Chandigarh. *Ekistics* 41 (249), August.

Shoup, Donald C. 1970. The Optimal Timing of Urban Land Development. *Papers of the Regional Science Association* 25.

—————. 1980. Financing Public Investment by Deferred Special Assessment. *National Tax Journal* 33(4), December.

Shoup, Donald C., and Ruth P. Mack. 1968. *Advance Land Acquisition by Local Governments.* Washington, D.C.: U.S. Government Printing Office.

Siegan, Bernard. 1972. *Land Use without Zoning.* Lexington, Mass.: D. C. Heath.

Smith, Roger S. 1974. Financing Cities in Developing Countries. *International Monetary Fund Staff Papers* (July).

Solaun, Mauricio, William L. Flinn, and Sidney Kronus. 1974. Renovation of a Squatter Settlement in Colombia. *Land Economics* 50(2), May.

Squire, Lyn, and Herman G. van der Tak. 1975. *Economic Analysis of Projects.* Baltimore, Md.: Johns Hopkins University Press.

Sudra, Thomasz. 1976. Low Income Housing Systems in Mexico City. Ph.D. dissertation. Massachusetts Institute of Technology.

Tipple, A. G. 1976. The Low-cost Housing Market in Kitwe, Zambia. *Ekistics* 41(244), March.

Tobin, James. 1969. A General Equilibrium Approach to Monetary Theory. *Journal of Money, Credit and Banking* (1), February.

Turner, John F. C. 1976. *Housing by People.* London: Marion Boyars.

Turvey, Ralph. 1957. *The Economics of Real Property.* London: Allen and Unwin.

U.N. Department of Economic and Social Affairs. 1971, 1975. *Urban Land Policies and Land Use Control Measures.* Vols. 1–6 and vol. 7, *Global Summary.*

United Nations, 1976. Report and Recommendations of the U.N. Habitat Conference, Vancouver. A/Conf 70/15. New York.

van der Harst, J. 1975. *Cost of Residing of Low-income Groups.* Joint Research Project IV, Urban Development and Slum Improvement. Karachi University and Free University of Amsterdam.

Vargha, Louis A. 1964. *An Economic View of Leasehold and Fee Simple Tenure of Residential Land in Hawaii.* Land Study Bureau Bulletin no. 4. Honolulu: University of Hawaii.

Varian, H. R. 1978. *Microeconomic Analysis.* New York: Norton.

Vernaz, George. 1973. Bogotá's Pirate Settlements: An Opportunity for Metropolitan Development. Ph.D. dissertation. University of California, Berkeley.

Walters, Alan A. 1968. *The Economics of Road User Charges.* Baltimore, Md.: Johns Hopkins University Press.

Ward, Peter. 1976. The Squatter Settlements as Slum or Housing Solutions: Evidence from Mexico City. *Land Economics* 52(3), August.

Watson, Peter L., and Edward P. Holland. 1978. *Relieving Traffic Congestion: The Singapore Area License Scheme.* World Bank Staff Working Paper no. 281. Washington, D.C.

Williamson, Oliver E. 1975. *Markets and Hierarchies: Analysis and Anti-trust Implications.* New York: Free Press.

Wong, John, ed. 1975. *The Cities of Asia: A Study of Urban Solutions and Urban Finance.* Singapore: Singapore University Press.

Woodruff, A. M., and L. L. Ecker-Racz. 1969. Property Taxes and Land Use Patterns in Australia and New Zealand. In Arthur Becker, ed. *Land and Building Taxes: Their Effect on Economic Development.* Madison: University of Wisconsin Press.

World Bank, 1974a. Sites and Services Projects. Washington, D.C.

———. 1974b. Economic Evaluation of Public Utility Projects. Department

Guideline Series, GAS 10. Washington, D.C.: World Bank, Electricity, Water and Telecommunications Department. Processed.

————. 1976. The Definition and Role of Marginal Cost in Public Utility Pricing: Problems of Application in the Water Supply Sector. Research Working Paper RES 6. Washington, D.C.: World Bank, Energy, Water and Telecommunications Department. Processed.

Index